May 2010

To Spyros,

with my sincere thanks
for all your help and support
throughout this doctoral
adventure!

Daphne

Intellectual Property and Traditional Cultural Expressions

To my parents, for their love, inspiration and unfailing support.

Intellectual Property and Traditional Cultural Expressions

Daphne Zografos

Lecturer in Law, University of Reading, UK

Edward Elgar
Cheltenham, UK • Northampton, MA, USA

Published by
Edward Elgar Publishing Limited
The Lypiatts
15 Lansdown Road
Cheltenham
Glos GL50 2JA
UK

Edward Elgar Publishing, Inc.
William Pratt House
9 Dewey Court
Northampton
Massachusetts 01060
USA

A catalogue record for this book is available from the British Library

Library of Congress Control Number: 2009937772

Mixed Sources
Product group from well-managed forests and other controlled sources
www.fsc.org Cert no. SA-COC-1565
© 1996 Forest Stewardship Council

ISBN 978 1 84844 406 5

Typeset by Cambrian Typesetters, Camberley, Surrey
Printed and bound by MPG Books Group, UK

Contents

Acknowledgements

My PhD thesis on *Origin Related Intellectual Property Rights as Best Policy Option for the Protection of Traditional Cultural Expressions* is at the origin of this book. I am obliged to the Herchel Smith bequest for funding my doctoral studies between 2004 and 2005. I am also obliged to the Queen Mary Intellectual Property Research Institute for funding my attendance at many conferences.

My sincerest thanks to both my PhD supervisors, Professor Michael Blakeney and Professor Spyros Maniatis, for supervising my thesis. Professor Blakeney guided me in the choice of the subject matter of my thesis and encouraged me in my research all along. Professor Maniatis helped me structure my thoughts and provided me with his constant support and wisdom.

I am also grateful to Professor John Phillips and Mr Wend Wendland for examining my thesis; Mr Malcolm Langley, for his help with my many bibliographical queries, and Dr Niko Iliadis, for his invaluable IT and moral support throughout our common doctoral adventure.

Finally, my thanks are due to my friends and colleagues at the Intellectual Property Unit of the Centre for Commercial Law Studies at Queen Mary, University of London: John Cahir, Alan Cunningham, Charlotte Knights, Florian Leverve, Muriel Lightbourne, Tina Loverdou, Viviana Munoz Tellez, Noam Shemtov and Ilanah Simon Fihma, for most interesting exchanges of thoughts and also their enjoyable company.

Figures

Tables

Abbreviations

AAC	Alaska Administrative Code
ANKAAA	Association of Northern Kimberly and Arnhem Aboriginal Artists
APEC	Asia-Pacific Economic Cooperation
ASEAN	Association of Southeast Asian Nations
ATO	alternative trade organisation
ATSI	Aboriginal and Torres Strait Islander
ATSIC	Aboriginal and Torres Strait Islander Commission
BIRPI	Bureaux Internationaux Réunis pour la Protection de la Propriété Intellectuelle
CCTV	Chinese Central Television
CTM	Community trade mark
ECJ	European Court of Justice
EEC	European Economic Community
EFTA	European Fair Trade Association
FBI	Federal Bureau of Investigation
FLO	Fair Trade Labelling Organisation International
GATT	General Agreement on Tariffs and Trade
GI	geographical indication
IACA	Indian Arts and Crafts Act
IACB	Indian Arts and Crafts Board
ICTSD	International Centre for Trade and Sustainable Development
IFAT	International Federation for Alternative Trade
IGC	Intergovernmental Committee on Intellectual Property and Genetic Resources, Traditional Knowledge and Folklore
IIED	International Institute for Environment and Development
ILO	International Labour Organisation
IP	intellectual property
IPONZ	Intellectual Property Office of New Zealand
IPR	intellectual property right
ISO	International Organisation for Standardisation
ITC	International Trade Centre
NAA	Native American Arts Inc.
NEWS	Network of European World Shops
NGO	Non-governmental organisation

NIAAA	National Indigenous Arts Advocacy Association
OAPI	African Intellectual Property Organisation
OHIM	Office for Harmonisation in the Internal Market
OIG	Office of Inspector General (US Department of the Interior)
OLP	origin labelled product
OTPDA	Organisme Tunisien de Protection des Droits d'Auteurs
OVOP	One Village One Product
PBU	Producer Business Unit
SODACT	Société des Auteurs et des Compositeurs de Tunisie
TCE	traditional cultural expression
TK	traditional knowledge
TRIPS	Trade-Related Aspects of Intellectual Property Rights
TTBA	Trademark Trial and Appeal Board
UNCTAD	United Nations Conference on Trade and Development
UNDP	United Nations Development Programme
UNESCO	United Nations Educational, Scientific and Cultural Organisation
UPOV	International Convention for the Protection of New Varieties of Plants
USPTO	United States Patent and Trademark Office
WIPO	World Intellectual Property Organisation
WTO	World Trade Organisation

Table of cases

Table of legislation

1. General introduction

Over the past few decades, the protection of traditional cultural expressions (TCEs) has generated lively debates within the international community and the questions of whether TCEs should be protected by intellectual property rights (IPRs), and if so how, have been of increasing practical concern for TCEs holders and national policy-makers in various countries. To date, however, work on the protection of TCEs has progressed slowly, and little has emerged in the way of concrete, binding law. Moreover, those instruments proposed as solutions appear unable to meet the whole range of concerns raised by TCEs holders and culturally-rich developing countries.

Concerns raised by TCEs holders can be classified into four main categories. First, they stress the difficulties they encounter in preventing and/or controlling the commercial use of their TCEs by third parties and in benefiting from this commercialisation themselves. Secondly, they express concerns about the inappropriate and offensive use of their TCEs. Thirdly, they wish to be attributed for their TCEs, as well as have the possibility to object to any false attribution. Finally, they emphasise the need to ensure the identification and preservation of existing TCEs, as well as their promotion, dissemination and continued evolution.

The protection of TCEs was initially envisaged on a copyright model, because of the similarity of subject matter between copyright law and TCEs. However, although copyright law seems well suited to meet some of the needs and objectives of TCEs holders, it is limited in its potential for protecting TCEs.

This study argues that 'origin related intellectual property rights', such as trade marks, certification and collective marks and geographical indications, as well as passing off and laws against misrepresentation, appear to be conceptually best suited for the protection of TCEs, because of their specific nature and characteristics. Such characteristics include the fact that they are usually produced within a community, which is often linked to a specific place, and according to traditional methods and know-how transmitted from generation to generation, often using raw material from sustainable resources. In addition, this method of protection also seems to accommodate the fact that TCEs are usually already in the public domain and to take into consideration some of the aims of TCEs holders, such as the fact that they would like a protection that is unlimited in time.

It will demonstrate that a system of protection based on origin related IPRs could offer practical advantages for TCEs holders since such category of rights used as such or with minor adaptations would enable them to obtain quick, practical and effective protection. In addition, there would be no need for the creation of a new *sui generis* intellectual property (IP) or IP related system, which would take a long time to establish and may not be politically feasible anyway. The proposed approach would admittedly not address all the concerns of TCEs holders, but it would provide a balanced and workable compromise solution that could satisfy most of their concerns and policy objectives.

In order to support this proposition, it is necessary (i) to identify the needs and expectations of TCEs holders; (ii) to examine and compare policy options that have been adopted at the national, regional and international levels for the protection of TCEs; and (iii) based on this information, to identify the policy approach that would satisfy those needs and expectations best.

Due to the multi-faceted nature of TCEs, their broad geographical reach and the wide range of concerns, which can vary from one traditional community to the other, it is not possible to provide an exhaustive study of all policy approaches or legal provisions that have been proposed or adopted, nor probably to find a one-size-fits-all approach to the protection of TCEs. In this view, the study presents a selection of case studies to better illustrate the main policy approaches. The case studies have been selected as test-sites for the proposition because they provide particularly significant illustrations of certain types of TCEs protection and because, together, they represent a wide range of perspectives, interests and concerns of TCEs holders.

Finally, it should be noted that it is not within the scope of this study to discuss whether or not TCEs should be protected but rather to identify what is the best option for their protection within IP or IP related systems.

1.1   TERMINOLOGY, DEFINITION AND CHARACTERISTICS OF TCES

Over the years, various terms have been used to describe the subject matter that is the object of this book. These include, but are not limited to, 'folklore', 'traditional cultural expressions', 'expressions of folklore', 'indigenous cultural and intellectual property', 'indigenous heritage' and 'traditional knowledge'.[1] The terminology used varies depending on the region and/or the traditional communities using it.

---

[1]   Terminological issues have been discussed by various academics and commentators. See for example Michael Blakeney, 'The Protection of Traditional

While this book uses the words 'traditional cultural expressions' as a working term,[2] it should be noted that this is not an internationally agreed term and that the terminology in this area is still under discussion in a number of national, regional and international fora.

Similarly, various definitions have been proposed at the national, regional and international level to describe the subject matter of TCEs. There is not, at the present time, an agreed legal definition of TCEs. Defining TCEs is a complex and subjective task, which varies depending on the region and the traditional community or body from which the definition emanates. Potentially, TCEs encompass a wide variety of customs, traditions, forms of artistic expressions, knowledge, beliefs, products and processes of production that originate from many societies throughout the world.[3]

Over the past few years, the Intergovernmental Committee on Intellectual Property and Genetic Resources, Traditional Knowledge and Folklore has continuously developed and refined a proposed definition of TCEs. Its current version is set out in Article 1 of the Substantive Provisions of the WIPO Revised Provisions for the Protection of Traditional Cultural Expressions/ Expressions of Folklore. It provides that:

(a) 'Traditional cultural expressions' or 'expressions of folklore' are any forms, whether tangible and intangible, in which traditional culture and knowledge are expressed, appear or are manifested, and comprise the following forms of expressions or combinations thereof:
   (i)   verbal expressions, such as stories, epics, legends, poetry, riddles and other narratives; words, signs, names, and symbols;
   (ii) musical expressions, such as songs and instrumental music;
   (iii) expressions by action, such as dances, plays, ceremonies, rituals and other performances;
   whether or not reduced to a material form; and

Knowledge under Intellectual Property Law' (2000) 22 *EIPR* 251–61; Terri Janke, *Our Culture: Our Future, Report on Australian Indigenous Cultural and Intellectual Property Rights* (report prepared for the Australian Institute of Aboriginal and Torres Strait Islander Studies and the Aboriginal and Torres Strait Islander Commission, 1998) 2–7; Marie Niedzielska, 'The Intellectual Property Aspects of Folklore Protection' (1980) *Copyright* 339–40; Stephen Palethorpe and Stefaan Verhulst, *Report on the International Protection of Expressions of Folklore under Intellectual Property Law* (report commissioned by the European Commission's Internal Market, October 2000) 6–8.

   2   At places, different terms may be used when discussing legal provisions using such terms. Similarly, this study uses both the terms 'TCEs holders' and 'indigenous or traditional communities', to designate the groups seeking TCEs protection.

   3   Although the protection of TCEs appears to be an issue that primarily concerns indigenous groups in developing countries, many indigenous communities in developed countries, such as Australia, New Zealand, Canada and the United States, maintain equally strong TCEs.

     (iv) tangible expressions, such as productions of art, in particular, drawings, designs, paintings (including body-painting), carvings, sculptures, pottery, terracotta, mosaic, woodwork, metalware, jewelry, baskets, needlework, textiles, glassware, carpets, costumes; handicrafts; musical instruments; and architectural forms;
         which are:

      (aa) the product of creative intellectual activity, including individual and communal activity;

      (bb) characteristic of a community's cultural and social identity and cultural heritage; and

      (cc) maintained, used or developed by such community, or by individuals having the right or responsibility to do so in accordance with the customary law and practices of that community.

(b) The specific choice of terms to denote the protected subject matter should be determined at the national and regional levels.

This definition draws upon the 1982 WIPO–UNESCO Model Provisions for National Laws for the Protection of Expressions of Folklore Against Illicit Exploitation and Other Prejudicial Action, the more recent 2002 Pacific Islands Regional Framework for the Protection of Traditional Knowledge and Expressions of Culture, as well as existing national copyright laws which provide *sui generis* protection for TCEs.

As highlighted in the proposed definition, TCEs refer to products of creative intellectual activity. It is generally accepted that TCEs have been handed down from one generation to another, reflect a community's history, values and cultural and social identity, and consist of characteristic elements of a community's heritage.[4] TCEs are often made using raw materials from sustainable resources and are constantly evolving and developing. In many cases, it is difficult or impossible to identify a specific author or authors, especially in relation to the oldest, pre-existing and collective TCEs. However, TCEs also include contemporary expressions of traditional culture, which are constantly recreated, reinterpreted and adapted by traditional communities and artists in response to their environment, and in relation to which it may be possible to identify an author. Often, however, these contemporary creations are regarded by a community as identifying and reflecting its traditions, values and beliefs, and thus as being owned by that community and falling within a shared sense of communal responsibility, identity and custodianship.[5]

---

[4]   See Documents WIPO/GRTKF/IC/6/3, 14–16 and WIPO/GRTKF/IC/13/4(b) Rev. Annex I, 4.

[5]   Ibid.

1.2 CONCERNS AND POLICY OBJECTIVES OF TCES HOLDERS

Initiatives for the protection of TCEs reflect a wide range of concerns and policy objectives, which may differ across regions and/or traditional communities.[6] The main concerns and policy objectives of TCEs holders may, however, be classified into the following categories.

1.2.1 Economic Interests and Commercial Use

TCEs holders stress the difficulties they encounter in preventing and/or controlling the commercial use of their TCEs by third parties and in benefiting from this commercialisation themselves. Although little statistical and economical data exists on the valuation of TCEs, it is generally accepted that they substantially contribute to the economy in a range of industries, such as arts and crafts, tourism, advertising, music, film, television and the export industry.[7] Many traditional communities rely on TCEs to generate income. They are concerned that allowing imitation products to compete in the marketplace may deprive them of a reliable source of income, and that the commercial use of TCEs on consumer products, when undertaken by others, may deny them that future use.

1.2.2 Inappropriate or Offensive Use

Inappropriate or offensive use may take various forms:

* **Distortion**: distortions of TCEs often occur when TCEs are adapted for marketing purposes without the consent of traditional communities. Such distortions are often considered inappropriate, disrespectful. and at times offensive.
* **Disclosure and sacred nature**: TCEs holders emphasise the often sacred and cultural significance of TCEs and the fact that using TCEs outside their traditional context, and in ways contrary to customary laws, may cause great offence and undermine the social organisation of traditional communities. In traditional communities, TCEs relating to sacred sites, objects, designs, religious ceremonies and initiation rituals

---

6   On concerns and policy objectives of TCEs holders, see WIPO, *Intellectual Property Needs and Expectations of Traditional Knowledge Holders, WIPO Report on Fact-Finding Missions on Intellectual Property and Traditional Knowledge (1998–1999)* (WIPO: Geneva, 2001).

7   See Palethorpe and Verhulst, *supra* note 1, 14.

are often an important element of the communities' social dynamic. The public disclosure of such materials, which may reach those not permitted for cultural reasons to know about or view such materials, may undermine the social organisation of such communities.

- **False connection**: in some industries, it has become common practice to promote non-indigenous products and businesses by using indigenous or traditional names or signs as brand names, trade marks and business names. TCEs holders are concerned that this practice misleads consumers by falsely suggesting a connection with the community and leads them to believe that the business is owned and run by indigenous people or that benefits flow back to indigenous or traditional communities. In addition, TCEs as such are often incorporated into souvenirs and other domestic consumer products ranging from items of clothing, wall hangings, etc., regardless of their significance to the beliefs of the originating culture.
- **Derogatory, libellous, defamatory or fallacious uses**: TCEs holders wish to object to any derogatory, libellous, defamatory or fallacious use of their TCEs.

1.2.3   Attribution

Traditional communities would like the right to be attributed for their TCEs, as well as the possibility to object to any false attribution. The latter issue arises, for example, where imitation products are presented as genuine TCEs in the marketplace. This phenomenon has increased in recent years as a result of a growing interest in the culture of traditional communities, the demand for their cultural products and the development of international travel and tourism.

The question of attribution also deals with another problem: the difference over property regimes. Most cases dealing with TCEs involve the concept of communal property over TCEs, whereas Western property theories tend to focus on the individual.

1.2.4   Identification, Preservation and Promotion

TCEs holders wish to ensure the identification and preservation of existing TCEs, as well as their promotion, dissemination and continued evolution. They fear that the gradual incorporation of TCEs into the cultures of others and their distortion from their original form might have potentially detrimental effects on their culture and may disrupt its continued evolution. Furthermore, they consider that TCEs are a valuable means of promoting a sense of cohesion and identity and should therefore be preserved.

1.3 CURRENT LEGISLATIVE BACKGROUND: THE PROTECTION OF TCES IN THE INTERNATIONAL ARENA

The protection of TCEs has generated lively debates within the international community and the questions of whether TCEs should be protected by intellectual property rights, and if so how, have been on the international agenda since the 1970s. The World Intellectual Property Organisation (WIPO) began to explore the field of TCEs in 1978.[8] It convened three meetings of experts in cooperation with the United Nations Educational, Scientific and Cultural Organisation (UNESCO) that led to the adoption in 1982 of the Model Provisions for National Laws on the Protection of Expressions of Folklore Against Illicit Exploitation and Other Prejudicial Actions ('the Model Provisions'). The Model Provisions were adopted following agreement that: (i) adequate legal protection of folklore was desirable; (ii) such legal protection could be promoted at the national level by model provisions for legislation; (iii) such model provisions should be so elaborated as to be applicable both in countries where no relevant legislation was in force and in countries where existing legislation could be further developed; (iv) the said model provisions should allow for protection by means of copyright and neighbouring rights where such form of protection could apply; and (v) the model provisions for national laws should pave the way for sub-regional and international protection of creations of folklore.[9]

The Model Provisions, which consist of 14 sections,[10] established a *sui*

---

[8] On WIPO's exploratory programme on TCEs, see Wend Wendland, 'Intellectual Property, Traditional Knowledge and Folklore: WIPO's Exploratory Program' (2002) 33 *IIC* 485–504 and 606–21.

[9] UNESCO and WIPO, *Model Provisions for National Laws on the Protection of Expressions of Folklore Against Illicit Exploitation and Other Prejudicial Actions* (UNESCO and WIPO, 1985), 7.

[10] Section 1 states the principle of protection. Section 2 defines 'expressions of folklore'. Section 3 specifies the utilisations which are subject to authorisation. Section 4 sets out the exceptions to the need for authorisation. Section 5 determines the way in which the source of the expression of folklore utilised must be indicated. Sections 6 to 8 deal with offences, sanctions and related measures. Section 9 determines the 'competent' and 'supervisory' authorities. Section 10 lays down the procedure for requesting and granting the required authorisation. Section 11 establishes the jurisdiction of courts. Section 12 expressly maintains copyright and other possible forms of applicable protection. Section 13 provides for the unhindered use and development of expressions of folklore where such use or development is 'normal'; and finally, section 14 determines the conditions under which expressions of folklore originating from a community in a foreign country are protected.

generis system of intellectual property-type protection[11] for expressions of folklore. Their aims reflected the necessity to maintain an appropriate balance between protection against abuses of expressions of folklore, on the one hand, and freedom and encouragement of their further development and dissemination on the other.[12] Following their adoption, some countries have used, to some or other degree, the Model Provisions as a basis for national legal regimes for the protection of folklore,[13] however the Model Provisions have not had an extensive impact on national legislation. Reasons for that include the use of the term 'expressions of folklore' and the scope of the term as used in the Model Provisions; the nature and scope of the rights granted over expressions of folklore by the Model Provisions, and the possibility that the Model Provisions may be out of date due to technological, legal, social, cultural and commercial developments since 1982.[14]

In April 1997, the UNESCO/WIPO World Forum on the Protection of Folklore was held in Phuket, Thailand. During the meeting, needs and issues related to intellectual property and folklore, as well as views and experiences were identified and discussed by the participants. The meeting adopted a Plan of Action which stated that:

---

[11]   The Model Provisions were criticised for addressing only one part of the problem of safeguarding folklore by concentrating on the sole use of IPRs as a tool of protection. See Janet Blake, *Preliminary Study into the Advisability of Developing a New Standard-Setting Instrument for the Safeguarding of Intangible Cultural Heritage: Elements for Consideration* (Paris, 2002) 19.

[12]   The Model Provisions were developed in response to concerns that expressions of folklore were susceptible to various forms of illicit exploitation and other prejudicial actions. In particular, it was feared that the dissemination of expressions of folklore might lead to improper exploitation of the cultural heritage of a nation and that any abuse of a commercial or other nature or any distortion of expressions of folklore was prejudicial to the cultural and economic interests of the nation. In addition, it was considered that protection of expressions of folklore had become indispensable as a means of promoting further development, maintenance and dissemination of those expressions. See Preamble to the Model Provisions.

[13]   These countries include Burkina Faso, Ghana, the Islamic Republic of Iran, Kenya, Mexico, Mozambique, Namibia, Panama, Senegal, Togo, the United Republic of Tanzania. Some other countries including Ghana, the United States and Venezuela, have stated that while their laws were not directly based on the Model Provisions, they coincided with the principles of the Model Provisions. See Detailed Statistics and Summary of Responses Received to the Questionnaire on National Experiences with the Legal Protection of Expressions of Folklore, Document WIPO/GRTKF/IC/3/10 ANNEX I, 2–3.

[14]   See Wend Wendland, 'Intellectual Property and the Protection of Cultural Expressions: The Work of the World Intellectual Property Organization (WIPO)' in Molengrafica Series 2002, *Intellectual Property Law, Articles on Cultural Expressions and Indigenous Knowledge* (Intersentia: Antwerp, 2002) 105. See also Document WIPO/GRTKF/IC/3/10, 45 and ANNEX I, 43–4.

The participants were of the view that at present there is no international standard protection for folklore and that the copyright regime is not adequate to ensure such protection. They also confirmed a need to define, identify, conserve, preserve, disseminate, and protect folklore which has been a living cultural heritage of great economic, social, and political significance from time immemorial. They emphasized the importance of striking a good balance of interests between the community owning the folklore and users of expressions of folklore. They were convinced that closer regional and international cooperation would be vital to the successful establishment of a new international standard for the protection of folklore.[15]

The Plan of Action suggested, *inter alia*, that a committee of experts be set up and that regional consultative fora should take place.[16] Following the Forum, in 1999 WIPO and UNESCO organised four Regional Consultations on the Protection of Folklore.[17] Each of the Regional Consultations adopted resolutions or recommendations which identified intellectual property needs and issues, as well as proposals for future work, related to TCEs.[18]

In 1998, WIPO began a new set of activities designed to explore the intellectual property aspects of the protection of TCEs with the objective 'to identify and explore the intellectual property needs and expectations of new beneficiaries, including the holders of indigenous knowledge and innovations, in order to promote the contribution of the intellectual property system to their social, cultural and economic development'.[19] To this end, WIPO conducted a series of fact-finding missions between 1998 and 1999 to identify the intellectual property related needs and expectations of traditional knowledge (TK) holders.[20]

---

[15]   See UNESCO and WIPO, *World Forum on the Protection of Folklore, Phuket, Thailand, April 8 to 10, 1997* (UNESCO and WIPO, 1998) 235.

[16]   Ibid.

[17]   The regional consultations were held for African countries in Pretoria, South Africa in March 1999; for countries of Asia and the Pacific region in Hanoi, Vietnam in April 1999; for Arab countries in Tunis, Tunisia in May 1999 and for Latin America and the Caribbean in Quito, Ecuador in June 1999.

[18]   Resolutions and recommendations were addressed to states, and to WIPO and UNESCO. For a detailed account of the resolutions and recommendations, see WIPO-UNESCO African Regional Consultation on the Protection of Expressions of Folklore, Document WIPO-UNESCO/FOLK/AFR/99/1; WIPO-UNESCO Regional Consultation on the Protection of Expressions of Folklore for Arab Countries, Document WIPO-UNESCO/FOLK/ARAB/99/1; WIPO-UNESCO Regional Consultation on the Protection of Expressions of Folklore for Countries of Asia and the Pacific, Document WIPO-UNESCO/FOLK/ASIA/99/1; and WIPO-UNESCO Regional Consultation on the Protection of Expressions of Folklore for Latin America and the Caribbean, Document WIPO-UNESCO/FOLK/LAC/99/1.

[19]   See Main Program 11, WIPO Program and Budget 1998–1999.

[20]   Nine fact-finding missions were conducted in 28 countries and indigenous and local communities, non-governmental organisations, governmental representatives, academies, researchers and private sector representatives were consulted on that occasion. See WIPO Report, *supra* note 6.

In September 2000, WIPO's Member States established an Inter-governmental Committee on Intellectual Property and Genetic Resources, Traditional Knowledge and Folklore ('the IGC'). The IGC met for the first time from 30 April to 3 May 2001 and held its 13th session from 13 to 17 October 2008. The initial mandate from the WIPO General Assembly required the IGC to meet semi-annually for two years to study and make recommendations for action to the General Assembly.[21] This mandate was subsequently renewed in 2003, 2005 and 2008.

Over the years, the IGC has extensively reviewed legal and policy options for the protection of TCEs. Its work has included a comprehensive analysis of existing national and regional mechanisms for the protection of TCEs[22] and surveys of policy frameworks available for the protection of TCEs, including conventional or general IP regimes, as well as new *sui generis* systems.[23] In addition, it has carried out and commissioned various case studies[24] and organised panel presentations on diverse national experiences.

The work of the IGC has led to the development of a set of draft provisions, which suggest possible international objectives and principles for the protection of TCEs.[25] The draft provisions draw upon a wide range of community,

---

[21]   See WIPO, WIPO General Assembly, Matters Concerning Intellectual Property and Genetic Resources, Traditional Knowledge and Folklore, Document WO/GA/26/6, 4.

[22]   At the first session of the IGC, Member States indicated a need for further information on national experience with the protection of TCEs. Accordingly, the Secretariat prepared and issued a Questionnaire on National Experiences with the Legal Protection of Expressions of Folklore, Document WIPO/GRTKF/IC/2/7. The questionnaire was completed by 64 states. See Final Report on National Experiences with the Legal Protection of Expressions of Folklore, Document WIPO/GRTKF/IC/3/10.

[23]   See Preliminary Systematic Analysis of National Experiences with the Legal Protection of Expressions of Folklore, Document WIPO/GRTKF/IC/4/3; and Consolidated Analysis of the Legal Protection of Traditional Cultural Expressions, Document WIPO/GRTKF/IC/5/3.

[24]   See for example Terri Janke, *Minding Culture: Case Studies on Intellectual Property and Traditional Cultural Expressions* (WIPO: Geneva, 2003); Valsala Kutty, *National Experience with the Protection of Traditional Cultural Expressions/ Expressions of Folklore: India, Indonesia, the Philippines* (WIPO: Geneva, 1999).

[25]   See WIPO, *Intellectual Property and Genetic Resources, Traditional Knowledge and Traditional Cultural Expressions/Folklore, Information Resources* (WIPO: Geneva, 2006). The draft provisions are also available as working documents for the IGC. The latest version of the draft provisions has been issued in Document WIPO/GRTKF/IC/11/4(c). A supplementary study describing how these objectives and principles have been adopted and implemented at regional and national levels is available in Document WIPO/GRTKF/IC/9/INF/4. In addition, a table of written comments on the revised draft objectives and principles provided between the ninth and tenth sessions of the IGC is available in Document WIPO/GRTKF/IC/11/4(b).

national and regional experiences, and have been developed over several years by and in consultation with WIPO Member States, indigenous people and other traditional communities, civil society organisations and a range cf other interested parties. While the draft objectives and principles have no formal status, they illustrate some of the perspectives and approaches that are guiding work in this area, and could suggest possible frameworks for the protection of TCEs against misappropriation and misuse. To date, the drafts have not been adopted or endorsed by the IGC, but may be developed further in future sessions of the IGC. More importantly, they are being used as points of reference in a range of national, regional and international policy discussions and standard-setting processes.[26]

---

[26]   See www.wipo.int/tk/en/consultations/draft_provisions/draft_provisions.html

2. The protection of traditional cultural expressions with copyright

2.1 INTRODUCTION

The legal protection of TCEs with intellectual property rights was first envisaged from a copyright perspective. At the national level, Tunisia was the first country to provide protection for TCEs within its copyright law in 1966. At the same time, the issue of TCEs was also brought up in the international agenda of the 1967 Stockholm Diplomatic Conference for the Revision of the Berne Convention for the Protection of Literary and Artistic Works ('the Berne Convention').

In the first part, this chapter will examine the attempts that have been made to achieve protection of TCEs through the copyright system in regional or international agreements, such as the Berne Convention, the 1976 Tunis Model Law on Copyright for Developing Countries and the 1977 Bangui Agreement. In the second part, it will present some case studies based on the experiences of Tunisia, Australia and China with the copyright protection of TCEs, to illustrate the extent to which copyright law may assist in preventing the unauthorised reproduction of TCEs.

2.2 A FEW MILESTONES IN PAST ATTEMPTS TO ACHIEVE INTERNATIONAL PROTECTION OF TCES THROUGH COPYRIGHT

At the international level, the first attempts to provide protection for TCEs included the protection of works of folklore as works of an unknown author in the Berne Convention, the provisions of the 1976 Tunis Model Law on Copyright for Developing Countries and the 1977 Bangui Agreement.

2.2.1 The Berne Convention

The issue of TCEs was first brought up in the international agenda of the 1967 Stockholm Diplomatic Conference for the Revision of the Berne Convention. An Indian proposal was brought before the Main Committee to include works of folklore in the list of works entitled to protection under the Berne Convention.[1] Following a favourable reception of the Indian proposal by the majority of delegations, a special Working Group was set up to consider what would be the most suitable place in the Convention for a provision dealing with works of folklore.[2]

The problems raised by the definition of folklore, the absence of an identifiable author or authors and the fact that they were often already in the public domain made it difficult for works of folklore to be included in the enumeration of literary and artistic works in Article 2(1) of the Berne Convention.[3] As a consequence, the Working Group decided that a work of folklore was, by definition, the work of an unknown author[4] and proposed the insertion in Article 15 of the following provision:[5]

(a) In the case of unpublished work where the identity of the author is unknown, but where there is every ground to presume that he is a national of a country of the Union, it shall be a matter for legislation in that country to designate the competent authority which shall represent the author and shall be entitled to protect and enforce his rights in the countries of the Union.

(b) Countries of the Union which make such designation under the terms of this provision shall notify the Director General by means of a written declaration giving full information concerning the authority thus designated. The Director General shall at once communicate this declaration to all other countries of the Union.

Due to definitional difficulties, the proposal of the Working Group did not mention the word 'folklore'. However the report of the Main Committee I stated that:

---

[1]   See WIPO, *Records of the Intellectual Property Conference of Stockholm, June 11 to July 14, 1967* (WIPO: Geneva, 1971) vol. I, 690–1 (Doc. S/73) and vol. II, 877 (Minutes of Main Committee I).

[2]   Ibid.

[3]   Sam Ricketson, *The Berne Convention for the Protection of Literary and Artistic Works: 1886–1986* (Centre for Commercial Law Studies, Queen Mary College and Kluwer: London, 1987) 314.

[4]   WIPO *Records, supra* note 27, vol. II, 917 (Minutes of the Main Committee I).

[5]   The proposal was subject to the following principles: (i) the work is unpublished; (ii) the author is unknown; (iii) there is every ground to presume that the author is a national of a country of the Union; (iv) if these three conditions are fulfilled, the legislation of that country may designate a competent authority to represent the author; (v) the competent authority is entitled to protect and enforce the rights of the author in all the countries of the Union; (vi) if such an authority is designated by a country, that country shall notify WIPO by means of a declaration in writing giving full information concerning the authority thus designated; WIPO shall then communicate this declaration to all other countries of the Union. Ibid. 1172–3 (report of the Main Committee I).

> [While] the provision applies to all works fulfilling the conditions indicated above
> … it is clear … that the main field of application of this regulation will coincide
> with those productions which are generally described as folklore.[6]

The Berne Convention was not successful in providing an adequate international framework of protection for TCEs. First, India was the only country to make the necessary notification to the Director General designating a national authority that would represent the author and enforce his rights according to Article 15(4)(b). Secondly, the Berne Convention does not provide for the protection of works that are already published and that are in the public domain.[7] Finally, the mechanisms provided by the Berne Convention do not offer the possibility to TCEs holders to exercise their rights directly.

2.2.2   The 1976 Tunis Model Law on Copyright for Developing Countries

The Tunis Model Law on Copyright for Developing Countries was adopted to provide developing countries with a text of a model law to assist them when framing or revising their national copyright legislation and to facilitate their adhesion to the Berne Convention and the Universal Copyright Convention, which required that their domestic law conform to the Convention rules.[8]

The Tunis Model Law goes a few steps further than the Berne Convention by explicitly including folklore in the list of protected works[9] and providing that works of national folklore are to be protected against improper exploitation.[10]

The drafters of the Tunis Model Law have made an exception to the fixation rule for works of folklore.[11] Indeed, according to the commentary by UNESCO and WIPO on the Tunis Model Law:

> The fixation requirement cannot possibly apply to works of folklore: such works
> form part of the cultural heritage of peoples and their very nature lies in their being
> handed on from generation to generation orally or in the form of dances whose steps
> have never been recorded.[12]

---

[6]   Ibid.

[7]   See Ricketson, *supra* note 3, 315.

[8]   WIPO, 'Tunis Model Law on Copyright' (1976) *Copyright* 165. The text of the Tunis Model Law can also be found in this article, as well as a commentary by the Secretary of UNESCO and the International Bureau of WIPO.

[9]   See section 1(3).

[10]   See section 6.

[11]   See section 5*bis*.

[12]   See WIPO, 'Tunis Model Law on Copyright', *supra* note 8, 167.

The Tunis Model Law also contains a definition of folklore[13] and a provision to the effect that works derived from folklore are also protected as original works.[14] Finally, the Tunis Model Law grants works of folklore a protection that is unlimited in time.[15]

During the preparatory works of the Committee of Governmental Experts on the Tunis Model Law, several delegates expressed the wish that a provision be introduced giving the destination of the remuneration derived from the exploitation of works of national folklore. This proposal was incorporated into section 17 entitled '*Domaine Public Payant*' (Paying Public Domain).[16] According to the *domaine public payant* system, 'a work that has fallen into the public domain may be used without restriction, subject to the payment of a fee calculated as a percentage of the receipts produced by the use of the work or its adaptations'.[17] The use to be made of the sums collected under this system is specified in section 17, which states that:

> The user shall pay to the competent authority . . . percent of the receipts produced by the use of works in the public domain or their adaptation, including works of national folklore. The sums collected shall be used for the following purposes:
> (i) To promote institutions for the benefit of authors [and of performers], such as societies of authors, cooperatives, guilds, etc.
> (ii) To protect and disseminate national folklore.

2.2.3　The 1977 Bangui Agreement

The Bangui Agreement, which governs intellectual property rights in the Member States of the African Intellectual Property Organisation (OAPI),[18] was adopted in 1977 and revised in 1999.[19] Its Annex VII, entitled 'Literary and Artistic Property', contains specific rules that provide for the protection of folklore. These can be found in Title I, which contains provisions on copyright and related rights, and also in Title II, which is concerned with the protection and promotion of the cultural heritage.

13　See section 18(iv).
14　See section 2(1)(iii).
15　See section 6(2).
16　WIPO, 'Committee of Governmental Experts to Prepare a Model Law on Copyright for Developing Countries' (1976) *Copyright* 142.
17　See WIPO, 'Tunis Model Law on Copyright', *supra* note 8, 179.
18　The 16 Member States of OAPI are Benin, Burkina Faso, Cameroon, Central African Republic, Chad, Congo, Côte d'Ivoire, Gabon, Guinea, Guinea-Bissau, Equatorial Guinea, Mali, Mauritania, Niger, Senegal and Togo.
19　The revised text of the Bangui Agreement can be found at www.oapi. wipo.net/accord_bangui_english.pdf

In Title I, folklore is included in the list of protected subject matter of copyright and related rights.[20] In addition, protection is also afforded to translations, adaptations, arrangements and other transformations of expressions of folklore and to collections of folklore.[21]

As with the Tunis Model Law, the Bangui Agreement contains a special provision for works that have fallen into the public domain. Article 59, entitled 'Paying Public Domain and Exploitation of Expressions of Folklore', provides that when the term of validity of copyright expires and works fall into the public domain, the exploitation of expressions of folklore shall be subject to the user entering into an undertaking to pay to the national collective rights administration body a relevant royalty, a part of which shall be devoted to welfare and cultural purposes.

Further protection of folklore is afforded in Title II. For the purpose of the Bangui Agreement, cultural heritage consists of all material or immaterial human productions that are characteristic of a nation over time and space. Such productions relate to folklore, sites and monuments or ensemble.[22] The system of protection of cultural heritage under the Bangui Agreement is based on the assumption that the protection, safeguard and promotion of the cultural heritage shall be the responsibility of the state, which shall carry out an inventory, determine, classify, place in security and illustrate the elements that make up the cultural heritage.[23]

The cultural heritage thus listed and classified is then protected against a series of prohibited acts. Article 73 states that '[i]t shall be prohibited to denature, destroy, exploit, sell, dispose of or transfer illegally any or a part of the property that makes up the cultural heritage'.

It further provides that, except where a special authorisation is issued by the national authority, it shall be prohibited to carry out for profit-making purposes:

> the publication, reproduction and distribution of copies of any cultural property, whether classified or not, listed or not, ancient or recent, and considered by this Act as part of the national cultural heritage ... any recitation, public performances, any transmission by wire or by wireless means and any other form of communication to the public of any cultural asset, whether classified or not, identified or not, ancient or recent and considered by this Act as an element of the national cultural heritage.

Furthermore, it is provided that any person who infringes Article 73 shall be punished by a term of imprisonment and a fine in accordance with the rele-

---

20   See Article 5(1).
21   See Article 6.
22   See Article 67.
23   See Article 72.

vant provisions of the national legislation, without prejudice to any damages.[24]

Finally, the Bangui Agreement has introduced fair use exceptions in relation to cultural heritage. According to Article 74, the prohibited acts listed in Article 73(2) shall not apply where the property that makes up the cultural heritage is used for 'teaching', 'illustration of the original work of an author on condition that the scope of such use remains compatible with honest practice' or constitutes 'borrowings for the creation of an original work from one or more authors'.

The Bangui Agreement is a complete body of legislation, which has not contented itself with copying foreign texts word for word, but has made generous allowances for provisions to meet the specific needs of the Member States of the OAPI.[25] The detailed rules on the protection of folklore and the depth of protection afforded to them are a good example of that.[26]

2.3　DEFINITIONAL CONSIDERATIONS

According to Article 2 of the Berne Convention, copyright protection is available for 'literary and artistic works'[27] as well as translations, adaptations, arrangements of music and other alterations of literary or artistic works, which shall be protected as original works, without prejudice to the copyright of the original work.[28] Many TCEs for which protection is sought are productions in the literary, scientific and artistic domain, and therefore, in principle, constitute the actual or potential subject matter of copyright law. Examples of TCEs that would fall within the subject matter of copyright include traditional music,

---

[24]　See Article 96(2).

[25]　B. Cazenave, 'The African Intellectual Property Organisation (OAPI) from Libreville to Bangui' (1989) *Industrial Property* 291–307.

[26]　Assafa Endeshaw, *Intellectual Property Policy for Non-Industrial Countries* (Dartmouth, 1996) 166.

[27]　According to Article 2(1) of the Berne Convention, '[t]he expression "literary and artistic works" shall include every production in the literary, scientific and artistic domain, whatever may be the mode or form of its expression, such as books, pamphlets and other writings; lectures, addresses, sermons and other works of the same nature; dramatic or dramatico-musical works; choreographic works and entertainments in dumb show; musical compositions with or without words; cinematographic works to which are assimilated works expressed by a process analogous to cinematography; works of drawing, painting, architecture, sculpture, engraving and lithography; photographic works to which are assimilated works expressed by a process analogous to photography; works of applied art; illustrations, maps, plans, sketches and three-dimensional works relative to geography, topography, architecture or science'.

[28]　See Article 2(3) of the Berne Convention.

songs, dances, plays, stories, ceremonies, rituals, drawings, paintings, carvings, pottery mosaic, woodwork, metalware, jewellery, basket weaving, needlework, textiles, carpets, costumes, musical instruments, architecture, sculptures, engravings, handicrafts, poetry and designs.[29] The protection provided by copyright seems well suited to accommodate some of the needs and expectations of TCEs holders. The economic rights to prevent or authorise, *inter alia*, the reproduction, adaptation and communication to the public could allow them to prevent or control the commercial use of their TCEs. The moral rights of paternity and integrity could allow them to prevent false claims to authenticity and distortion of their TCEs. Finally, the possibility under copyright to be compensated for the use of TCEs either through receiving royalties or through damages for infringement could allow them to benefit from the commercialisation of their TCEs and support their economic development.

In the following paragraphs, this chapter examines attempts that have been made, at the national level, to provide protection for TCEs through the copyright system. These include the protection of 'works inspired by folklore' as a subject matter of copyright law in Tunisia and the establishment of an authorisation mechanism for the commercial exploitation of folklore against payment of a fee; a series of Australian decisions as well as a Chinese decision that examine the extent to which copyright law may assist in preventing the unauthorised reproduction of TCEs.

2.4   THE TUNISIAN EXPERIENCE

2.4.1   Introduction

Many countries have attempted to protect TCEs through their copyright laws, either by referring to TCEs as a form of copyright work,[30] or by including provisions specifically designed for TCEs within their copyright legislation.[31]

---

[29]   See WIPO, *Consolidated Analysis of the Legal Protection of Traditional Cultural Expressions/Expressions of Folklore* (WIPO: Geneva, 2003) 35.

[30]   Examples include the Islamic Republic of Iran (1970), Côte d'Ivoire (1978), Barbados (1982), Indonesia (1997) and Ukraine (2001).

[31]   Examples include Tunisia (1966 and 1994), Bolivia (1968 and 1992), Morocco (1970), Algeria (1973), Senegal (1973), Kenya (1975), Mali (1977), Burundi (1978), Sri Lanka (1979), Guinea (1980), Cameroon (1982), Congo (1982), Madagascar (1982), Burkina Faso (1984), the Central African Republic (1985), Ghana (1985), Nigeria (1988), Togo (1991), Niger (1993), Namibia (1994 and 2000), Viet Nam (1995), Mexico (1997), the United Republic of Tanzania (1999) and Mozambique (2001).

The reason that guided the choice of Tunisia for this case study is the fact that Tunisia was the first country ever to provide protection for TCEs within a copyright law in 1966, which allows an analysis of the efficiency of its provisions over a longer period of time.[32]

2.4.2   Tunisia's Folklore

The wealth of the Tunisian cultural heritage is due to its exceptional situation. Due to its geographical location to the extreme North of the African continent and at the doorstep of Europe, Tunisia has been at the crossroads of the Phoenician, Roman, Punic, Vandal and Arabic civilisations. As a result, it has accumulated layers of cultural heritage linked to different historical periods. As Boubaker Ben Fraj, Director General at the Institut National du Patrimoine (The National Institute of the Cultural Heritage), in Tunis, explained:

> What's particular about Tunisia is that we have remaining traces of all those civilisations and we recognise all of them. We consider that each historical period is one that has made us who we are today.[33]

Tunisia's folklore consists mainly of traditional music, folk stories, writings, dances and handicrafts, including carpets and tapestries, hand-crafted and painted ceramics and pottery, wrought-iron works, mouth-blown glass objects, as well as a diversity of copper, leather and wood artisan works.

2.4.3   Tunisia's Copyright History

In Tunisia, the history of copyright protection starts at the time when the former colonial powers extended their national legislation to their colonies, protectorates or dependent territories. Consequently, most of the former colonies reached independence with copyright laws inherited from colonial governments, which they either confirmed at the time national sovereignty

---

[32]   On the Tunisian experience with the protection of TCEs, see Claude Joubert, 'Comments on the New Tunisian Law on Artistic and Literary Ownership' (1966–67) 50 *RIDA* 180–223; Nébila Mezghani, 'The New Tunisian Body for the Protection of Authors' Rights' (1997) 31 *Copyright Bulletin* 30–8; Nébila Mezghani, 'A New Tunisian Law Relating to Literary and Artistic Property' (1995) 29 *Copyright Bulletin* 26–34; Nébila Mezghani, 'Letter from Tunisia: Development of the Law on Literary and Artistic Property in Tunisia' (1984) *Copyright* 265–72; Daphne Zografos, 'The Legal Protection of Traditional Cultural Expressions: The Tunisian Experience' (2004) 7 *JWIP* 229–42.

[33]   'A Crash Course in 3000 Years of World History', *Washington Times*, 10–14 July 2000.

was recovered or replaced by new laws drawn up by the national legislator. Even though it was common for the colonial powers to adjust their own legislation to the particular economic and social situation of their overseas possessions, not much attention was paid to the preservation and legal protection of local folklore, and practically all the former colonies attained independence without legislative protection of folklore. Thus, the first Tunisian copyright law, which was inherited from the French Protectorate, namely, the Tunisian Law on Literary and Artistic Property of 15 June 1889, did not mention folklore.

Following their independence, most former colonies drafted and adopted their own copyright legislation. In Tunisia, the Tunisian Law on Literary and Artistic Property of 15 June 1889 was replaced by Law No. 66-12 of 14 February in 1966 ('the Law of 1966')[34] and later, by Law No. 94-36 of 24 February in 1994 ('the Law of 1994').[35] Together with the Law of 1994, Tunisia also adopted its Code du Patrimoine, which was enacted by Law No. 94-35. The Code du Patrimoine protects the archaeological, historic and traditional heritage of Tunisia and applies to movable goods, cultural and archaeological sites, historic monuments and agglomerations of monuments such as villages or cities.

In August 1963, the first African working party on copyright was held in Brazzaville under the auspices of UNESCO and Bureaux Internationaux Réunis pour la Protection de la Propriété Intellectuelle (BIRPI). This international meeting, which brought together delegates from African countries, international experts and representatives of international organisations, resulted in the drafting of a model bill for African countries. The Brazzaville meeting was also the first international meeting to examine the legal problems associated with the protection of folklore and to adopt a recommendation regarding folklore. It was decided that the best means to safeguard the integrity of African heritage and to protect it from exploitation would be for local governments to adopt appropriate legislation.[36] Tunisia was the first country to endorse the recommendation on folklore of the Brazzaville meeting and to introduce a special protection for folklore and works inspired by folklore within its copyright law. Following this meeting, Tunisia adopted Law

---

34   An English translation of this law can be found in (1967) *Copyright* 23–7.

35   An English translation of this law can be found in Copyright and Neighbouring Rights Laws and Treaties, 1995/10/No. 1-01.

36   Samantha Sherkin, 'A Historical Study on the Preparation of the 1989 Recommendation on the Safeguarding of Traditional Culture and Folklore' in *Safeguarding Traditional Cultures: A Global Assessment* (UNESCO and Smithsonian Center for Folklife and Cultural Heritage, 2001) 45.

No. 66-12 of 14 February 1966. Whereas most of the new Tunisian law was patterned on this bill, especially drawn for African countries, the Tunisian legislator tried to be original, either by departing from the model bill, or by adding some complements that were deemed useful.[37]

Interestingly, the adoption of the Law of 1966 was shortly followed by the adoption of the Stockholm Act of the Berne Convention in 1967, which constituted the first specific attempt to provide protection for works of folklore at an international level.[38] The question whether there is a relationship between articles 1 and 6 of the Law of 1966 and Article 15(4) of the Stockholm and Paris Acts of the Berne Convention must, however, be answered negatively. Whereas the Law of 1966 provides for a system of authorisation from the Department in charge of cultural affairs in order to be allowed to exploit folklore commercially, as well as for a definition of folklore, the Working Group which came up with Article 15(4) took as its starting point the principle that a work of folklore was, by definition, the work of an unknown author, and therefore proposed an amendment to Article 15, which treated them as a special category of anonymous work within the meaning of that article.[39] Furthermore, Article 15(4), which only applies to works of an unknown author, ceases to apply in the event that a work is published.[40] Finally, Article 15(4) does not even mention the word folklore.[41]

---

[37]   See Joubert, *supra* note 32, 180–1.

[38]   See *supra* para. 2.2.1. During the discussions of the Working Group set up by the Main Committee to decide what would be the most suitable place in the Convention for a provision dealing with works of folklore, Tunisia pointed out that it agreed with the Indian proposal to include works of folklore in the list of works entitled to protection under the Berne Convention. It referred to the system of protection of folklore provided by the Law of 1966 and highlighted that it only applied in the Tunisian territory and therefore, it suggested that 'to remedy that defect, the Conference might … provide in a third paragraph of Article 15, for instance, that where the copyright in any works inspired by folklore had been vested in the State in a country of the Union, that vesting should be recognised in the other countries of the Union' (see WIPO, *Records of the Intellectual Property Conference of Stockholm, June 11 to July 14, 1967* (WIPO: Geneva, 1971), Document S/73, 876).

[39]   See Ricketson, *supra* note 3, 314.

[40]   Ibid. 315.

[41]   The reason given by the Working Group for not mentioning the word 'folklore' was that they considered it extremely difficult to define. However, the Report of the Main Committee makes it clear that the main field of application of Article 15(4) coincides with those productions which are generally described as folklore. See WIPO, *Records, supra* note 1, vol. II, 1173 (Report of the Main Committee I).

2.4.4 Tunisia's Copyright Law

Rationale for the protection of folklore in Tunisia

In Tunisia, folklore is considered to be a source of creativity and innovation and it is believed that it has contributed to the social and economic development of the country. Consequently, the aim of Tunisia is to prevent the erosion of its folklore and to further enrich it by allowing its lawful exploitation. According to Mohamed Kheireddine Abdel Ali, Managing Director of the Organisme Tunisien de Protection des Droits d'Auteurs (OTPDA) (Tunisian Body for the Protection of Author's Rights):

> To protect Tunisia's cultural heritage does not mean to freeze it, for this cultural heritage should be able to be exploited, to develop and to evolve. We inherited it, but this legacy should not be frozen. It is important that the memory of our cultural heritage be protected as it is, in its original form, but it is also important that we let it develop.[42]

This rationale was also reflected in a commentary of President Ben Ali:

> We have brought the preservation of our heritage and its revitalisation together to create a key factor for social progress and development, and a fundamental inspiration for cultural production.[43]

On the other hand, Tunisia also wishes to prevent the unlawful exploitation of its folklore. A famous example of such unlawful exploitation can be found in the registration, in Japan, of the design of the Sidi Bou Said birdcage, which brought to an end export agreements of birdcages between Tunisia and the United States, resulting in a loss of trade and source of income for the Sidi Bou Said craftsmen.[44]

The Sidi Bou Said birdcage is one of the most famous examples of Tunisian handicrafts. Sidi Bou Said birdcages, which are completely hand-made by Tunisian craftsmen, are spherical cages made of metal volutes on a square wood basis, which are filled with C and S shaped iron motives. They are inspired from the design of the wrought iron windows that can be found on the palaces of the old Tunis and by the traditional Tunisian wrought-iron work that is generally used to decorate gates, doors, windows and various other objects.

---

[42] Author's translation from French following an interview in October 2003.

[43] See *Washington Times, supra* note 33.

[44] Information provided by the OTPDA in October 2003. The case of the Sidi Bou Said birdcage was also referred to WIPO during its fact-finding missions to the Arab countries on intellectual property and traditional knowledge in 1999. See WIPO, *Intellectual Property Needs and Expectations of Traditional Knowledge Holders*, WIPO Report on Fact-finding Missions on Intellectual Property and Traditional Knowledge (1998–99), WIPO, Geneva, 2001, 167.

Figure 2.1   Sidi Bou Said birdcages

'Works inspired by folklore' as a subject matter of copyright law
Article 1 of the Law of 1994 deals with the subject matter of copyright protection. It states that copyright shall subsist in all original literary, scientific or artistic works whatever their value, purpose, mode or form of expression and provides a non-exhaustive list of protected works, which includes 'works inspired by folklore'.[45]

---

[45]   Article 1 of the Law of 1994 provides that 'Copyright shall subsist in all original literary, scientific or artistic works whatever their value, purpose, mode or form of expression, as also in the title of works. It shall apply equally to a work in its original form and in any form derived from the original.

The works in which copyright subsists shall include: written or printed works such as books, pamphlets and other written or printed works; works created for the theatre or for broadcasting (sound or visual), whether dramatic, dramatico-musical, choreographic or of dumbshow; musical compositions with or without words; photographic works, to which shall be assimilated for the purpose of this Law works expressed by a process analogous to photography; cinematographic works, to which shall be assimilated for the purposes of this Law works expressed by a process producing visual effects analogous to those of cinematography; works executed by painting, drawing, lithography, etching or woodcutting and other works of like nature; sculpture of all kinds; works of architecture, comprising also designs, models and the mode of construction; tapestries and articles of artistic handwork, including both the drawings

The list of protected works can be classified into three categories:

- works that are customarily covered by the definition of works eligible for copyright protection;
- works associated with Tunisian tradition;
- works resulting from the evolution of modern technology.[46]

'Works inspired by folklore', together with 'tapestries and articles of artistic handwork, including both the drawings or models and the work itself' belong to the second category of works, that is, works associated with Tunisian tradition.

In Tunisia, folklore is generally described as having the following characteristics:

- it is passed on from generation to generation in unfixed form;
- it is a community-oriented creation in that its expression is regulated by local traditions, standards, and expectations;
- its expressions are often not attributable to individual authors; and
- it is being continually utilised, developed and innovated by the communities in which it lives.[47]

Tunisia uses the words 'cultural/popular heritage' and 'folklore' in order to designate TCEs.[48] The reason why the legislator used the words 'works inspired by folklore' instead of 'works of folklore' in the list of protected works in article 1 of both the Copyright Laws of 1966 and 1994, needs to be examined, all the more so since these laws dedicate an entire article to the protection of folklore.

The rationale behind the use of the words 'works inspired by folklore' has been interpreted differently by commentators on these laws. For Claude Joubert, the inclusion of 'works inspired by folklore' in the list of protected works in article 1 is merely a way to 'stress the desire of the African people to draw attention to the value of their traditional cultural patrimony'[49] and not a direct reference to works of folklore as such. According to him, by stating the obvious fact that, as long as they were original, works inspired by folklore

---

or models and the work itself; maps, as also drawings and graphic and three-dimensional reproductions of a scientific or artistic nature; works inspired by folklore; software; translations and arrangements or adaptations of the aforementioned works.'

46   See Mezghani, 'A New Tunisian Law', *supra* note 32, 31.
47   WIPO Report, *supra* note 44, 160.
48   This is reflected in the Tunisian Copyright Act of 1994 and in the Code du Patrimoine of 1994.
49   See Joubert, *supra* note 32, 184–5.

could benefit from copyright protection, the legislator wanted to attrac⁻ attention to the value it attributed to traditional cultural patrimony:

> If it includes an element of originality, the work patterned either on folklore, the copyright of which has more generally lapsed, or on a work, the copyright of which has not run out, must benefit by the statute of protection linked to copyright, as every arrangement or adaptation *'lato sensu'*.[50]

For Nébila Mezghani, on the other hand, the reference to 'works inspired by folklore' should be understood as meaning works of folklore:

> We fail to understand why the Tunisian legislator chose not to mention 'works of folklore' as such. For it is Tunisian folklore itself that is the subject of protection, not works inspired by it. The latter works are of course protected, but in the same way as any derived work, namely as long as they embody an element of originality.[51]

In this more logical perspective, considering also the existence of art⁻cle 7, which deals specifically with folklore, 'works inspired by folklore' should be understood as meaning 'works of folklore', and works inspired by folklore should rather be assimilated to translations and arrangements or adaptations of the works.

The protection of folklore in Article 7 of the Law of 1994

Article 7 of the Law of 1994 provides that:

> Folklore forms part of the national heritage and any transcription of folklore with a view to exploitation for profit shall require authorisation from the Ministry responsible for culture against payment of a fee for the benefit of the welfare fund of the Copyright Protection Agency established pursuant to this Law.

Authorisation from the Ministry responsible for culture is also required for the production of works inspired by folklore, for the full or partial assignment of copyright in a work inspired by folklore, or for an exclusive licence with respect to such work.

Folklore within the meaning of this Law includes any artistic her⁻itage bequeathed by preceding generations and bound up with customs and traditions and any aspect of folk creation, such as folk stories, writings, music and dance.

Article 7(1) provides that 'folklore forms part of the national heritage' of Tunisia. Indeed, as there are practically no indigenous communities in Tunisia,

---

50 Ibid.
51 See Mezghani, 'Letter from Tunisia', *supra* note 32, 267.

folklore belongs to what is called *le domaine public de l'Etat*, the public domain of the state,[52] which should not be mistaken for *le domaine public*, the public domain. Whereas works that are in the public domain can be appropriated by anyone, works that are in the public domain of the state belong to the collective memory of the people of Tunisia, which means that they cannot be appropriated by any individual and are protected for an unlimited period of time.

Article 7(1) further provides that 'any transcription of folklore with a view to exploitation for profit shall require authorisation from the Ministry responsible for culture against the payment of a fee for the benefit of the welfare fund of the Copyright Protection Agency'. As Mohamed Kheireddine Abdel Ali pointed out:

> The State does not intend to exploit the cultural heritage for its own profit. For this reason, it has decided to set up a system of authorisation that allows the Ministry responsible for culture to decide, through a system of authorisations, which people are able to exploit the cultural heritage, as there is a minimum of knowledge and know-how that one must have in order to be allowed to exploit the Tunisian folklore.[53]

The Law of 1966 used to provide an exception to the system of authorisation in favour of public national organisations having the status of legal entities, such as the Tunisian Radio and Television, or the Tunisian cinema industry. However, this exception was not taken over by the Law of 1994.

The fee that has to be paid in return for the authorisation to exploit the works of folklore is set by the OTPDA according to the same table that is used for collecting copyright royalties and following a global assessment of each situation. The usual fee for the exploitation of works of folklore is 20 dinars a year, renewable every year, for an unlimited period of time. As Mohamed Kheireddine Abdel Ali commented, '[w]e didn't want this fee to be too high so that people would be able to access works of folklore. This is a practical aspect of the system'.[54]

---

[52]   This is also expressed in article 1 of the Code du Patrimoine of 1994, which states that the cultural heritage belongs to the public domain of the state. During the WIPO fact-finding missions on intellectual property and traditional knowledge which took place from 27 February to 13 March 1999, the understanding that the property rights in cultural heritage and folklore should be vested in the state was identified as being common to the Arab countries which the mission visited during that period, namely the Sultanate of Oman, the State of Qatar, the Arab Republic of Egypt and the State of Tunisia.

[53]   Author's translation from French following an interview in October 2003.

[54]   Author's translation from French following an interview in October 2003.

An application for authorisation can be made for many works at a time. The authorisations are not exclusive, different people can be granted an authorisation for the same work of folklore at the same time.

The fact that an authorisation is required in the case of exploitation with a gainful intent seems to exclude the fixation of folklore with a view to a non-commercial exploitation. According to Nébila Mezghani, '[t]he text does not seem to oppose such fixation; the fixation of folklore by an individual, for his personal pleasure, or by a body, without gainful intent, is therefore permitted'.[55]

Article 7(2) provides that an authorisation from the Ministry responsible for culture is also required for the production of works inspired by folklore, as well as for the full or partial assignment of copyright in a work inspired by folklore or for an exclusive licence with respect to such work. This is an improvement to the Law of 1966, which did not require an authorisation for the production of works inspired by folklore, but only for their total or partial assignment, or for the grant of an exclusive licence relating to a work inspired by folklore. This provision is understandable since folklore, which is the source of the work, cannot itself be fixed for exploitation with gainful intent without the prior authorisation of the Ministry responsible for culture.

Finally, contrary to the Law of 1966, which defined 'a work inspired by folklore' as a 'work composed with the aid of elements borrowed from the cultural traditional patrimony of the Tunisian Republic', the Law of 1994 gives a non-exhaustive definition of 'folklore' as 'any artistic heritage bequeathed by preceding generations and bound up with customs and traditions and any aspect of folk creation such as folk stories, writings, music and dance'. This definition, which is very broad, leaves room for interpretation.

Infringement

Article 51 of the Law of 1994 deals with infringement of copyright. It states that:

> Any person who infringes recognised copyright in any protected work as set out in Article 2 of this Law shall be required to pay to the owner of such right damages of which the amount shall be determined by the competent court.
>
> Infringement of copyright shall be deemed proven where the user of the work is unable to furnish the authorisation referred to in Article 2 of this Law.

Consequently, any person who infringes article 7, and who does not have an authorisation from the Ministry responsible for culture, could be liable to pay damages to the owner of the copyright. Since there is not one single copyright

---

[55] See Mezghani, 'Letter from Tunisia', *supra* note 32, 267.

owner in the case of folklore, but the copyright belongs to the collective memory of the people of Tunisia, and in the absence of any known precedent, it is presumed that the damages would be awarded to the social fund of the OTPDA (see below).

2.4.5   The Tunisian Body for the Protection of Authors' Rights

The Organisme Tunisien de Protection des Droits d'Auteurs (OTPDA) (Tunisian Body for the Protection of Authors' Rights) was set up by article 48 of the Law of 1994. It replaces the Société des Auteurs et des Compositeurs de Tunisie (SODACT) (Society of the Authors and Composers of Tunisia). The role performed by SODACT since its establishment in 1968 did not prove very effective on either the national or the international scene. This was a result of the extreme inadequacy of the resources made available to it. For this reason, the legislator set up a new copyright body to replace it.[56] However, even though the establishment of the OTPDA was planned in the Law of 1994, the OTPDA only came into existence in 1999.

The OTPDA is a public establishment of an industrial and commercial nature that enjoys legal personality and financial autonomy. It is under the authority and the supervision of the Ministry responsible for culture and consists of a Board, a Managing Director, an Advisory Committee and members. The OTPDA is responsible for defending and handling author's rights and safeguarding the moral and economic interests of authors. In addition, as Mohamed Kheireddine Abdel Ali indicated, 'the aim of the OTPDA is also to make public opinion become sensitive to the issues of copyright protection'.[57]

The powers and structure of the OTPDA were set up by Decree No. 96-2230 of 11 November 1996 establishing the Administrative and Financial Functioning Organisation of the Tunisian Copyright Office ('the Decree'). Its functioning, on the other hand, was established by the OTPDA's Rules of Procedure that were drawn up by the governing board of the OTPDA and approved by the Minister of Culture.

Articles 23 and 24 of the Decree provide for the establishment of a social and cultural fund that should be made up, amongst other things, of income derived from the exploitation of folklore belonging to the national heritage, in pursuance of article 7 of the Law of 1994. They further provide that the OTPDA shall be in charge of administering the rights, the proceeds of which are paid into the social and cultural fund. The organisation, administration and conditions under which the royalties may be used on behalf of the creators and

---

[56]   See Mezghani, 'The New Tunisian Body', *supra* note 32, 30.
[57]   Author's translation from French following an interview in October 2003.

their heirs are laid down by the Rules of Procedure. They establish, amongst other things, the fixing of the amounts of royalties, the method of collecting royalties and the rules for the apportionment of the royalties and the various schedules for their periodic distribution.

2.4.6 Documentation and Conservation of Folklore

In Tunisia, the protection of folklore operates at two levels. On the one hand, there is the legal protection of folklore, described above, and on the other, there is the material protection of folklore. The material protection of folklore, which is mainly achieved through a documentation process, has a dual function:

- the effective protection of folklore from illicit exploitation;
- the safeguarding of Tunisian cultural identity, historical continuity and social community in a time of rapid modernisation.[58]

The documentation and conservation of Tunisian folklore is carried out by various institutions, which come under the authority of the Ministry for Culture, Youth and Leisure. Their main tasks are to carry out studies and research on Tunisia's cultural heritage, collect data and ensure the fixation of the cultural heritage in order to allow its exploitation as a source of creativity and enrichment.[59]

The Institut National du Patrimoine is in charge of organising and performing the excavation and inventory of the archaeological and historical heritage of Tunisia, and of collecting the traditional cultural heritage and popular arts, making an inventory of them, and displaying them.[60] In addition, the Institut National du Patrimoine has played an important role in the identification and documentation process of traditional Tunisian clothes and jewellery.

The Centre de Musiques Arabes et Méditerranéennes Ennejma Ezzahra (the Centre of Arab and Mediterranean music Ennejma Ezzahra), in Sidi Bou Said, is in charge of contributing to the protection of the musical heritage of Tunisia (works and musical instruments). It is entrusted with collecting, recording and managing the national sound archives.[61] The Centre, which was established in

---

[58] See WIPO Report, *supra* note 44, 162 and Document WIPO/GRTKF/IC/4/INF/3.

[59] Document WIPO/GRTKF/IC/4/INF/3.

[60] Article 3 of Decree No. 93-1609 of 26 July 1993, which lays down the functions and organisation of the Institut National du Patrimoine.

[61] As provided for in Decree No. 94-2137 of 10 October 1994, which lays down the functions and organisation of the Centre de Musiques Arabes et Méditerranéennes Ennejma Ezzahra.

1991, is a public establishment enjoying legal personality and financial autonomy. Its main objectives are the documentation and conservation of expressions of traditional Arabic and Mediterranean music, the establishment of a
database comprising an extensive and almost exhaustive set of recordings of
traditional Tunisian music, the publication and making available of such music
to the public, the publication of studies and research on traditional Tunisian,
Arabic and Mediterranean music, and the organisation of concerts.[62]

Finally, the Bibliothèque Nationale (the National Library), is in charge of
collecting the written, printed, photocopied or otherwise recorded national
cultural heritage and to ensure its restoration and conservation.[63]

2.4.7   Conclusion

Tunisia has been praised for being the first country to introduce an article dealing specifically with the protection of folklore in its copyright law in 1966.
However, it was not until the adoption of the Law of 1994, and the setting up
of the OTPDA, that the system for the protection of folklore was properly
established.

Since its creation in 1999, the OTPDA has reported that only a few applications for authorisation were made for the transcription of folklore with a
view to exploitation for profit or for the production of works inspired by folklore, for the assignment of copyright in these works, or for the grant of an
exclusive licence with respect to these works.[64] These applications were
usually successful. In fact, no precise criteria for the refusal of an application
were given, other than the fact that the applicant needed to seem able to exploit
folklore, that is, 'to have a minimum of knowledge and know-how'.[65] In addition, the annual royalty that has to be paid to the social fund of the OTPDA,

---

[62]   WIPO Report, *supra* note 44, and Document WIPO/GRTKF/IC/5/3.

[63]   As provided for in Decree No. 94-559 of 15 March 1994, which lays down
the functions and organisation of the Bibliothèque Nationale.

[64]   Although most examples relate to applications filed by Tunisian nationals,
one application to use Tunisian folklore was brought by Microsoft Ltd London. In
2000, Microsoft Ltd London required authorisation from the Ministry of Culture to use
a fragment of Nouba Dhil, which is a category of music that belongs to Tunisia's musical cultural heritage, in order to insert it in its series of 'Encarta Interactive World
Atlas'. The Ministry of Culture agreed, in principle, in return for an exploitation
contract. The contract was drafted in French by the staff of the OTPDA. Microsoft Ltd
London requested an English translation that was not provided by the OTPDA. This
resulted in the application procedure being brought to an end. However, this example
shows that, although in the end it did not result in a successful authorisation, article 7
of the Law of 1994 was taken into account by a foreign company. Information provided
by the OTPDA in October 2003.

[65]   Ibid.

20 dinars, is a derisory compensation for the exploitation with gainful intent of a work of folklore.

Despite the fact that Tunisia is the country with the longest tradition in the copyright protection of TCEs, its experience in this field is still very recent, and because of the lack of case law and the relatively modest amount of practical experience in this area, it is still early to draw conclusions as to the efficiency of the Tunisian system for the legal protection of folklore. However, in view of the rapid progress that the country experienced in the area of copyright protection, and the development of adequate administrative infrastructure to manage folklore that has been set up over the past few years, it remains to be seen whether the Tunisian regime for the protection of TCEs will prove to be efficient.

2.5   THE AUSTRALIAN EXPERIENCE

2.5.1   Introduction

In Australia, over the past decades, there has been a proliferation of Aboriginal designs being reproduced without the consent of the artist or relevant clan group, resulting in an increased commodification of native culture and sometimes causing great offence. In recent years, indigenous artists have had some success in taking action for copyright infringement in court. This part will present the most relevant Australian cases, which have raised awareness in the indigenous arts industry, and have helped reduce copyright infringements.

2.5.2   Australian Case Law

Since the High Court's recognition, in *Mabo and Ors v State of Queensland*,[66] of the capacity of the common law to recognise traditional Aboriginal land law, there have been increasing demands for legislation to acknowledge the validity of other aspects of traditional Aboriginal law.[67] One of these aspects relates to reproductions of traditional Aboriginal designs, which are of significance to Aboriginal religious beliefs and cultural identity, on a number of products aimed at the tourist industry, ranging from tea-towels and T-shirts to carpets and wall hangings.

---

[66]   *Mabo and Ors v State of Queensland* (1992) 175 CLR 1. In this case, the legal fiction that Australia was uninhabited when the Europeans invaded it was overturned, and the court found that indigenous customary law existed at that time.

[67]   See Michael Blakeney, 'Protecting Expressions of Australian Aboriginal Folklore under Copyright Law' (1995) 9 *EIPR* 442.

One of the earlier cases, *Foster v Mountford*,[68] concerned a situation where an anthropologist had collected information from the Pitjantjatjara people in central Australia in the 1940s, including information concerning sacred sites and objects, stories and secrets, paintings and drawings, and published it in a book in 1976. An action was brought by the Pitjantjatjara Council on behalf of the community to try to prevent the sale of the book. The Supreme Court of the Northern Territory found that the information was of deep religious and cultural significance and that its publication amounted to breach of confidence. The court granted an injunction to prevent the sale of the book. In particular, it noted that the revelation of the secrets to their women, children and uninitiated men might undermine the religious stability of their hard-pressed community.[69]

However, this case concerned information obtained in confidence, and the law relating to breach of confidence cannot be invoked to prevent the unauthorised dissemination or reproduction of Aboriginal designs which are already in the public domain.

The following cases deal with the extent to which copyright law may assist in preventing the unauthorised reproduction of such designs.

Bulun Bulun v Nejlam Pty Ltd[70]

In this case, a painting by Mr Johnny Bulun Bulun, a successful Aboriginal artist, was reproduced on T-shirts, without his knowledge or permission. Subsequently, a revised version of the T-shirt was created, which drew on another one of Mr Bulun Bulun's paintings, as well as the original painting. This adapted version also incorporated a number of minor design features taken from works of other artists, without their permission. The T-shirt designs were called 'At the Waterhole', this being the name used in association with a number of Mr Bulun Bulun's *Waterhole* works. In 1989, Mr Bulun Bulun initiated legal proceedings against the T-shirt manufacturer for infringement of copyright under the Copyright Act 1968 and breaches of the Trade Practices Act 1974 in the Federal Court in Darwin.[71]

In his affidavit,[72] Mr Bulun Bulun deposed that he was the author of the works in question, and that they were original works. He explained the signif-

---

68   *Foster v Mountford* (1976–78) 29 FLR 233.
69   Ibid. 236.
70   *Bulun Bulun v Nejlam Pty Ltd*, Federal Court of Australia, Darwin, 1989 (unreported). On this case, see Colin Golvan, 'Aboriginal Art and Copyright: The Case for Johnny Bulun Bulun' (1989) 11 *EIPR* 346–55.
71   Ibid. 347.
72   This affidavit was prepared for the interlocutory injunction stage of the proceedings but it was not actually relied upon. Ibid. 347.

icance of the imagery in his paintings and exposed his suffering due to the unauthorised reproduction of his artwork:

> [I] never approved of the reproduction of any of my artworks on T-shirts, and never approved the mass reproduction of any of my artwork, other than the reproduction of photos of my works in art books … Had [the respondents] sought my permission, I would not have given it.

> My work is closely associated with an affinity for the land. This affinity is at the essence of my religious beliefs. The unauthorized reproduction of artworks is a very sensitive issue in all Aboriginal communities. The impetus for the creation of works remains their importance in ceremony, and the creation of artworks is an important step in the preservation of important traditional customs … It is also the main source of income for my people, both in my tribe and for people of many other tribes …

> The reproduction has caused me great embarrassment and shame, and I strongly feel that I have been the victim of the theft of an important birthright. I have not painted since I learned about the reproduction of my artworks, and attribute my inactivity as an artist directly to my annoyance and frustration with the actions of the respondents in this matter.[73]

The manufacturers and two Darwin tourist shops which sold the T-shirts gave undertakings to the court agreeing to cease manufacturing and selling T-shirts, and to deliver up all remaining stocks of T-shirts. The case was eventually settled before trial in an agreement which required the T-shirt manufacturers to withdraw all infringing T-shirts from sale and pay a substantial amount in damages.

The outcome of this case was described as a landmark for Aboriginal artists as their rights in their work were formally recognized by means of undertakings given to a court.[74]

Yumbulul v Reserve Bank of Australia[75]
This pre-*Mabo* case concerned the issue by the Reserve Bank of Australia of a special AUS$10 banknote to commemorate the first European settlement in Australia that reproduced elements of Aboriginal artworks, including the reproduction of a design of a Morning Star Pole created by Terry Yumbulul, an Aboriginal artist. The reproduction was made under a sub-licence of the copyright in the work granted to the bank by the Aboriginal Artists Agency Ltd, which, in turn, had an exclusive licence from Mr Yumbulul.[76]

---

73 Ibid. 348.
74 Ibid. 347.
75 *Yumbulul v Reserve Bank of Australia* (1991) 21 IPR 481.
76 Ibid.

Following the reproduction of the Morning Star Pole by the bank, Mr Yumbulul came under considerable criticism from within his community for allowing that to happen.[77] Poles have a central role in Aboriginal ceremonies commemorating the death of important persons, and inter-clan relationships, and the makers of poles have a cultural obligation to ensure that a pole is not used or reproduced in a way which offends against their perceptions and significance.

Mr Yumbulul brought an action against the Aboriginal Artists Agency Ltd and the Reserve Bank of Australia claiming that his copyright had been infringed by an unauthorised reproduction of his artistic work. In addition, he claimed that the licence to the Aboriginal Artists Agency was invalid because he had not understood the nature of the agreement and that, because of that, the licence was granted as a result of false, misleading or unconscionable conduct.[78]

The court found the pole to be an original artistic work of Mr Yumbulul, within the meaning of the Copyright Act 1968, and that the artist's copyright had been validly assigned.[79] It rejected Mr Yumbulul's claims and found that he had not granted the licence as a mistake. French J recognised that:

[This case] demonstrates difficulties that arise in the interaction of traditional Aboriginal culture and the Australian legal system relating to the protection of copyright and the commercial exploitation of artistic works by Aboriginal people.[80]

It may [...] be [the case] that Australia's copyright law does not provide adequate recognition of Aboriginal community claims to regulate the reproduction and use of works which are essentially communal in origin.[81]

However, he concluded that:

The question of statutory recognition of Aboriginal communal interests in the reproduction of sacred objects is a matter for consideration by law reformers and legislators.[82]

Milpurrurru and Ors v Indofurn Pty Ltd and Ors[83]

The Federal Court decision in *Milpurrurru and Ors v Indofurn Pty Ltd and Ors* was the first post-*Mabo* case to consider the extent to which copyright law may assist in preventing the unauthorised reproduction of Aboriginal designs.

---

[77]   Ibid. 490.
[78]   Ibid. 481.
[79]   Ibid. 484.
[80]   Ibid. 482.
[81]   Ibid. 490.
[82]   Ibid. 492.
[83]   *Milpurrurru and Ors v Indofurn Pty and Ors* (1994–95) 30 IPR 209. On this case, see Blakeney, *supra* note 67.

It concerned the importation into Australia and sale of carpets manufactured in Vietnam that reproduced the works of several prominent Aboriginal artists. The claimants were three living artists and the public trustee of the Northern Territory, representing the estates of five deceased artists. The respondents were Mr Bethune, an Australian entrepreneur, Indofurn, a Perth-based import company through which Mr Bethune carried on business, and the company's two directors. The artworks were owned by the Australian National Gallery, other museums, commissioned or otherwise exhibited nationally and internationally. They had been reproduced in a portfolio of Aboriginal art published by the Australian Information Service and a portfolio of artworks and calendar published by the Australian National Gallery.[84] In each of these publications, the reproductions of the artworks were published over the name of the artist and with the artist's permission. The carpets reproduced seven of the eight artworks in identical form and colour, while the eighth artwork was substantially reproduced, although in a simplified form.[85]

Each carpet was affixed with a swing tag that read:

> These unique wall hangings and rugs have been designed by Aboriginal artists from areas throughout Australia. These artists are paid royalties on every carpet sold … As carpet weaving is not a tradition of the Aboriginal people, the rugs are produced in Vietnam where we can combine the artistic skills of the Aboriginal people with the weaving traditions of the Vietnamese … [W]e have achieved a blending of the talents of these people to produce original artistic creations.[86]

However, the defendant had no agreement with the Aboriginal artists whose paintings he copied, did not have their authorisation to reproduce the artworks, and did not pay them any royalties.

The subject matter of the artworks concerned creation stories and dreamings of spiritual and sacred significance to the applicants and the cultures of the groups to which the artists belonged. Evidence was tendered that illustrated their significance and the importance that they be portrayed accurately:

> Those stories are represented in ceremonies of deep significance, and are often secret and sacred, known only to a few senior members of the clan … Painting techniques, and the use of totemic and other images and symbols are in many instances, and almost invariably in the case of important creation stories strictly controlled by Aboriginal law and customs. Artworks are an important means of recording these stories, and for teaching future generations. Accuracy in the portrayal of the story is of great importance. Inaccuracy, or error in the faithful reproduction of an artwork, can cause deep offence to those familiar with the dreaming.[87]

---

[84]　Ibid. 209.
[85]　Ibid. 213.
[86]　Ibid. 248.
[87]　Ibid. 214.

Evidence was further provided to describe the system of traditional collective ownership that applies to such artworks and the consequences of their unauthorised reproduction:

> The right to create paintings and other artworks depicting creation and dreaming stories, and to use pre-existing designs and well recognised totems of the clan, resides in the traditional owners (or custodians) of the stories or images ... [w]ho together have the authority to determine whether the story and images may be used in an artwork, by whom the artwork may be created, to whom it may be published, and the terms, if any, on which the artwork may be reproduced.[88]
>
> If unauthorised reproduction of a story or imagery occurs, under Aboriginal law it is the responsibility of the traditional owners to take action to preserve the dreaming, and to punish those considered responsible for the breach ... If permission has been given by the traditional owners to a particular artist to create a picture of the dreaming, and that artwork is later inappropriately used or reproduced by a third party, the artist is held responsible for the breach which has occurred, even if the artist had no control, or knowledge, of what occurred.[89]

While the authorised display of such artworks in art galleries or publication for educational purposes could be acceptable when carried out with appropriate sensitivity, the reproduction of these artworks in circumstances where the dreaming would be walked on could cause great offence and result in the punishment of the artist. Such punishment could include the removal of the right to reproduce paintings of a given story, or being outcast from the community.[90]

The claimants sued for copyright infringement claiming that they had a valid copyright in the paintings and that Indofurn had violated their exclusive rights under the Copyright Act 1968 by importing and selling in Australia carpets that reproduced and/or adapted each of the artworks or substantial parts of them. The court agreed with the claimants and found infringement of copyright in each of the eight artworks, as well as contravention in the Trade Practices Act 1974.

When assessing remedies, Von Doussa J noted that statutory remedies did not normally recognise the infringement of ownership rights of the kind which reside under Aboriginal law in the traditional owners of dreaming and creation stories. In a typical copyright case, the measure of damages would be related to the depreciation of the value of the copyright. Von Doussa J accepted that in the present case, the action of the company did not cause economic loss to the artists, since they had no intention of commercialising the works. On this basis, a modest award of damages was made to reflect the damaging effect of

---

88   Ibid.
89   Ibid.
90   Ibid. 215.

the carpets on the reputation of the artworks and their loss of 'freshness'.[91] However, his Honour noted that in that case, the damages sustained extended beyond the commercial potential for monetary return, particularly in the case of the living artists. He noted that the infringements had caused personal distress and potentially exposed the artists to embarrassment and contempt within their communities, if not to the risk of diminished earning potential and physical harm. Finally, the court also awarded additional damages on the basis that the firm had been guilty of a particularly flagrant disregard of the artist's rights.

Bulun Bulun and Anor v R&T Textiles Pty Ltd and Anor[92]

In this case, the defendant, R&T Textiles Pty Ltd, imported and sold printed clothing fabric into Australia, which reproduced a painting of Mr Bulun Bulun entitled 'Magpie Geese and Water Lilies at the Waterhole'. The claimants, Mr Bulun Bulun and Mr Milpurrurru, were both renowned artists and senior members of the Ganalbingu people of Arnhem Land in the Northern Territory. Mr Bulun Bulun painted the work in 1978 with the permission of senior members of the Ganalbingu people.[93]

Mr Bulun Bulun sued R&T Textiles Pty Ltd as the legal owner of the copyright in the painting and sought remedies for infringement under the Australian Copyright Act 1968. The defendant admitted infringement of copyright in the artistic work, withdrew the infringing fabric from sale and consented to final declarations that they had infringed Mr Bulun Bulun's legal title to the copyright in the artistic work and comprehensive permanent legal injunctions against future infringement.[94]

Mr Milpurrurru, acting in his own right and as a representative of the Ganalbingu tribe, claimed that the traditional Aboriginal owners of Ganalbingu country were the equitable owners of the copyright subsisting in the painting.[95] In its defence against Mr Milpurrurru's claims, the defendant argued that as Mr Bulun Bulun's claim had been satisfied, it was unnecessary to consider the question of the equitable ownership of the copyright. Mr Milpurrurru sought to continue the action as a test case on communal

---

[91] Ibid. 243.

[92] *Bulun Bulun and Anor v R&T Textiles Pty and Anor* (1998) 41 IPR 513. On this case see Michael Blakeney, 'Communal Intellectual Property Rights of Indigenous Peoples in Cultural Expressions' (1998) 1 *JWIP* 985–1002; Michael Hall, 'Case Note: Bulun Bulun v R & T Textiles' (1998) 16 *Copyright Reporter* 124–35; Terri Janke, *Minding Culture: Case Studies on Intellectual Property and Traditional Cultural Expressions* (WIPO: Geneva, 2003) 50–68.

[93] *Bulun Bulun and Anor, supra*, note 92, 513.

[94] Ibid. 515–16.

[95] Ibid. 515.

intellectual property rights of indigenous Australian peoples arising from copyright infringement.[96]

Mr Milpurrurru's submissions reflected a wide-ranging search for a way in which the communal interests of the traditional Aboriginal owners in cultural artworks might be recognised under copyright law. In particular, the court had to consider whether these communal interests created binding legal or equitable obligations on persons outside the relevant Aboriginal community.[97]

On the issue of legal obligation, while the court recognised that customary Aboriginal laws relating to the ownership of artistic work survived the introduction of the common law of England in 1788, they were abolished when the law of copyright was codified in Australia. Von Doussa J noted that the exclusive domain of the Copyright Act 1968 in Australia was expressed in section 8, namely that 'copyright does not subsist otherwise than by virtue of the Act', making it impossible for Australian common law to recognise a legal obligation in the communal interests of traditional Aboriginal owners in cultural artwork. Von Doussa J found that to conclude that the Ganalbingu people were communal owners of the copyright in the existing work would ignore the provisions of section 8 of the Copyright Act, and involve the creation of rights in indigenous people which are not otherwise recognised by the legal system of Australia.[98]

On the issue of equitable obligation, it was submitted that copyright subsisted in the artistic work as a fiduciary and/or alternatively on trust.[99] In particular, it was contended that:

> These rights arise because Mr [M] and those he represents have the power under customary law to regulate and control the production and reproduction of the corpus of ritual knowledge. It is contended that the customs and traditions regulating this use of the corpus of ritual knowledge places Mr Bulun Bulun as the author of the artistic work in the position of a fiduciary, and, moreover, make Mr Bulun Bulun a trustee for the artwork, either pursuant to some form of express trust, or pursuant to a constructive trust in favour of the Ganalbingu people.[100]

The court found that there was no evidence of an express or implied trust created in respect of Mr Bulun Bulun's art. Von Doussa J held that this was a question of evidence and that Mr Bulun Bulun's behaviour did not indicate an

---

[96]   Ibid. 516.
[97]   Ibid. 524.
[98]   Ibid. 524–5.
[99]   Ibid. 526.
[100] Ibid.

intention to create a trust, nor was there any practice among the Ganalbingu people whereby artworks were held in trust.[101]

In the absence of an express trust, Von Doussa J examined the existence of a fiduciary relationship between Mr Bulun Bulun and the Ganalbingu people. He quoted a passage from the judgment of Mason J in *Hospital Products Ltd v US Surgical Corporation*[102] that described the essential characteristics of fiduciary relationships:

> The critical feature of [fiduciary] relationships is that the fiduciary undertakes or agrees to act for or on behalf of or in the interests of another person in the exercise of a power or discretion which will affect the interests of that other person in a legal or practical sense. The relationship between the parties is therefore one which gives the fiduciary a special opportunity to exercise the power or discretion to the detriment of that other person who is accordingly vulnerable to abuse by the fiduciary of his position ... It is partly because the fiduciary's exercise of the power or discretion can adversely affect the interests of the person to whom the duty is owed and because the latter is at the mercy of the former that the fiduciary comes under a duty to exercise his power or discretion in the interests of the person to whom it is owed.[103]

Applying this principle, Von Doussa J found the subsistence of a fiduciary relationship between Mr Bulun Bulun and the Ganalbingu people. He said that this relationship arose out of the trust and confidence placed in Mr Bulun Bulun by the Ganalbingu people, which was manifested by the use with permission by Mr Bulun Bulun of ritual knowledge of the Ganalbingu people in accordance with their the law and customs, and the embodiment of that knowledge within the artistic work.[104]

Von Doussa J held that equity imposed obligations on Mr Bulun Bulun not to exploit the artistic work in a way contrary to the laws and customs of the Ganalbingu people, and, in any event of infringement by a third party, to take reasonable and appropriate action to restrain and remedy infringement of the copyright in the artistic work. However, the existence of these obligations did not vest an equitable interest in the ownership of the copyright in the Ganalbingu people. Instead, the primary right, in the event of breach of obligation by the fiduciary was a right *in personam* to bring action against the fiduciary to enforce the obligation.[105]

In the present case, Mr Bulun Bulun had successfully taken action against the respondent to obtain remedies in respect of the infringement, so there was

---

[101]   Ibid. 526–7.
[102]   *Hospital Products Ltd v US Surgical Corporation* (1984) 156 CLR 41
[103]   See *Bulun Bulun and Anor, supra* note 92, 528.
[104]   Ibid. 529–30.
[105]   Ibid. 531.

no occasion for the intervention of equity to provide additional remedy to the beneficiaries of the fiduciary relationship.

2.5.3   Conclusion

The Federal Court decision in *Milpurrurru and Ors v Indofurn Pty Ltd and Ors* was the first post-*Mabo* case to consider the extent to which copyright law may assist in preventing the unauthorised reproduction of Aboriginal designs. It represents a step forward from previous case law. Indeed, *Bulun Bulun v Nejlam Pty Ltd* only constituted an implicit victory, as the case was settled before trial. As for *Yumbulul v Reserve Bank of Australia*, although the court recognised that Australia's copyright law did not provide adequate recognition of Aboriginal community claims in relation to the reproduction and use of works which are communal in origin, it concluded that this was a matter for consideration by law reformers and legislators.

In *Milpurrurru*, the court recognised that the claimant had a valid copyright and that damages, especially in the case of living artists, extended beyond the commercial potential for monetary return. In particular, infringement could cause personal distress, expose the artists to embarrassment and contempt within their communities, and to the risk of diminished earning potential and physical harm. In *Bulun Bulun and Anor v R&T Textiles Pty Ltd and Anor*, the court found the subsistence of a fiduciary relationship between the claimant artist and his tribe, which imposed obligations on the artist not to exploit an artistic work in a way contrary to the laws and customs of the tribe and to take reasonable and appropriate action to restrain and remedy infringement of the copyright in the work.

While some of these cases show that copyright law may, to some extent, assist in preventing the unauthorised reproduction of Aboriginal artistic works and help reduce copyright infringements, it should be noted that this will only be possible if the Aboriginal artists and the artistic works in question comply with the conditions of protection of the Copyright Act. For example, whereas the court recognised that the claimants had a valid copyright in *Milpurrurru* and *Bulun Bulun*, this would not be the case if the artistic works that were reproduced were already in the public domain.[106]

---

[106]   The limitations of the copyright system to protect TCEs are discussed in detail *infra* para. 2.7.

2.6   THE CHINESE EXPERIENCE

2.6.1   Introduction

The treatment of TCEs in the countries comprising East and Southeast Asia has been extremely diverse and derives mainly from existing intellectual property laws in each jurisdiction. None of these countries has passed a new *sui generis* law on the protection of TCEs and there have been no cooperative efforts amongst the countries of Southeast Asia for the establishment of a common policy on the protection of TCEs despite their common membership in the Association of Southeast Asian Nations (ASEAN). Instead there have been some attempts, at the national level, to protect TCEs.

Some countries have attempted to protect TCEs within their copyright laws, either by referring to TCEs as a form of copyright work, or by including provisions specifically designed for the protection of TCEs within their copyright legislation.

In Indonesia, TCEs are simply referred to as a form of copyright work within the part on works of unknown authors. Article 10 of the Law of the Republic of Indonesia No. 19 Year 2002 Regarding Copyright provides that the state shall hold the copyright in prehistoric remains, historical and other national cultural objects.[107] The article further provides that:

> The State shall hold the Copyright for folklores and works of popular culture that are commonly owned, such as stories, legends, folk tales, epics, songs, handicrafts, choreography, dances, calligraphies and other artistic works.[108]

To publish or reproduce those works, any person who is not a citizen of Indonesia shall, first, seek permission from the institution related to the matter.[109]

In Vietnam, Law No. 50-2005-QH11 on Intellectual Property contains a provision, within its part on copyright and related rights, on the protection of folklore and folk artworks. It states that:

> Folklore and folk work means a collective creation based on the traditions of a community or individuals reflecting the ambitions of such community and expressed in a form appropriate to the cultural and social characteristics, standards and values of such community which have been handed down by imitation or other modes.[110]

---

[107]   Law of the Republic of Indonesia No. 19 Year 2002 Regarding Copyright, art. 10(1).
[108]   Ibid. art. 10(2).
[109]   Ibid. art. 10(3).
[110]   Law No. 50-2005-QH11 on Intellectual Property, art. 23(1).

The provision goes on to give a non-exhaustive list of such works, including for example folk tales, lyrics and riddles, folk songs and melodies, folk dances, plays, rites and games, folk art products including graphics, paintings, sculpture, musical instruments, architectural models and other artistic expressions in any material form.[111] Finally, it provides that:

> Organisations and individuals using folklore and folk artworks must cite the origins of the folklore and folk artworks, and must ensure that the authentic value of such folklore and folk artworks is preserved.[112]

While these provisions recognise that TCEs should, to some extent, be protected within national copyright law, the level of protection afforded to them is very limited. The Indonesian law does not recognise the ownership of TCEs by indigenous communities. Instead, it implies that TCEs belong to the national heritage of the state and form part of the public domain of the state. As a consequence, TCEs, which are commonly owned, can be appropriated and exploited by any citizen of Indonesia. The protection afforded by the Vietnamese law, on the other hand, is equally limited as it simply consists of a moral right of paternity and does not recognise any economic rights over folklore or folk works nor does it provide any defence against their adaptation or unauthorised exploitation.

In China, a recent case highlighted the importance of the concept of 'derivative work' in relation to modern adaptations of traditional music.

2.6.2   The 17 December 2003 Decision of the Beijing Higher People's Court in Case No. 246 (2003) (final)

In 2003, the Beijing Higher People's Court issued a decision in a case involving a dispute between a modern composer of a traditional ethnic minority song and the ethnic Hezhe minority.[113]

In 1962, Guo Song conducted a field study in the area where the ethnic Hezhe lived and collected a number of folk songs. Based on these songs, Guo Song and two others composed the contemporary song known as 'Wusuli Chantey'. This was reported in a number of separate publications of traditional folk song collections, which stated that 'Wusuli Chantey' was a song of the ethnic Hezhe minority but was composed by Guo Song and two colleagues.

---

[111]   Ibid. art. 23(2).
[112]   Ibid. art. 23(3).
[113]   See 17 December 2003 Decision of the Beijing Higher People's Court in Case No. 246 (2003) (final) (2006) 37 *IIC* 482–7.

On 12 November 1999, the local government of Nanning City and the Chinese Central Television (CCTV) organised an international folk song festival, which featured the performance of the song 'Wusuli Chantey' by Guo Song. After the performance, a presenter announced that although the song had previously been presented as an adaptation from traditional Hezhe folk songs, it was actually an original composition. In addition, the CDs containing the songs of the festival did not mention that 'Wusuli Chantey' was an adaptation either.

The local government of the ethnic Hezhe people, which was given standing by the Beijing People's Second Intermediate Court, to litigate on behalf of the ethnic Hezhe minority[114] claimed that the folk songs on which 'Wusuli Chantey' was based had been transmitted from generation to generation, belonged collectively to the ethnic Hezhe and should be protected under copyright law.[115] The court agreed with an appraisal of the Chinese Music Copyright Association, that while the beginning and ending of 'Wusuli Chantey' were new compositions, the rhythm element of the main part of that song was similar to several traditional Hezhe folk songs.[116] The court held that 'Wusuli Chantey' should be identified as an adaptation rather than an original composition and that when using that song in the future, Guo Song and CCTV should state that it is an adaptation of the folk songs of the ethnic Hezhe. In addition, any product or broadcast involving the songs should recognise their contribution.[117] On 17 December 2003, the Beijing Higher People's Court confirmed the judgment of the first instance.[118]

This is an important decision, the impact of which should not be underestimated. It recognises that an ethnic group whose traditional musical work has been adapted within a modern song by a third party has valid claims to have authorship attributed to it for the use of the folk song within a modern work. Although the court found no infringement on the part of the modern adapter, where the adapter failed to recognise the contribution of the ethnic group's folk song in the modern work, it provided a form of civil protection over the use of folklore,[119] by establishing that it is unfair to adapt a traditional song, even if the song was in the public domain, and recognised the moral right of paternity of a collective group over a traditional song.

---

114 Ibid. 482–3.
115 Ibid. 482.
116 Ibid.
117 Ibid. 483.
118 Ibid. 487.
119 See Bryan Bachner, 'Comment on the 17 December 2003 Decision of the Beijing Higher People's Court in Case No. 246 (2003) (final)' (2006) 37 *IIC* 488.

In addition, the court established that despite the fact that copyright law does not set out clearly who controls proprietary rights over folkloric works and the difficulty of identifying the author of such works, the administrative unit that governs an ethnic group may represent that ethnic group in defending copyright infringement claims over its folk works.[120] It is interesting to note that on this point, the court's view was in line with the position taken by the Berne Convention, that due to the problems raised by the definition of folklore, the absence of an identifiable author or authors, and the fact that they were often already in the public domain, it was difficult for works of folklore to be included in the enumeration of literary and artistic works in Article 2(1) of the Berne Convention.[121] As a consequence, a work of folklore is considered to be, by definition, the work of an unknown author and it is a matter for legislation in each country to designate the competent authority which shall represent the author and shall be entitled to protect and enforce their rights. In effect, while not explicitly mentioning international law, the court followed Article 15(4) of the Berne Convention by allowing a governmental unit to represent the interests of unknown authors of folkloric works.[122]

2.6.3 Conclusion

Despite this encouraging outcome, it should be noted that: (i) the court found no infringement on the part of the modern adapters, where they failed to recognise the contribution of an ethnic group's folk song in a modern work; (ii) no damages were awarded for the lack of acknowledgement of such contribution; (iii) the court left open the question of economic rights of an ethnic group over its works of folklore; and (iv) the court did not recognise the right of an ethnic group to defend its folklore against unauthorised uses.

This court's decision, which was based on articles 6[123] and 12 of the 1990 Copyright Law of the People's Republic of China, as amended in 2001, was recently reinforced by the 2006 amendment to the Chinese Copyright Law. Former article 12 provided that:

> Where a work is created by adaptation, translation, annotation or arrangement of a pre-existing work, the copyright in the work thus created shall be enjoyed by the adapter, translator, annotator or arranger, provided that the exercise of such copyright does not prejudice the copyright in the pre-existing work.

---

120   Ibid.
121   See *supra* para. 2.2.1.
122   See Bachner, *supra* note 119.
123   Article 6 provided that measures for the protection of copyright in works of folk literature and art should be formulated separately by the State Council. The State Council, however, never implemented those measures.

It was replaced by a more explicit provision to the effect that:

> A performance by a performer of a pre-existing work or folklore shall be protected as an independent work. Protection of a performance shall not affect the copyright in the pre-existing work.[124]

2.7 CONCLUSION: EFFICIENCY AND LIMITATIONS OF COPYRIGHT LAW TO PROTECT TCES

2.7.1 Limitations Relating to the Conditions for the Grant of Copyright

In order for a work to be protected by copyright law, several criteria must be fulfilled, which may vary from one jurisdiction to the other. However, because of their nature, in many instances TCEs appear unable to fulfil the conditions for the grant of copyright protection.[125]

Originality
In order to be protected by copyright law, literary and artistic works must be original. Although this requirement is not explicitly stated in the Berne Convention, it has nonetheless become a generally accepted principle. According to Ricketson, the necessity of 'intellectual creation' is implicit in the notion of literary and artistic work. However, there are no guidelines as to the degree of intellectual creation that is needed for protection, which is a matter for national legislation to establish.[126] While both the civil law and common law systems require a work to be original in order to be protected by copyright, the level of creativity required by common law jurisdictions is relatively low.[127]

---

[124] Copyright Law of the People's Republic of China (as amended on 30 May 2006), art. 7*bis*.

[125] On the limitations of copyright law to protect TCEs, see Agnès Lucas-Schloetter, 'Folklore' in Silke von Lewinski (ed.), *Indigenous Heritage and Intellectual Property* (Kluwer Law International: London, 2004) 291–8.

[126] See Ricketson, *supra* note 3, 900–1.

[127] See for example *Feist Publications, Inc. v Rural Telephone Service Co. Inc.*, 499 US 340; 18 USPQ.2d 1275; (1990–91) 20 IPR 129, 132 where O'Connor J stated that '[o]riginal, as the term is used in copyright, means only that the work was independently created by the author (as opposed to copied from other works), and that it possesses at least some minimal degree of creativity … To be sure, the requisite level of creativity is extremely low; even a slight amount will suffice. The vast majority of works make the grade quite easily.'

The question whether TCEs are original is to be assessed in relation to each individual work. TCEs are usually produced within a community, according to traditional methods that are transmitted from generation to generation. Accordingly, works that are unoriginal imitations or reproductions of pre-existing TCEs are unlikely to meet the originality requirement. On the other hand, contemporary works inspired by or building upon pre-existing TCEs may meet the originality requirement, at least as far as common law countries are concerned. This can be seen in the Australian cases of *Milpurrurru & Ors v Indofurn Pty Ltd & Ors*[128] and *Yumbulul v Reserve Bank of Australia,*[129] which were discussed above,[130] where the court had no difficulty in holding that the works in question were original.

Fixation

Some jurisdictions require that copyright works be fixed in a material form in order for them to be protected. It is a matter for legislation in each country to prescribe that works in general or any specified categories of works shall not be protected unless they have been fixed in some material form. In general, civil law countries do not require that a work be fixed in a material form in order to receive protection. Some common law countries, however, such as the United Kingdom and the United States, do require fixation, because it proves the existence of works and provides a clearer and more definite basis for rights.[131] While this requirement will not be a problem for tangible TCEs such as paintings, sculptures or handicrafts, many TCEs such as folk tales, dances or songs are not fixed in a tangible medium and are transmitted orally. This requirement therefore considerably reduces the scope of application of copyright law to TCEs in countries which require fixation.[132]

---

[128]   Discussing the application of the Copyright Act to Aboriginal artworks based on pre-existing tradition and images, Von Doussa J said that '[t]he problem was whether works incorporating them satisfied the requirement of originality so as to attract copyright protection … Although the artworks follow traditional Aboriginal form and are based on dreaming themes, each artwork is one of intricate detail and complexity reflecting great skill and originality'. See *Milpurrurru and Ors v Indofurn Pty Ltd and Ors, supra* note 83, 216.

[129]   'In the sense relevant to the Copyright Act 1968 (Cth), there is no doubt that the pole was an original artistic work, and that [Yumbulul] was its author, in whom copyright subsisted.' See *Yumbulul v Reserve Bank of Australia, supra* note 75, 484.

[130]   See *supra* para. 2.4.2.

[131]   See Ricketson, *supra* note 3, 242–3.

[132]   Section 5*bis* of the Tunis Model Law provides an example of the fixation requirement being waived for works of folklore as it was considered incompatible with their very nature. See *supra* para. 2.2.2.

Identifiable author

In order for a work to be protected by copyright law, its author must be identifiable.[133] This requirement will usually not be a problem in respect to contemporary TCEs, as can be seen in the Australian case law. However, due to the fact that TCEs are the result of an evolutionary process and are often communal in nature, it will be difficult, if not impossible in the case of pre-existing TCEs, to identify a specific individual or group of individuals as author or authors.

In that case, there is the possibility of using Article 15(4) of the Berne Convention for protection of works where the identity of the author is unknown and to designate an authority which shall represent the author and shall be entitled to protect and enforce his rights.[134] Even though India was the only country to designate such an authority, a similar approach was taken by the Beijing People's Second Intermediate Court when it gave standing to the local government of the Hezhe people to litigate on behalf of the ethnic Hezhe minority in relation to folk songs which had been transmitted from generation to generation, belonged collectively to the ethnic Hezhe and for which there was no identifiable author.[135]

2.7.2　Other Copyright Limitations

In addition to the limitations relating to the conditions for the grant of copyright, other limitations include the limited term of protection and the difficulty of copyright to provide defensive protection mechanisms to TCEs.

Limited term of protection

Copyright law is limited in time. Its duration usually extends to 50 years[136] after the death of the author, or 70 years in some jurisdictions, as for example in the Member States of the European Union. However, many TCEs are already in the public domain. In addition, TCEs holders would like the term of protection of TCEs to be unlimited in time. In that respect, the copyright system does not meet their needs and seems incompatible with the very nature of TCEs.

---

[133]　Article 7(3) of the Berne Convention provides protection for anonymous and pseudonymous works for 50 years after the work has been lawfully made available to the public. However, the countries of the Union will not be required to protect anonymous or pseudonymous works in respect of which it is reasonable to presume that their author has been dead for 50 years.

[134]　See *supra* para. 2.2.1.

[135]　See *supra* para. 2.6.2.

[136]　Article 7(1) of the Berne Convention provides that copyright protection should extend to the life of the author and 50 years after his death.

Inability to provide defensive protection

The copyright system does not prevent third parties from acquiring copyright over contemporary TCEs incorporated into derivative works, such as compilations or adaptations. In addition, where copyright subsists in TCEs, limitations and exceptions allowed under copyright law may undermine customary rights. For example, such exceptions might, under certain conditions, allow third parties to access and use the copyrighted TCEs without permission from the TCEs holders, thus leaving aside the principle of prior authorisation.

2.7.3   Economic and Moral Rights

Once TCEs qualify for copyright protection, two categories of rights arise: economic rights and moral rights. Some of these may be helpful to meet some of the concerns and policy objectives of TCEs holders.

Economic rights

The economic rights are designed to give the author or other right owner the opportunity to control and participate in the benefits of the use of the work. The main types of economic rights are those of reproduction, adaptation, distribution and communication. Other economic rights include the public performance right, the rental or lending right, and the right to authorise others to carry out these activities. Economic rights allow TCEs holders to benefit from the commercialisation of their TCEs and to prevent other parties from carrying out any of the afore-mentioned activities.

Moral rights

The moral rights protect an author's non-economic interests. They relate to the protection of the personality of the author and the integrity of his work. Article 6*bis* of the Berne Convention gives authors the right to 'claim authorship of the work and to object to any distortion, mutilation, or other modification of, or other derogatory action in relation to the said work, which would be prejudicial to his honour or reputation'. These rights, otherwise known as the right of paternity or right of attribution, the right of integrity and the right of divulgation or publication, relate to the personality of the author, subsist independently to the author's economic rights and can potentially be exercised for a longer period or time.

   Some of these rights appear able to meet some of the concerns and policy objectives of TCEs holders:

* The right of paternity is the right of the author to be identified as the author of the work. It is relevant in relation to the attribution of TCEs, but also in the authentication process as it allows consumers to identify genuine TCEs and thus reduce the sale of imitation products.

- In some jurisdictions, the right of paternity also includes the right to object to a false attribution of authorship. Such right can be used against false connection claims, which may mislead consumers by falsely suggesting a connection with a community.
- The right of integrity is relevant in relation to concerns over inappropriate uses of TCEs, such as distortion or derogatory uses.
- Finally the right of publication or divulgation may address TCEs holders' concerns over the disclosure of sacred works and thus also reduce the possibility of inappropriate use of TCEs.

In conclusion, the rights granted by copyright law seem to address some of the concerns and policy objectives of TCEs holders. In particular, it was shown in the case studies that copyright law may, to some extent, assist in preventing the unauthorised reproduction of TCEs. However, the application of copyright law to TCEs has important limitations as it requires that the conditions for the grant of copyright be satisfied. Such limitations relate to the requirements of originality, fixation and identifiable author, as well as the limited term of protection and the inability of copyright to provide defensive protection. Therefore, whereas copyright protection would be available to tangible, contemporary TCEs or intangible contemporary TCEs, in countries not requiring fixation, by applying general principles of copyright law, copyright appears to be inappropriate for the protection of pre-existing TCEs.

This view was also taken by the participants at the UNESCO-WIPO World Forum on the Protection of Folklore in Phuket in 1997, where the participants stated in the Phuket Plan of Action that '[they] were of the view that at present there is no international standard protection for folklore and that the copyright regime is not adequate to ensure such protection'.[137]

The following chapters will move on to examine the possibility of protecting TCEs with origin related intellectual property rights, such as trade marks, certification and collective marks, fair trade labelling, geographical indications as well as passing off and laws against misrepresentation.

---

[137] See UNESCO and WIPO *World Forum on the Protection of Folklore, Phuket, Thailand, April 8–10, 1997* (UNESCO and WIPO, 1998) 235.

3. The protection of traditional cultural expressions with trade marks

3.1 INTRODUCTION

Over the past decades there has been an increasing use, in the course of trade, of traditional words, designs and symbols by indigenous and non-indigenous entities as a result of a growing trend in 'ethnicity'. Many well publicised examples of unauthorised use of words, designs and symbols can be found in various parts of the world. To take only a few, in Canada, names of First Nations, such as Algonquin, Mohawk, Haida and Cherokee, as well as symbols such as Indian heads, tepees or tomahawks are used as trade marks by many non-Aboriginal companies to market products ranging from firearms and axes to tobacco, gasoline and cars.[1] In the United States, over the years, more than 2,600 high school, college or professional teams have used Native American names and images as mascots, logos and team names[2] and most professional teams and many college teams have registered them as trade marks. Finally, in New Zealand, Maori text and imagery have been extensively used in relation to various products such as toys, video games, cars, sports apparel, as well as in the fashion industry.

These practices have raised concerns amongst indigenous people and traditional communities that traditional signs are used in the course of trade and registered as trade marks by non-indigenous entities without proper consent being sought from the indigenous communities. In particular, they are concerned that some trade marks are offensive and degrading and that they themselves might be restricted in their use of trade mark laws to protect their TCEs. In addition, indigenous people and traditional communities fear that, since trade marks serve to indicate the commercial origin of products and distinguish one product from another, such unauthorised use could potentially

---

[1]   See Michael Cassidy and Jock Langford, *Intellectual Property and Aboriginal People, A Working Paper* (Minister of Indian Affairs and Northern Development: Ottawa, 1999) 22.

[2]   See Kristin E. Behrendt, 'Cancellation of the Washington Redskins' Federal Trademark Registrations: Should Sports Team Names, Mascots and Logos Contain Native American Symbolism?' (2000) 10 *Seton Hall J Sport L* 396.

cause confusion in the minds of consumers as to the true origin of the products concerned.

As a consequence, it is becoming increasingly relevant to examine the protection of TCEs within the trade mark law system. The aim of this chapter is to
demonstrate how indigenous communities can use the trade mark system as a
defensive tool to prevent the unauthorised registration of traditional words,
designs and symbols that are considered offensive, but also as a practical instrument to promote TCEs and benefit commercially from them. In order to do so,
this chapter examines whether TCEs can constitute the subject matter of trade
mark law and then moves on to present two case studies based on the experiences
of New Zealand and the United States with the trade mark protection of TCEs.

3.2 THE 'ORIGIN RELATED' ELEMENT

The essential and primary function of a trade mark is to indicate the source or
the trade origin of the goods or services in respect of which it is used. The
concept that trade marks denote origin is accepted in both civil law and
common law jurisdictions.[3]

Within the European Union, the 'origin related' function of a trade mark
underlies the whole body of law relating to registered trade marks. The
seventh recital of the Community Trade Mark Regulation states:

> Whereas the protection afforded by the Community trade mark, the function of
> which is in particular to guarantee the trade mark as an indication of origin.[4]

Similar wording can be found in the tenth recital of the Trade Mark Directive.[5]
It is also made clear in the Memorandum on the Creation of an EEC trade
mark which states:

> Both economically and legally the function of the trade mark as an indication of
> origin is paramount. It follows directly from the concept of a trade mark as a distinc-
> tive sign, that it serves to distinguish trade marked products originating from a
> particular firm or group of firms from the products of other firms.[6]

---

[3]   On the origin function of trade marks, see Anselm Kamperman Sanders and
Spyros Maniatis, 'A Consumer Trade Mark: Protection Based on Origin and Quality'
(1993) 11 *EIPR* 406; Jeremy Phillips, *Trade Marks Law: A Practical Anatomy* (Oxford
University Press: Oxford, 2003) 21–8.
[4]   Council Regulation (EC) 40/94 on the Community Trade Mark.
[5]   Council Directive 89/104/EEC of 21 December 1988 to approximate the laws
of the Member States relating to trade marks.
[6]   Commission of the European Communities, Memorandum on the Creation of

There are two sorts of origins that a trade mark can denote: (i) the actual physical origin of the goods, and (ii) the identity of origin of the goods. The idea that a trade marks indicates the physical origin of the goods dates back to ancient times where traders used to apply marks to their goods to indicate origin. Examples of such practices include hallmarking of precious metals and cattle branding or earmarking of sheep. However, at the beginning of the twentieth century, this conception became obsolete[7] as it was considered to be incompatible with the trading conditions of the modern world where licensing and outsourcing of products are usual and often necessary practices. On the other hand, the concept of identity of origin implies that the trade mark gives information about a particular firm, producer or group of producers and refers to goods that originate under the control of a single undertaking. It acts as a guarantee of the identity of the origin of the marked products to enable consumers or end users to distinguish those products or services from others which have a different origin.

This is also the preferred approach of the European Court of Justice (ECJ), which was outlined in *Unilever plc v OHIM*. The Court of First Instance said that:

> It is not necessary for a mark to convey exact information about the identity of the manufacturer of the product or the supplier of the services. It is sufficient that the mark enables members of the public concerned to distinguish the product or service that it designates from those which have a different trade origin and to conclude that all the products or services that it designates have been manufactured, marketed or supplied under the control of the owner of the mark and that the owner is responsible for their quality.[8]

Other functions of trade marks include the guarantee of quality function and the advertising function. The guarantee of quality function implies a guarantee to the consumer that the quality of the goods or services, be it good or bad, will be consistent with that to which the consumer has become accustomed. The advertising function, on the other hand, relates to the image of the goods or services and to the aura associated with them. The distinction between the various functions of a trade mark is clearly described in the Memorandum on the Creation of an EEC trade mark:

---

an EEC Trade Mark Adopted by the Commission on 6 July 1976, SEC(76)2462 Final, *Bulletin of the European Communities*, Supplement 8/76, para. 68.

7   Frank I. Schechter, *The Historical Foundation of the Law Relating to Trade Marks* (Columbia University Press: New York, 1925).

8   *Unilever plc v OHIM*, Case T-194/01, 5 March 2003 (unreported), para. 43. On the advertising function of trade marks, see also *Parfums Christian Dior SA and Anor v Evora BV*, Case C-337/95 [1998] ETMR 26, 38–40.

From [the origin function] of the trade mark are derived all the other functions which the trade mark fulfils in economic life. If the trade mark guarantees that the commercial origin is the same, the consumer can count on a similarity of composition and quality of goods bearing the trade mark; and the advertising value of the trade mark requires that between the trade marked goods and the owner of the trade mark there is a definite legal relationship. Although the quality function predominates in the mind of the consumer and the publicity function predominates in the mind of the producer, so far as the legal aspect is concerned the decisive criterion is the function of the mark as an indication of origin. Only if the proper purpose of the trade mark is maintained, namely to distinguish the trade marked goods from goods of different origin, can it fulfil its further role as an instrument of sales promotion and consumer information; and only then does the trade mark right perform its function of protecting the proprietor against injury to the reputation of his trade mark.[9]

3.3   DEFINITIONAL CONSIDERATIONS

Generally speaking, a trade mark can be described as being a sign which is capable of being represented graphically and which distinguishes particular goods or services of one undertaking from the goods or services of other undertakings in the course of trade. According to Article 2 of the Trade Mark Directive:

A trade mark may consist of any sign capable of being represented graphically, particularly words, including personal names, designs, letters, numerals, the shape of goods or of their packaging, provided that such signs are capable of distinguishing the goods or services of one undertaking from those of other undertakings.

The Trade Mark Directive does not provide a definition of what constitutes a sign. The use of the words 'may consist of any sign' and 'particularly' indicate that the list provided by Article 2 of the types of signs that can constitute a trade mark is non-exhaustive. According to Jacob J, a sign is 'anything which can convey information'.[10] In a similar vein, the Board of Appeal of the Office for Harmonisation in the Internal Market (OHIM) said that the notion of a sign is to be interpreted as 'a very broad, open, and general term encompassing all conceivable types of marks (including, for example, sound marks and three-dimensional marks)'.[11] Therefore, it has been alleged that the expression 'sign' should be understood as a general term which is wide enough to include

---

[9]   See Commission of the European Communities, *supra* note 6, para. 68.

[10]   See *Philips Electronics NV v Remington Consumer Products Ltd (No. 1)* [1998] RPC 283, 298; [1998] ETMR 124. See also *Dyson Ltd v Registrar of Trade Marks* [2003] EWHC 1062 (Ch); [2003] ETMR 77.

[11]   See *Wm. Wrigley Jr Co.'s Trade Mark Application*, Case R-122/98-3 [1999] ETMR 214, para.17.

Table 3.1   Applications and registrations of Community trade marks classified by type of mark

Type of mark	1996–2007 applications	2008 applications	1997–2007 Registered trade marks	2008 Registered trade marks
Word mark	406 514	50 888	265 756	47 830
Figurative	235 897	35 787	157 999	33 059
3D	4834	444	2281	329
Colour	604	105	112	41
Other	524	82	204	30
Sound	82	21	47	23
Hologram	10	–	3	–
Olfactory	7	–	1	–
Total	648 472	87 327	358 248	81 312

Note: Chart compiled from statistics on Community trade marks available at http://oami.europa.eu/ows/rw/resource/documents/OHIM/statistics/ssc009-statistics_of_community_trade_mark_2008.pdf

all possible trade marks, including a wide range of unusual marks, such as marks consisting of a single colour, a smell, a sound or a moving image.[12]

TCEs can consist of verbal expressions, musical expressions, expressions by action or tangible expressions. Since a sign can be 'anything which can convey information', trade mark law may apply to TCEs provided they fulfil the requirements of the definition of a trade mark, i.e. that they constitute a sign, which is capable of being represented graphically and which is distinctive.

According to OHIM statistics on Community trade marks (CTMs), trade marks have been registered under the following categories: word marks, figurative marks, three-dimensional marks, colour marks, sound marks, hologram marks, olfactory marks, and others (see Table 3.1). Therefore, TCEs which consist of verbal expressions, such as words, signs, names and symbols, could be registered as word marks; TCEs which consist of musical expressions, such as songs and instrumental music, could be registered as sound marks; TCEs which consist of expressions by action, such as dances, plays, ceremonies, rituals could be registered as movement marks or holograms; and TCEs which consist of tangible expressions, such as drawings, designs, paintings, sculp-

---

12   See David Kitchin *et al.*, *Kerly's Law of Trade Marks and Trade Names* (14th edn, Sweet & Maxwell: London, 2005) 13.

tures, jewellery, costumes or handicrafts could be registered as figurative or three-dimensional marks.[13] However, if this assumption is easily verified in relation to the registration of verbal expressions as word marks or to a certain extent for tangible expressions as figurative or three-dimensional marks, the registration of musical expressions as sound marks and expressions by action as hologram marks raises more complex issues.

3.3.1 The Registration of Verbal Expressions

There are several well-publicised examples of registration of verbal expressions as trade marks. Some of the most famous include the registration of the word mark CHEROKEE[14] by car manufacturer Daimler Chrysler and the word mark REDSKINS[15] by the Washington professional football team.

3.3.2 The Registration of Musical Expressions

In *Shield Mark*,[16] the ECJ established that sounds can be registered as trade marks provided they are capable of being regarded as trade marks, of distinguishing the goods or services of one undertaking from those of other undertakings and of being represented graphically. It reaffirmed the general requirements set out in *Sieckmann*[17] to be satisfied by any graphical representation, in particular, that a trade mark may consist of a sign which is not in itself capable of being perceived visually, provided that it can be represented graphically, particularly by means of images, lines or characters, and that its representation is clear, precise, self-contained, easily accessible, intelligible, durable and objective. The ECJ emphasised that in order to register a sign as a sound mark, the applicant has to state in the application for registration that the sign in question must be understood as a sound sign so as to prevent applications from being examined as if they were a word and/or figurative mark. Furthermore, it held that the requirement of graphical representation is not satisfied when the sign is represented graphically by means of a description using the written language, such as an indication that the sign consists of the notes going to make up a musical work, or the indication that it is the cry of

---

[13] Issues relating to the registration of signs involving Maori words, symbols, sounds or smells were also examined by the Maori Trade Marks Focus Group. See *infra* para. 3.6.3.

[14] Registration No. 2,704,632 issued 26 June 2001.

[15] Registration No. 1,085,092 issued 7 February 1978.

[16] *Shield Mark BV v Joost Kist H.O.D.N. Memex*, Case C-283/01 [2004] RPC 17; [2004] ETMR 33.

[17] *Ralf Sieckmann v Deutches Patent- und Markenamt*, Case C-273/00 [2003] RPC 38; [2003] ETMR 37.

an animal, or by means of a simple onomatopoeia, without more, or by means of a sequence of musical notes, without more. On the other hand, the court held that those requirements are satisfied where the sign is represented by a stave divided into measures and showing, in particular, a clef, musical notes and rests whose form indicates the relative value and, where necessary, accidentals.

Most of the audible Community trade marks that have been registered so far are for advertising jingles and consist of a melody or a sequence of notes represented in notated form, some of them with harmony in the form of a score, and some even in the form of a proper movement for an entire orchestra. Some of the applications also contained indications as to the key and the beat or provided the words to be sung.[18] As illustrated in Table 3.1 however, there are relatively few examples of registered sound marks, and no known practice of registering traditional musical expressions as sound marks.

Would it nonetheless be possible to register musical expressions as sound marks? As with any other sound signs, it is possible to represent musical expressions graphically. However, it is less clear to what extent musical expressions can operate as trade marks and to what extent they are capable of distinguishing goods and services. The acceptability of such signs will depend on their capacity of being regarded as trade marks and whether the sound is or has become a distinctive sign, that is, whether the average consumer will perceive the sound as meaning that the goods or services are exclusively associated with one undertaking. However, if short sequences of musical expressions can acquire a distinctive character, it is questionable whether whole songs or longer pieces of instrumental music could be regarded as trade marks, as it would be difficult to establish the distinctive character of the mark.

3.3.3   The Registration of Expressions by Action

It is generally accepted, as with sound marks, that marks involving movement or holograms can be registered as trade marks, provided they are capable of being regarded as trade marks, that is, of distinguishing the goods or services of one undertaking from those of other undertakings and of being represented graphically. Movement marks refer to those kinds of marks in which a change in appearance caused by a certain movement is part of the mark for which protection is being sought.[19] They can be represented graphically by a series of still images which show the movement and the change in the mark's appearance, provided it is made clear that the mark is a moving image, what the

---

[18]   See Stefan Völkwe, 'Registering New Forms under the Community Trademark' (2002) 152 *Trademark World* 29.
[19]   Ibid. 30.

image depicts, how many images are involved in the complete sequence of movement, what the sequential order of the images is and the fact that there is a single sequence of movement. Hologram marks, on the other hand, are marks which give the appearance of motion. Applicants will be required to show each of the various views depicted in the hologram so that all the material features of the mark can be discerned.

As with sound marks, there are very few examples of registered movement marks or hologram marks (see Table 3.1), and no known practice of registering expressions by actions as trade marks. It is to be expected that the registration of expressions by action, such as dances, ceremonies or rituals, as trade marks would face technical problems due to the length and complexity of the movement. In addition, it is questionable whether long or complex sequences of action can acquire a distinctive character and be able to indicate origin.

3.3.4 The Registration of Tangible Expressions

There are numerous examples of registration of tangible expressions, such as drawings and designs, as figurative marks. In the United States, the image of an Indian head alone has been registered as a figurative mark for products as diverse as tobacco, firearms, motor oils, automobiles, brewing companies, moccasins, slippers and boots, and sports teams. Similarly, as of 2003, 65 trade mark applications which included images of Aboriginal people were listed on the Australian trade mark register. Of these, many old ones were removed. However, 24 current trade marks incorporate images of Aboriginal people.[20]

In addition, three-dimensional product shapes may be protected as trade marks, either through the registration of the product shape itself or through the registration of a two-dimensional trade mark which could be infringed by its unauthorised reproduction in three-dimensional form. As a consequence, it is possible to register tangible expressions such as sculptures or handicrafts as trade marks.

3.4   PROTECTION AGAINST OFFENSIVE USE

A sign is registrable as a trade mark, provided that it satisfies the criteria of registrability which are laid down by the law. Some signs may be subject to absolute bars to registration and therefore be inherently unregistrable. Absolute bars to registration can be found in most countries' legislations. They

---

[20]   See Terri Janke, *Minding Culture: Case Studies on Intellectual Property and Traditional Cultural Expressions* (WIPO: Geneva, 2003).

either relate to the form which the trade mark takes, or to its meaning. Bars relating to the form of a trade mark are concerned with the questions whether it constitutes a sign, whether it can distinguish goods or services, and whether it is capable of being graphically represented. On the other hand, bars relating to the meaning of a trade mark are concerned with the questions whether its meaning is descriptive or generic, whether it is deceptive, whether it is the same as or similar to a work which has been reserved exclusively for non-trade mark use, and most importantly for TCEs, whether the trade mark is contrary to public policy or morality.[21]

3.4.1   Signs which are Contrary to Public Policy and Morality

Article 6*quinquies* of the Paris Convention provides for refusal or invalidity of registration in relation to trade marks that are 'contrary to morality or public order and, in particular, of such a nature as to deceive the public'.[22]

Corresponding rules can be found in the law or practice of most countries, although sometimes with a different wording.[23] At the European Union level, for example, Article 7(1)(f) of the Community Trade Mark Regulation provides that 'trade marks which are contrary to public policy or to accepted principles of morality' shall not be registered.[24] Article 1052 of the Lanham Act, on the other hand, provides that:

> No trademark by which the goods of the applicant may be distinguished from the goods of others shall be refused registration on the principal register on account of its nature unless it (a) consists of or comprises immoral, deceptive, or scandalous matter; or matter which may disparage or falsely suggest a connection with persons, living or dead, institutions, beliefs, or national symbols, or bring them into contempt, or disrepute.

3.4.2   The Concepts of 'Contrary to Morality' and 'Contrary to Public Order'

The concepts of 'contrary to morality' or 'contrary to public order' are very broad concepts which require a value judgement to be made by the relevant trade mark registries. Generally speaking, offence may relate to words and/or

---

21   See Phillips, *supra* note 3, 61–2.
22   Paris Convention for the Protection of Industrial Property, Art. 6*quinquies*.
23   The corresponding rule at the European Union level can be found in Art. 7(1)(f) of Council Regulation (EC) 40/94 on the Community Trade Mark. It provides that 'trade marks which are contrary to public policy or to accepted principles of morality' shall not be registered.
24   Council Regulation (EC) 40/94 on the Community Trade Mark, Art. 7(1)(f).

images and may be caused on matters of race, sex, religious beliefs, or general matters of taste and decency.[25] According to the UK Trade Marks Registry Work Manual, marks which are 'contrary to public policy or to accepted principles of morality' fall into three types: those with criminal connotations, those with religious connotations, and explicit/taboo signs.[26] In addition, this type of provisions is concerned with the intrinsic quality of the mark itself, and not the personal qualities of the applicant for registration, such as circumstances relating to conduct or identity.[27]

The terms 'public policy' or 'public order' are intended to deny protection to marks which could induce public disorder, or increase the likelihood of criminal or other offensive behaviour. According to the *Work Manual*, caution should be taken, amongst other things, where marks exhibit racial, religious or discriminatory characteristics. 'Accepted principles of morality', on the other hand, are more difficult to define. Some guidance was provided in *Ghazilian's Trade Mark Application* as to how the degree of censure involved should be assessed:

> Each case must be decided on its own facts. The dividing line is to be drawn between offence which amounts only to distaste and offence which would justifiably cause outrage or would be the subject of justifiable censure as being likely significantly to undermine current religious, family or social values. The outrage or censure must be amongst an identifiable section of the public and a higher degree of outrage or censure amongst a small section of the community will no doubt suffice just as lesser outrage or censure amongst a more widespread section of the public will also suffice.[28]

Some useful guidance regarding trade marks that are 'contrary to public policy or to accepted principles of morality' is also provided by Article 8.7 of the OHIM examination guidelines. They provide that:

> If a trade mark is contrary to public policy or to accepted principles of morality within the Community the examiner must object. Words or images which are offensive, such as swear words or racially derogatory images, or which are blasphemous are not acceptable. There is a dividing line between this and trade marks which might be considered in poor taste. The latter do not offend against this provision.

---

25   See Kitchin *et al.*, *supra* note 12, 212–13.
26   See Patent Office, *Trade Mark Registry Work Manual* (Patent Office: Newport, 1994–) ch. 6, section 39.1.
27   See *Durferrit GmbH v OHIM*, Case T-224/01 [2004] ETMR 124, paras 67–71, 75, 76: Art. 7(1)(f) of Council Regulation (EC) 40/94 on the Community Trade Mark does not cover the situation in which the applicant acts in bad faith. An overall reading of the various subparagraphs of Art. 7(1) of the Community Trade Mark Regulation shows that they refer to the intrinsic qualities of the mark claimed and not to circumstances relating to the conduct of the person applying for the trade mark.
28   *Ghazilian's Trade Mark Application* [2002] RPC 33, 628; [2002] ETMR 57.

3.4.3 The Perception of the Public

Trade mark law is usually concerned with the perception of the consumers of the goods or services concerned. However, when assessing if a mark is contrary to morality or public order, one has to examine the public as a whole, since offensive marks may be viewed by people other than those who purchase the goods. In addition, this type of provision is not concerned with political correctness but with principles of morality. The test is therefore an objective one, using the concept of the 'right-thinking member of the public'.

The question of what the public must see in order for a mark to be barred from registration on immorality grounds has been approached in different ways by the appeal bodies of OHIM and the UK registry. In *Dick Lexic Ltd's Application*,[29] the OHIM Board of Appeal took a strictly objective approach and decided that the examiner had to try and establish what the applicant is trying to tell consumers through using the mark, and whether they will detect this message. In *Basic Trademark SAC Application*,[30] the UK Lord Chancellor's Appointed Person took the more unpredictable approach to look at the reaction of the public to the mark, rather than to conduct a semantic examination of the mark in the abstract. The test was therefore whether the mark would be 'seriously troubling' in terms of the public interest in the prevention of disorder or the protection of morals.

3.5 PROTECTION AGAINST DECEPTIVE USE

Another absolute bar to registration which is relevant in the context of TCEs is in relation to deceptive marks. As with signs that are contrary to public policy and morality, provisions regarding deceptive marks can be found in most countries' legislations.

The Trade Mark Directive provides that trade marks shall not be registered if they are of 'such a nature as to deceive the public, for instance as to the nature, quality or geographical origin of the goods or services'.[31] The prohibition will usually apply to marks which, though distinctive, contain some kind of suggestion or allusion that is inaccurate. The risk of deception, however, must be a real one and fanciful trade marks will be accepted even though they might be deceptive. Indeed, according to the ECJ, the provision presupposes

---

29 *Dick Lexic Ltd's Application*, Case R-111/2002-4 [2005] ETMR 99.
30 *Basic Trademark SAC Application* [2005] RPC 25.
31 Council Directive 89/104, Art. 3(1)(g).

'the existence of actual deceit or of a sufficiently serious risk that the consumer will be deceived'.[32] This risk will be assessed from the viewpoint of the consumer who is reasonably well-informed, observant and circumspect. The aim of the provision is to protect the public, i.e. the consumers of the product for which registration is sought.

According to the OHIM Examination Guidelines, if the trade mark is of such a nature as to deceive the public, for instance as to the nature, quality or geographical origin of the goods or services, then the examiner must object. A trade mark which suggests that goods are made of a particular material, where the material would be a significant factor for the purchaser and where the purchaser would be likely to draw the conclusion that this would be its composition, must be objected to if the list of goods is not specific on this point. If, for example, the trade mark gives rise to a real expectation that the goods come from a particular locality and the list is not specific on this point, then the examiner must object.[33]

Similarly, if the trade mark seems to suggest that the good or service has an indigenous origin, where such origin would be a significant factor for the purchaser, and this is not actually the case, the trade mark must be objected.

3.6 THE NEW ZEALAND EXPERIENCE

Over the past few years, an increasing number of companies, in New Zealand and overseas, have started using Maori imagery and text in order to increase the commercial value of their products. In addition, a growing quantity of imitation products, mass-produced outside New Zealand, or by non-Maori artists, have appeared on the New Zealand market, mainly in the field of the tourism industry, to the detriment of local authentic works.

In response to growing Maori concerns about the inappropriateness of existing intellectual property laws to protect their traditional knowledge (TK) and TCEs, and in an attempt to take into account Maori needs and perspectives, the New Zealand government has entered into a process of reconsideration of its intellectual property laws. In this perspective, it has taken steps to amend its Trade Marks Law of 1953 to incorporate a mechanism by which the interests of sections of the community, particularly Maori, can be taken into account during the trade mark registration process. Similarly, in other intellectual

---

[32] See *Formaggio Gorgonzola v Käserei Champignon Hofmeister GmbH*, Case C-87/97 [1999] ETMR 454, para. 41.
[33] See OHIM Examination Guidelines, para. 8.8.

property fields, such as patents and plant varieties rights, the Ministry of Economic Development has recently published two discussion papers in which it respectively considers the possibility to amend the Patent Act of 1953 to ensure that consultation with Maori occurred when patent applications were made for inventions based on TK or indigenous genetic material[34] and to amend the Plant Varieties Act of 1987 in a similar way.[35]

This case study will first set out the New Zealand intellectual property context and the relation between Maoris and the intellectual property system. It will give specific examples of what could be interpreted as misappropriation of Maori TCEs and it will then move on to analyse how the New Zealand Trade Marks Act 2002 has attempted to provide protection for a particular aspect of Maori TCEs, namely Maori imagery and text.

3.6.1   Maori and Intellectual Property

According to Maori lawyer Maui Solomon:

> [T]here is a fundamental clash between the ideological underpinnings of the intellectual property rights system and the philosophical underpinnings of indigenous people's rights and obligations.[36]

This often results in the inability for Maori to obtain intellectual property rights to enable them to protect and commercially exploit their TK or TCEs because of the requirement of originality, the different conceptions of ownership of intellectual property, and the inappropriate term of protection of traditional intellectual property rights. In addition, the intellectual property rights system can also have negative effects for Maori through the granting of intellectual property rights to third parties for creations or inventions based on Maori traditional knowledge or traditional cultural expressions, the inappropriate exploitation of Maori TK and TCEs, and the lack of benefit sharing resulting from that commercialisation.

The Treaty of Waitangi
The Treaty of Waitangi was signed on 6 February 1840 by representatives of

---

34   Ministry of Economic Development, *Review of the Patents Act 1953: Boundaries to Patentability, A Discussion Paper* (Regulatory and Competition Policy Branch, Ministry of Economic Development: Wellington, March 2002) 24.

35   Ministry of Economic Development, *Review of the Plant Variety Rights Act 1987, A Discussion Paper* (Regulatory and Competition Policy Branch, Ministry of Economic Development: Wellington, March 2002) 24.

36   Maui Solomon, 'Intellectual Property Rights and Indigenous Peoples Rights and Obligations', available at www.inmotionmagazine.com/nztrip/ms1.html

Queen Victoria and many Maori chiefs.[37] It is the founding document of the relationship between Maori and the British Crown and it is considered to be of constitutional significance to New Zealand.[38] The Treaty of Waitangi is a short document which consists of three articles. It was originally written and signed in both Maori and English languages, the result being that today, there are two official versions of the Treaty. Even though the terms of the two versions are, in certain respects, conflicting, both versions represent an agreement in which Maori ceded to the British Crown the power to govern in New Zealand and to develop British settlements, while the Crown promised to protect Maori chiefly authority, including their rights to their lands and other possessions and to extend to Maori the same rights and privileges as British citizens.

Article the Second of the Treaty is the most relevant article to intellectual property. The English version of Article the Second provides that Maori leaders and people were confirmed and guaranteed:

> [T]he full exclusive and undisturbed possession of their Lands and Estates, Forests, Fisheries and other properties which they may collectively or individually possess so long as it is their wish and desire to retain the same in their possession.

In the Maori version, however, Maori were guaranteed '*te tino rangatiratanga*'[39] – the unqualified exercise of their chieftainship over their lands '*wenua*', villages '*kainga*', and all their treasures '*taonga katoa*'. While neither the English nor the Maori version of Article the Second refer to intellectual property as such, commentators consider that it is clear that many of

---

[37]   At the time the Treaty was signed, the Maori population numbered approximately 115,000 people, compared to a British migrant population of about 2,000 people. Today, Maori comprise approximately 15 per cent of New Zealand's population of 4 million people. See www.stats.govt.nz/domino/external/web/prod_serv.nsf/htmldocs/Population.

[38]   Unlike most countries, New Zealand does not have a single written constitution that overrides other law, but rather a collection of legislation and customs, which together, establish the framework of New Zealand government. Even though the Treaty by itself cannot be described as a constitution, it is considered to be an integral part of New Zealand's constitutional arrangements. This was also suggested by the Waitangi Tribunal (*Ngai Tahu Report* (1991) 272) which said that the Treaty must be seen as a 'basic constitutional document'. For more information see Te Puni Kokiri, *A Guide to the Principles of the Treaty of Waitangi as Expressed by the Courts and the Waitangi Tribunal* (Te Puni Kokiri: Wellington, 2002) 14–16.

[39]   There are different meanings for '*te tino rangatiratanga*' and the concept itself is part of a rich and ongoing debate in Maori society. The word '*tino*' is an intensifier of the word '*rangatiratanga*', which broadly speaking, relates to the exercise of chieftainship. Other translations include self-determination, absolute sovereignty and Maori independence. See http://aotearoa.wellington.net.nz/back/intro.htm

the things covered by traditional intellectual property might be considered to be *taonga*,[40] which can be translated as 'treasures'.[41]

The difference between the Maori and the English versions of the Treaty have led to different understandings of the meaning of the Treaty. These differences, coupled with the need to apply the Treaty in contemporary circumstances, have resulted in the Parliament referring to the 'Principles of the Treaty' in legislation rather than to the Treaty texts themselves. As a consequence, when interpreting legislative references to the Treaty, the courts have considered the principles inspired by the Treaty texts, rather than the texts themselves. The Waitangi Tribunal, on the other hand, has a more general jurisdiction to consider the texts of the Treaty, when considering whether the Crown has acted in a manner which is inconsistent with its principles.[42] Broadly speaking, both the courts and the Waitangi Tribunal recognise the existence of three major principles: the principle of partnership,[43] the principle of active protection,[44] and the principle of redress.[45] A broader approach

---

[40]   Susy Frankel and Geoff McLay, *Intellectual Property in New Zealand* (LexisNexis Butterworths: Wellington, 2002) 103.

[41]   '*Taonga*' was translated by Prof. Sir Hugh Kawharu, a scholar and former member of the Waitangi Tribunal, as 'treasures'. See modern English translation of the Treaty of Waitangi by Prof. Sir Hugh Kawharu, available at www.mfat.govt.nz/support/kpm/framework.html. This definition was later accepted by the Privy Council in *New Zealand Maori Council v Attorney-General* [1994] 1 NZLR 513 (PC) (the 'Broadcasting Assets' case) 517. In its early reports, the Waitangi Tribunal noted that *taonga* included 'all valued resources or tangibles such as fishing grounds, harbours and foreshores, as well as intangible valuables such as the Maori language and the mauri (or life-force) of a river' (see the *Motunui-Waitara Report* (1983), the *Kaituna River Report* (1984), the *Manukau Report* (1985) and the *Te Reo Maori Report* (1986)). The Tribunal later added that the word '*taonga*' was used in a metaphorical sense to cover a variety of possibilities, rather than itemised specifics (see the *Muriwhenua Fishing Claim Report* (1988) 174). It also clearly stated that language and Maori customary knowledge were *taonga* (*Wananga Capital Establishment Report* (1999) xii). For more information see Te Puni Kokiri, *supra* note 38, 60–4.

[42]   Te Puni Kokiri, *supra* note 38, 75–7.

[43]   The principle of partnership is often used to describe the relationship between the Crown and Maori. It implies fiduciary duties as an aspect of the partnership, and is often considered, both by the courts and the Waitangi Tribunal, to emphasise a duty on the parties to act reasonably, honourably and in good faith.

[44]   The principle of active protection encompasses the Crown's obligation to take positive steps to ensure that Maori interests are protected. This principle was elaborated by the Waitangi Tribunal as part of its understanding of the exchange of sovereignty for the protection of Maori chieftainship over their lands. The Tribunal explicitly referred to the Crown's obligation to protect Maori capacity to retain tribal authority over tribal affairs, and to live according to their cultural preferences.

[45]   It has been acknowledged by the courts and by the Waitangi Tribunal that the Crown has an obligation to remedy past breaches of the Treaty. Whereas the courts see

to these principles, which would take into account intellectual property concerns, would also include the right of Maori to self-management, to maintain Maori culture, to control their resources, and the fact that the Treaty should be implemented in a broad and generous spirit that takes cultural differences into account.[46]

The Waitangi Tribunal and the Wai 262 claim to indigenous flora and fauna and cultural and intellectual heritage rights and obligations

The Waitangi Tribunal   The Waitangi Tribunal was established in 1975 by an Act of Parliament, the Treaty of Waitangi Act 1975.[47] The Tribunal, which does not function as an adversarial court, but as a permanent commission of inquiry, is a quasi-judicial body, with jurisdiction to hear claims brought by Maori. Its proceedings are by way of inquiry or report. As it is a specialist body, members of the Waitangi Tribunal are chosen for their knowledge and experience in the different aspects of the matters that are likely to come in front of the Tribunal. The Tribunal comprises up to 16 members and a chair person at a time, who are equally chosen between Maori and *Pakeha* (non-Maori) as a reference to the partnership of the Treaty of Waitangi.

The Tribunal has exclusive authority to determine the meaning and effect of the Treaty of Waitangi, as embodied in both the Maori and English texts and to decide issues raised by the differences between them. Its main function is to inquire into claims submitted by Maori relating to actions or omissions of the Crown, which breach the promises made in the Treaty of Waitangi and to determine whether they are well-founded.[48] Where the Tribunal finds a claim to be well-founded, it may recommend to the Crown that action be taken to

---

this principle as arising from the principle of partnership and from the fiduciary obligations inherent to the principle of partnership, the Waitangi Tribunal considers that the principle of redress arises from the Crown's duty to act reasonably and in good faith as a Treaty partner. For more information on the principles of the Treaty of Waitangi, as expressed by the courts and the Waitangi Tribunal, see Te Puni Kokiri, *supra* note 38, 74–106.

[46]   Frankel and McLay, *supra* note 40, 103.

[47]   For information on the Waitangi Tribunal, see its official website: www.waitangi-tribunal.govt.nz/ or, Waitangi Tribunal, *Guide to the Practice and Procedure of the Waitangi Tribunal* (Waitangi Tribunal: Wellington, 2000) available at www.waitangi-tribunal.govt.nz/doclibrary/GuidetoPracticeandProcedure.pdf

[48]   The role of the Waitangi Tribunal includes inquiring into and making recommendations upon any claim properly submitted to the Tribunal, examining and reporting on any proposed legislation referred to the Tribunal by the House of Representatives or a Minister of the Crown, and making recommendations or determinations in respect of certain Crown forest land, railway land, state-owned enterprise land and land transferred to educational institutions.

compensate, remove the prejudice or prevent other persons from being similarly affected in the future. Even though the powers of the Tribunal are only recommendatory, successive governments have tended to take its recommendations seriously. Indeed, the Waitangi Tribunal Reports frequently set the tone for negotiations between *iwi* (tribes) and the Crown over the return of assets, and have helped set the parameters for future governmental policy agenda.[49]

The Wai 262 claim to indigenous flora and fauna and cultural and intellectual heritage rights and obligations   The Wai 262 claim to indigenous flora and fauna and cultural and intellectual heritage rights and obligations (the Wai 262 claim)[50] was brought against the New Zealand Crown in 1991[51] by the members of six tribes (Ngati Kuri, Ngati Wai, Te Rarawa, Ngati Porou, Ngati Kahungunu and Ngati Koata). The Wai 262 claim relates to:

> [T]*e tino rangatiratanga o te iwi* Maori in respect of indigenous flora and fauna *me o ratou taonga katoa* (and all their treasures) including but not limited to *matauranga, whakairo, waahi tapu*, biodiversity, genetics, Maori symbols and designs and their use and development and associated indigenous, cultural and customary heritage rights in relation to such *taonga*.[52]

The claimants argue that some of the government's legislation and policies are in breach of the Treaty of Waitangi and have resulted in the impossibility for Maori to exercise their political authority with respect to knowledge of native flora and fauna, as well as other traditional knowledge and cultural and intellectual property rights. Indeed, one of the foundations of the claim is that:

> [T]he Declaration of Independence and the Treaty of Waitangi clearly reaffirm that the authority of *te tino rangatiratanga o te iwi* Maori is unable to be subordinated to any other sovereign power, and that any actions, inactions and policies of the Crown which seek to so subordinate it are in breach of the Treaty of Waitangi.[53]

---

[49]   Graeme W. Austin, 'Re-Treating Intellectual Property? The Wai 262 Proceeding and the Heuristics of Intellectual Property Law' (2003) 11 *Cardozo J Int'l and Comp L* 347.

[50]   The Wai 262 claim was named after its Tribunal registration number.

[51]   The Wai 262 claim was later amended in 1997.

[52]   Amended Statement of Claim of the Wai 262 claim.

[53]   The paramountcy of *rangatiratanga* as the basis for Treaty-based claims was also reaffirmed by national *hui* (workshop) such as the Hirangi *hui* in January 1995. According to the 1995 *hui* resolutions, the following were reaffirmed as basis for *tino rangatiratanga*: (i) the Treaty of Waitangi is the constitution of New Zealand; (ii) from 1840 the right of the Crown to exercise *kawanatanga* depended on not breaching *tino rangatiratanga* reserved perpetually to Maori; (iii) the right of the government to exercise *kawanatanga* (the power of sovereignty) is lost if *tino rangatiratanga* is not

According to the Statement of Claim, *te tino rangatiratanga o te iwi* Maori incorporates the following things:

- decision-making authority over the conservation, control of, and proprietorial interests in natural resources, including indigenous flora and fauna *me o ratou taonga katoa*;
- the right to determine indigenous cultural and customary heritage rights in the knowledge and use of indigenous flora and fauna *me o ratou taonga katoa*;
- the right to participate in, benefit from and make decisions about the application of existing and future technological advances as they relate to the breeding, genetic manipulation and other processes relevant to the use of indigenous flora and fauna;
- the right to control and make decisions about the propagation, development, transport, study, or sale of indigenous flora and fauna;
- the right to protect, enhance and transmit the cultural, medicinal and spiritual knowledge and concepts found in the life-cycles of indigenous flora and fauna;
- a right to environmental well-being dependent upon the nurturing and wise use of indigenous flora and fauna;
- the right to participate in, benefit from and make decisions about the application, development, uses and sale of *me o ratou taonga katoa*; and
- the right to protect, enhance and transmit the cultural and spiritual knowledge and concepts found in *me o ratou taonga katoa*.

The Wai 262 claim is extremely broad and since the claim was first filed, its scope was further extended by evidence and by filing of multiple amended statements of claim. The major issues raised by the claim can be divided into the following points:

Protection and retention of Maori traditional knowledge: As guaranteed in Article the Second of the Treaty of Waitangi, Maori claim the full, exclusive and undisturbed possession of their traditional knowledge, which includes, amongst others, arts, carving, history, oral traditions, music, medicinal and therapeutic treatments and healing, and environmental management ethics. They characterise these as '*taonga*' on the basis that they contribute to the continued preservation and development of Maori identity and well-being.

---

provided for; and (iv) any change to *tino rangatiratanga* or *kawanatanga* as provided for by the Treaty requires prior consent of all *iwi*. For more information, see M H Durie and S Asher (eds), *The Hirangi Hui: A Report Concerning the Government's Proposals for the Settlement of Treaty of Waitangi Claims and Related Constitutional Matters* (Turanga, 1995) para. 9.32.

Article the Second guarantees control, access to and the rights of guardianship, maintenance, documentation, storage, housing and development of these *taonga*.[54] As a consequence, the claimants voice their concerns about the protection and retention of such traditional knowledge, especially in the light of the adoption by the Crown of some intellectual property conventions, as they consider that these are in breach of the Crown's obligations under Article the Second of the Treaty.

Maori intellectual and cultural property rights: The claimants' concerns over intellectual and cultural property rights are threefold.

First, they are concerned about the unsuitable nature of intellectual property rights for the protection of Maori traditional knowledge and cultural property and the resulting difficulty for Maori to obtain intellectual property rights to enable them to protect or commercially exploit their traditional knowledge. This is due to the fundamental differences between the Western intellectual property rights system and the nature of indigenous traditional knowledge. For example, whereas indigenous people seek protection in perpetuity and do not want sacred information to be disclosed to the public, traditional intellectual property rights are usually limited in duration and involve disclosure to the public. In addition, other requirements, such as novelty or the identification of an individual or commercial entity as author or creator of a work or invention make it difficult for indigenous people to have access to intellectual property protection. Secondly, they are worried about the adverse effects intellectual property rights can have on traditional knowledge, cultural property and biological resources. Concerns include the granting of intellectual property rights to third parties for creations and inventions based on traditional knowledge and the resulting commercialisation of these creations and inventions, especially where sacred knowledge is involved, as well as the lack of equitable benefit sharing in the event of successful commercialisation. Specific concerns include the patenting of life forms and the inappropriate registration of trade marks based on Maori imagery and text. Finally, the claimants express concerns that their intellectual property rights are affected by New Zealand's intellectual property legislation and international obligations.

Protection of indigenous flora and fauna: The claimants allege that the Crown failed to fulfil its obligation under Article the Second of the Treaty to actively protect Maori's exercise of their chieftainship and protection over the indigenous flora and fauna. Also, they claim that it breached its obligations under the Treaty by agreeing to various international agreements that affect indigenous flora and fauna, such as the International Convention for the Protection of New Varieties of Plants (UPOV) and the TRIPS Agreement.

---

54   Austin, *supra* note 49, 35–3.

Specific concerns include bio-prospecting and access to indigenous flora and fauna, biotechnological developments involving genetic material, ownership claims to resources and species, Maori participation in decision-making on these matters and the right to benefit commercially from their traditional knowledge and their indigenous flora and fauna.

The Wai 262 claim was filed in 1991, but hearings didn't begin until 1998. The claimants' evidence was completed in March 2001, and the Tribunal also heard evidence from claimant expert witnesses and Tribunal commissioned researchers. The Crown filed its Statement of Response in June 2002 and the Tribunal produced a Statement of Issues based on the Statements of Claim and the Crown's Statement of Response in July 2006, which set the parameters of the Tribunal's inquiry.[55] Hearings of Tribunal expert witnesses, claimants, third parties and the Crown itself took place between September 2006 and June 2007 and the closing submissions took place in June 2007. The inquiry is currently at the report writing phase and the decision of the Tribunal is expected by the end of 2009.

The Wai 262 claim raises important issues. First, it challenges the right of the Crown to set cultural policies in areas that affect the interests of Maori. Indeed, the claim not only challenges policies that the Crown has adopted in the past, but also calls for recognition of the right of Maori to participate in the determination of the future direction of cultural policy in New Zealand. This should lead the Tribunal to question the appropriateness of removing control of important aspects of cultural policy development from the scrutiny of central government.[56] Secondly, the Tribunal will need to question the legitimacy of the current assumption that English law rules, doctrines and presumptions apply unless Maori can prove customary associations and entitlements. It has been argued that it should be the responsibility of the Crown to provide the Tribunal with evidence as to how, if at all, the relationships of the *tangata whenua*, the people of the land, with the indigenous flora and fauna have been subsumed lawfully and consistently with the Treaty so as to support claims to full ownership of such resources now being vested in the Department of Conservation, Crown Research Institutes, as well as patent, copyright or trade mark holders.[57] Finally, the outcome of the claim might have implications on the future content of intellectual property rights in New Zealand. Indeed, there are fundamental ideological differences between Maori traditional knowledge and the rights and obligations it involves, on the one hand, and traditional

---

55 The status of current inquiries before the Waitangi Tribunal is available at www.waitangi-tribunal.govt.nz/inquiries/floraandfaunawai262/

56 Austin, *supra* note 49, 357–8.

57 David Williams, *Matauranga Maori and Taonga* (Waitangi Tribunal Publication: Wellington, 2001) 11.

intellectual property regimes, on the other. Therefore, it is expected that one of the outcomes of the Wai 262 claim will be to lead to an adjustment of intellectual property laws, so that they can be consistent with the requirement of *te tino rangatiratanga*.[58]

The Mataatua Declaration on Cultural and Intellectual Property Rights of Indigenous Peoples

The Mataatua Declaration on Cultural and Intellectual Property Rights of Indigenous Peoples ('the Mataatua Declaration') was passed at the end of the First International Conference on the Cultural and Intellectual Property Rights of Indigenous Peoples in June 1993, the United Nations International Year for the World's Indigenous Peoples.[59] The conference, which was convened by the Nine Tribes of Mataatua in the Bay of Plenty Region of Aotearoa New Zealand, examined a range of issues, including the value of indigenous knowledge, biodiversity and biotechnology, customary environmental management, arts, music, language and other physical and spiritual cultural forms. The Mataatua Declaration is one of the first initiatives by indigenous peoples to promulgate their self-determination rights in relation to cultural and intellectual property, and even though it has not been adopted in any legal sense, it acts as a benchmark and can be used as a template for future initiatives.[60]

The Mataatua Declaration states that as a result of their right to self-determination, indigenous peoples must be recognised as the exclusive owners of their cultural and intellectual property. Also, it recognises the fact that indigenous peoples are capable of managing their traditional knowledge themselves.

---

[58]   As a result of the Wai 262 claim, the claimants had a small measure of influence on government policy. In 1994, they narrowly failed to obtain a Treaty of Waitangi protection mechanism in the legislation giving effect to the TRIPs Agreement. See Solomon, *supra* note 36.

[59]   One of the results of the United Nations International Year for the World's Indigenous Peoples was the promulgation of a Draft Declaration on the Rights of Indigenous Peoples (available at www.unhchr.ch/indigenous/main.html). Note that intellectual property plays an important role in the draft, thus showing the importance that intellectual property issues have gained for indigenous peoples throughout the world. The Draft Declaration states that indigenous peoples have the right to practise and revitalise their cultural traditions and customs, which include the right to maintain, protect and develop the past, present and future manifestations of their cultures (Art. 12). In addition, Art. 29 provides that 'indigenous peoples are entitled to the recognition of the full ownership, control and protection of their cultural and intellectual property. They have the right to special measures to control, develop and protect their sciences, technologies and cultural manifestations, including human and other genetic resources, seeds, medicines, knowledge of the properties of fauna and flora, oral traditions, literatures, designs and visual and performing arts'.

[60]   Solomon, *supra* note 36.

The Mataatua Declaration formulates various recommendations to indigenous peoples, as well as to states, national and international agencies. It states amongst other things that indigenous peoples should define themselves and their intellectual and cultural property, develop and maintain their traditional practices and sanctions for the protection, preservation and revitalisation of their traditional intellectual and cultural properties, establish a body with appropriate mechanisms to preserve and monitor the commercialisation of indigenous cultural properties in the public domain, advise and encourage indigenous peoples to take steps to protect their cultural heritage, and allow a mandatory consultative process with respect to any new legislation affecting indigenous cultural and intellectual property rights.[61] It also recommends that states and national and international agencies must recognise that indigenous peoples are the guardians of their customary knowledge and have the right to protect and control dissemination of that knowledge, that indigenous peoples have the right to create new knowledge based on cultural traditions, and that they should develop an additional cultural and intellectual property rights regime, in cooperation with indigenous peoples, which should incorporate:

- collective (as well as individual) ownership and origin;
- retroactive coverage of historical as well as contemporary works;
- protection against debasement of culturally significant items;
- cooperative rather than competitive framework;
- first beneficiaries to be the direct descendants of the traditional guardians of that knowledge; and
- multi-generational coverage span.

Finally, it recommends that both indigenous peoples and states, national and international agencies, should note that existing protection mechanisms are insufficient for the protection of indigenous peoples' cultural and intellectual property rights.

3.6.2 Exploitation of Maori Imagery and Text

There are a large number of examples of exploitation of Maori imagery and text by third parties in the commercial or show business context. Two of the most well-known examples that have prompted heated debates are the use of Maori and Polynesian names for a range of toys by Lego and the use of Maori imagery by Sony Playstation in a game called the 'Mark of Kri'.

---

[61] See section 1.

In 2001, Danish toy company Lego launched a new game called 'Bionicle', which was challenged by Maori tribes for using Maori and Polynesian names, such as *tohunga*, a spiritual healer.[62] The storyline of 'Bionicle' is said to be based on stories told by the Rapa Nui people, who live on Easter Island.[63] It features a range of action figures who inhabit an imaginary island called Mata Nui, which has fallen under the control of an evil spirit. The mission of the six heroes, called the Toa (meaning an especially brave Maori warrior) with names such as Whenua (land) or Pohatu (stone), is to liberate the inhabitants of the island. Maori groups approached Lego saying they considered the use of the Maori language by Lego to be inappropriate and offensive. After initially claiming that it had not done anything illegal, Lego later admitted it had drawn partly on Polynesian culture for inspiration and had borrowed names from the Maori culture to spice up its toys.[64] The company said that 'future launches of Bionicle sets will not incorporate names from any original culture'. Furthermore, it added that it 'will seek to develop a code of conduct for cultural expressions of traditional knowledge'.[65]

In March 2003, Sony PlayStation released a game called the 'Mark of Kri', featuring Rau, a warrior wearing a facial tattoo and carrying a *taiaha* (an ancient Maori weapon). The game was criticised by Maori intellectual property campaigners for its 'inappropriate and upsetting usage of New Zealand Maori imagery'. In addition, they thought that Rau was promoted as a violent barbarian, thus portraying Maori in a negative manner to the international audience and linking them with stereotyped violence.[66] Indeed, the hero of the 'Mark of Kri' has been said to look and feel 'like a brutal, blood-thirsty Conan character from New Zealand has broken into a Disney film and gone wild' by IGN entertainment gaming magazine.[67] Sony replied that while the game was somewhat Maori inspired, it was not intended to be directly Maori. According to Jeff Merghart, the game's art designer, the creators tried to keep the imagery as ethnically neutral as possible. 'The geographical look of the game is supposed to represent a world that never really existed but looks like it could

---

[62]   On the Lego case, see also the response of New Zealand to the WIPO Questionnaire on National Experiences with the Legal Protection of Expressions of Folklore, available at www.wipo.int/tk/en/questionnaires/ic-2-7/newzealand.pdf

[63]   Andrew Osborn, 'Maoris Win Lego Battle', *Guardian Unlimited*, 31 October 2001.

[64]   Ibid.

[65]   Ibid.

[66]   As recounted by Maori intellectual property campaigner Kingi Gilbert in a letter to Sony Computer Entertainment dated 28 March 2003, available at www.aocafe.com/forums/

[67]   Interview with Jeff Merghart, the 'Mark of Kri's art designer by Douglass C. Perry, available at http://ps2.ign.com/articles/365/365290p1.html

have'.[68] When asked to comment on the actual designs, tattoos and markings on the characters themselves, Merghart said that:

> [T]hey were a variation of Polynesian, Celtic, Greek, etc. designs ... but we tried not to replicate anything specific. It was hard because everyone liked the Polynesian flavour that the game was taking on so we tried to make things with a more contemporary or inventive Polynesian twist where we could.[69]

Whereas Sony denies any plagiarism, the company's own promotional websites describes the game as 'set in an ancient Maori-inspired world of swords and sorcerers'[70] and promotes it with the slogan 'strip to the waist and cover yourself in Maori-esque tattoos, because after watching our gore-drenched vid barbarian chic will be all the rage'.[71]

Other examples of commercial exploitation of Maori imagery and text include the use of a Maori style tattoo on the boot of a Ford truck,[72] the use of a kiwi, which is an indigenous bird of New Zealand, and other Maori imagery and text in relation to rugby boots,[73] and the use of Maori imagery in the fashion industry.[74]

---

68   Ibid.

69   Ibid.

70   See http://uk.playstation.com/games/gamesinfo04_game.jhtml?localeTitleId=1040798

71   See http://uk.playstation.com/news/newsStory.jhtml?storyId=103161_en_GB_NEWS&linktype=GRS

72   On a promotional website, Ford Motor Company said that the hard-core, tattooed appearance of the Ford F-150 Lightning truck was inspired by the resurgence of rock-and-roll and the current fascination with body art and admitted that the tattoo on the boot of the truck was inspired by the Maori. It explained that in Maori culture, a tattooed face was a great source of pride to a warrior, for it made him fierce in battle. Ed Golden, the Executive Director of North American Ford Brand Design further added that 'the F-150 has a great history and has consistently been the leader among full-size pick-ups – it is certainly fierce in battle'. See www.fast-autos.net/ford/fordrod.html

73   In 2002, sports apparel manufacturer Canterbury of New Zealand released a new range of rugby boots on the New Zealand market. While three of the eight new boot designs incorporated explicit *koru*-based designs (*koru* means a fern frond that symbolises life, growth, strength and peace) in the form of differently coloured leather decorations on the outside of the boot, all eight boots were given names such as *Rangatira* (chiefly person), *Tane-Toa* (champion), *kaha* (strength), *whetu* (star), *moko* (tattoo), *toa* (warrior), *hiko* (flash, zigzag, shine) and *haka* (posture dance). For more information, see Peter Shand, 'Scenes from the Colonial Catwalk: Cultural Appropriation, Intellectual Property Rights, and Fashion' (2002) 3 *Cultural Analysis* 74–7.

Canterbury of New Zealand was not the only sports apparel manufacturer to draw its inspiration from the exoticism or reputation of indigenous or cultural symbols. In 1999,

In addition to the commercial exploitation of Maori imagery and text, many personalities have recently been subject to a growing fascination for the Maori culture. Celebrities such as rock star Robbie Williams or boxer Mike Tyson have exhibited Maori-style tattoos, and soccer player Eric Cantona appeared on the cover of British style magazine *GQ* with a *moko*[75] painted on his face.

Over the past few years, attempts have been made in New Zealand to protect some aspects of Maori TK and TCEs through traditional intellectual property rights such as copyright, trade marks or patents. These, however, were not always successful because of the fundamental divergences between the aim and essence of the intellectual property rights system and the needs of Maori.

In 1999, Wellington's Ngati Toa Iwi applied to trade mark[76] *Te Rauparaha's Haka*, the haka posture dance, mainly known through rugby as the dance performed by the All Blacks.[77] The tribe claimed ownership of the haka, saying that it had been written by their ancestor Te Rauparaha, while hiding from pursuers, and that as a consequence it should be protected as identifiable cultural property because it did not belong to everyone. While the trade mark application for the registration of Te Rauparaha's haka is still pending, many doubt that it will be successful. They consider that its registration is against the purpose of a trade mark, which is to distinguish a product or a service in the course of trade. According to New Zealand intellectual property lawyer, John Hackett, 'the haka would be classified as a song or a chant or a

---

Adidas' advertisement campaign included the image of a Maori warrior wearing a *moko*. Similarly, it is interesting to note that the name and logo of the Nike company come from Greek mythology. Indeed, the company, which was first known as Blue Ribbon Sports in 1964, changed its name to Nike, after the Greek goddess of victory, in 1968. In the same way, the Nike SWOOSH logo, created in 1971 by Caroline Davidson, represents the wings of the Greek goddess Nike.

[74]   Examples include the use of interlocking curvilinear *koru* designs on women's swimsuits by New Zealand swimwear manufacturer Moontide in 1998, and Paco Rabanne's Spring 1998 collection featuring two models wearing metal outfits reproducing a stylised *moko*.

[75]   '*Ta Moko*' is the Maori form of a tattoo tradition which extends throughout the islands of Polynesia.

[76]   Trade mark applications No. 305166, 305167 and 305168 filed by researcher Oriwa Solomon.

[77]   The *Ka mate!* haka has been performed by the All Blacks, correctly or incorrectly, for over 100 years and it has come to symbolise the power and invincibility of the All Blacks and their place in world rugby. Ironically, on many occasions, foreign companies and journalists seeking information about the haka have contacted the New Zealand Rugby Team, and when debate erupted within the Maori community over the use of the haka in a foreign commercial, the production company argued that they had sought advice from the New Zealand Rugby Union on its use. See Wira Gardiner, *Haka: A Living Tradition* (Hodder Moa Beckett Publishers Ltd: Auckland, 2001) 91–4.

challenge, rather than a trade mark. As such it comes under the Copyright Act.'[78]

Despite that, he added that it was unlikely that copyright would apply to the original haka either, since copyright in New Zealand only exists for 50 years after the death of the original author. He suggested that the only way to get intellectual property protection would be for the iwi to develop a new and original haka, which would then be protected by copyright.[79]

3.6.3 The New Zealand Trade Marks Act 2002

The New Zealand Trade Marks Act 2002 replaced the New Zealand Trade Marks Act 1953 and introduced some major changes to New Zealand trade mark law. One of its purposes is to address the concerns of Maori relating to the registration of trade marks containing a Maori sign, including imagery and text.[80] It does so mainly by allowing trade mark registration to be denied on the grounds of cultural offence to significant sections of the community, particularly Maori, and by creating an Advisory Committee to help the Commissioner of Trade Marks (the Commissioner) assess the potential offensiveness of a trade mark.

Legislative background
The adoption of the new provisions was the result of a process that began in 1990, when the Ministry of Commerce[81] released a general discussion paper entitled *Review of Industrial Property Rights, Patents, Trade Marks and Designs: Possible Options for Reform, Volume One*[82] with the intention to undertake a broad-ranging and integrated review of New Zealand's intellectual property rights legislation. In 1991, the Ministry of Commerce proposed a number of changes to the 1953 Act in an options paper entitled *Reform of the Trade Marks Act 1953.*[83] However, following concerns expressed by Maori that the proposed reforms to the 1953 Act did not adequately protect their cultural and intellectual property, work on the legislation was suspended in order to undertake consultation with Maori. In 1994, four national *hui* (workshops)

---

[78]   See www.ajpark.co.nz/content/news/haka_not_trademark.htm
[79]   Ibid.
[80]   Trade Marks Act 2002, s. 3(c).
[81]   Now Ministry of Economic Development.
[82]   Ministry of Commerce, Competition Policy and Business Law Division, *Review of Industrial Property Rights, Patents, Trade Marks and Designs: Possible Options for Reform, Volume One* (Ministry of Commerce: Wellington, 1990).
[83]   Ministry of Commerce, Competition Policy and Business Law Division, *Reform of the Trade Marks Act 1953* (Ministry of Commerce: Wellington, 1991).

were held, resulting in the establishment of the Maori Trade Marks Focus Group ('the Focus Group'). The task of the Focus Group was to discuss issues related to the registration of signs involving Maori 'words, symbols, sounds or smells'.[84] The Focus Group met in 1995 and 1996 and produced a background paper in 1997,[85] which reported the outcome of its deliberations. Eight further *hui* were then held around the country to discuss the issues arising from the paper. The work of the Focus Group and subsequent consultations formed the basis of recommendations to Cabinet in April 1999, concerning measures to be included in the future Bill.

The Focus Group recommended that Maori words, symbols, sounds or smells should be registrable by 'any person' who was able to satisfy the requirements of source, consent and cultural appropriateness. Within the context of trade mark application procedure, it recommended the establishment of a consultative group to include Maori people with expertise in the registration process and in Maori arts or language. Finally, the Focus Group agreed with a former proposal of the Ministry of Commerce to reform the 1953 Act by replacing the Commissioner's residual discretion under section 16 to refuse to register a matter that is considered 'scandalous' or 'contrary to morality' with discretion to refuse to register a trade mark that would cause offence to a significant section of the community.[86]

Taking into account the 1991 Recommendations for Reform of the Trade Marks Act 1953 of the Ministry of Commerce proposing a modern law of trade marks, the amendments which had already been made in 1994 in order to comply with the TRIPS requirements, the results of the consultation with Maori and the recommendations of the Focus Group, the government issued a Trade Marks Bill in 2001 and adopted the revised Trade Marks Act in 2002.

Offensive trade marks   Under the New Zealand Trade Marks Act 2002, a trade mark can be registered provided that there are no absolute or relative grounds for refusing to register it. One of those absolute bars to registration can be found in section 17(1)(b)(ii). It provides that:

---

84   Ministry of Commerce and Maori Trade Marks Focus Group, *Maori and Trade Marks: A Discussion Paper* (Ministry of Commerce: Wellington, 1997) 12–13.

85   Ibid.

86   However, in its Discussion Paper, the Focus Group put emphasis on the Commissioner's discretion to refuse to register a trade mark that was 'culturally inappropriate', as opposed to one that could cause offence. It pointed out that 'offensiveness' was difficult to define and that it didn't cover use that was inappropriate while not necessarily being offensive. For more information on the recommendations of the Focus Group, see Morgan Owen, 'Protecting Indigenous Signs and Trade Marks: The New Zealand Experiment' (2004) 1 *Intellectual Property Quarterly* 66–7.

The Commissioner must not … register a trade mark or part of a trade mark if the Commissioner considers that its use or registration would be likely to offend a significant section of the community, including Maori.[87]

The 'offence' provision of section 17(1)(b)(ii) represents a significant development for the protection of TCEs. Indeed, there is no exact equivalent to section 17(1)(b)(ii) in either the 1953 Act or in jurisdictions other than New Zealand. Section 17(1)(b)(ii) has replaced the well-known tests of 'scandalous matter' and 'contrary to morality' of section 16(1) of the 1953 Act, which was almost identical to the former 1938 UK Trade Marks Act.[88] Section 16(1) of the 1953 Act provided that:

> It shall not be lawful to register as a trade mark or part of a trade mark any scandalous matter or any matter the use of which would be likely to deceive or cause confusion or would be contrary to law or morality or would otherwise be disentitled to protection in a Court of justice.

Section 3(3)(a) of the UK Trade Marks Act 1994, on the other hand, which is in line with Directive 89/104,[89] provides that '[a] trade mark shall not be registered if it is contrary to public policy or to accepted principles of morality'.

Whereas provisions of a similar nature to that of section 3(3)(a) of the UK Trade Marks Act 1994 can be found in the law or practice of most countries, though sometimes with a different terminology,[90] section 17(1)(b)(ii) is unique in its unprecedented attempt to provide protection to Maori imagery and text.

The original text of section 17(1)(b)(ii) in the Trade Marks Bill provided that the Commissioner should not register a trade mark if he considers 'on reasonable grounds' that its use or registration would be likely to offend a significant section of the community, including Maori. However, the words 'on reasonable grounds' were omitted from the text of section 17(1)(b)(ii), in order to remove any suggestion that the Commissioner does not have a duty to act reasonably in respect of other powers of decision contained in the Act. In addition, it was thought that the omission of these words helped retain the duty of the Commissioner to determine registrability of trade marks independently of the Advisory Committee's advice.[91]

---

[87] Trade Marks Act 2002, s. 17(1)(b)(ii).

[88] New Zealand's trade mark law has historically been identical to that of the United Kingdom's. Although recently the United Kingdom's trade mark law has taken a European orientation, the core principles remain the same.

[89] See Council Directive 89/104/EEC to approximate the laws of the Member States relating to trade marks, Art. 3(1)(f). See also Council Regulation (EC) 40/94 on the Community Trade Mark, Art. 7(1)(f).

[90] See Phillips, *supra* note 3.

[91] Commerce Select Committee, 'Trade Mark Bill as Reported from the

Section 17(1)(b)(ii) contains three important elements:

(1) **'The Commissioner considers':** The use of these words reinforces the assumption that it is the Commissioner's decision and not the Advisory Committee's decision that determines the question of registrability of a trade mark.

(2) **'Likely to offend':** Section 17(1)(b)(ii) provides that the Commissioner must not register trade marks that 'would be likely to offend' a significant section of the community, including Maori. The Commissioner does not need actual proof that the registration of a trade mark would offend. A likelihood to offend is sufficient. Whereas one of the main reasons for replacing 'scandalous matter' and 'contrary to morality' by 'likely to offend' was that the previous terms were subjective, it should be noted that 'likely to offend' also requires the Commissioner to make a subjective judgement as to what he considers would be likely to offend. According to the Commerce Select Committee that issued a report on the Trade Marks Bill in March 2002, the change was seen as best meeting the needs of modern New Zealand society. Indeed, one of the advantages of using the phrase 'likely to offend' is to avoid risks associated with using more prescriptive criteria that would become outdated and inflexible as a basis for assessing the appropriateness of particular trade marks.[92]

There is no definition of what should be considered likely to 'offend' in the Act. As a consequence, commentators on the law have attempted to provide guidance as to its meaning. For Susy Frankel, one of the possible meanings of 'offensive' is that the trade mark uses a word or image of cultural significance in a manner that ignores or defiles the purpose for which the image or word is traditionally used.[93] According to Owen Morgan, on the other hand, words should be given effect in their ordinary and natural meaning. Accordingly, on the basis of the online edition of the *Oxford English Dictionary*, he considers that the use or registration of a trade mark is likely to be offensive in relation to an act that causes annoyance or disgust.[94]

According to the Practice Guidelines of the Intellectual Property Office of New Zealand (IPONZ) on section 17 of the Trade Marks Act 2002, a distinc-

---

Commerce Committee', 3, available at www.clerk.parliament.govt.nz//content/643/142bar2.pdf

[92]   Ibid.

[93]   In order to illustrate this, she gives the example of the reproduction of various New Zealand icons, such as a *hetiki* (greenstone pendant personifying a human ancestor) on a paper mat produced by McDonald's which is used in their restaurants to cover food trays (in this example, however, the *hetiki* was not used as a trade mark). See Susy Frankel, 'Third Party Trade Marks as a Violation of Indigenous Cultural Property: A New Statutory Safeguard', paper presented at the Twelfth Fordham Annual Conference on International Intellectual Property Law and Policy, 15 April 2004, 6 and 12.

[94]   Owen, *supra* note 86, 71–2.

tion should be drawn between marks that are offensive and marks that would be considered by some to be in poor taste. Section 17(1)(b)(ii) only prohibits the registration of marks that are likely to offend a significant section of the community. Therefore, it does not prohibit the registration of marks that are in poor taste. In addition, the Practice Guidelines provide that a mark should be considered likely to offend a significant section of the community where it is likely to cause a significant section of the community to be outraged and/or a significant section of the community is likely to feel that the use or registration of the mark should be subject to censure.[95]

(3) **'Significant section of the community, including Maori':** The terms 'significant section of the community' were chosen to allow for changes in New Zealand's social and demographic patterns, and shifts in the mix and significance of identifiable groups, values and beliefs to be recognised over time.[96] According to the Practice Guidelines, the significant section of the community may be a minority that is nevertheless substantial in number. In addition, a higher degree of outrage or censure among a smaller section of the community, or a lesser degree of outrage or censure among a larger section of the community, may suffice.[97]

The statute provides that the significant section of the community includes Maori. According to the Commerce Committee, the aim of this provision was to balance the interests of Maori and persons seeking to register a trade mark, and the specific reference to Maori signals the intent to recognise concerns of Maori with regard to intellectual property law. However, since Maori already constitute a significant section of the community, it is unclear whether a section of the Maori community would also qualify. In its Discussion Paper, the Focus Group considered that 'significant' was a relative term, and that therefore, it should be defined. However, it argued that the word 'significant' might mean an extended family or a tribe. As a consequence one can assume that a significant section of the Maori community could qualify under section 17(1)(b)(ii). Finally, even though the Act specifically refers to Maori, it is clear that sections of the community other than Maori may also invoke the provision.

During the consultation period of the Trade Marks Bill, criticisms of the future law included concerns that section 17(1)(b)(ii) could give rise to a considerable increase in objections to trade mark applications and result in

---

[95] IPONZ Trade Mark Practice Guidelines, 'Section 17 of the Trade Marks Act 2002, Absolute Grounds: General', 34, available at www.iponz.govt.nz/pls/web/dbssiten.main

[96] Commerce Select Committee, *supra* note 91, 3.

[97] IPONZ Trade Mark Practice Guidelines, 'Section 17', *supra* note 95, 34. See also *Ghazilian's Trade Mark Application*, *supra* note 28.

increasing numbers of trade mark applications being rejected. Also, it was argued that the words 'offend a significant section of the community, including Maori' were untested judicially and ultimately, when taken in conjunction with the Advisory Committee, would cause delay and increased costs for the IPONZ.[98] According to officials of the IPONZ, however, out of approximately 2,000 trade mark applications they received each month, only 12 to 15 contained Maori imagery and text. As a consequence, they did not consider that the new provisions would result in an increase in the number of applications, or that there would be cost impacts as a result of the new provisions.[99]

Invalidity of registration of a trade mark   Section 73(1) of the Act provides that:

> The Commissioner or the Court may, on the application of an aggrieved person (which includes a person who is culturally aggrieved), declare that the registration of a trade mark is invalid to the extent that the trade mark was not registrable under Part 2 at the deemed date of its registration.

Section 73(1), which gives standing to an aggrieved person to apply to declare a registration invalid, is related to section 17(1)(b)(ii) by the fact that it explicitly provides that aggrieved persons include persons who are culturally aggrieved and that it directly refers to the registrability provisions of Part 2.

This section raises the question whether any aggrieved person could apply for the registration of a trade mark to be declared invalid or whether this person has to represent 'a significant section of the community'. It should be presumed that the aggrieved person should represent 'a significant section of the community' or, in other words, that the person should be aggrieved because the registration is likely to offend a significant section of the community, the risk being that otherwise any person, who would not normally be given standing under section 17(1)(b)(ii) because they do not represent 'a significant section of the community', would be able later to declare the registration of a trade mark invalid.

In addition, it should be noted that this provision does not have a retrospective effect. Indeed, it is considered that the question of registrability must be judged 'at the deemed date of its registration'.[100] This means that, for example, it would not be possible for an aggrieved person to apply to declare the registration of a culturally offensive trade mark invalid if that trade mark has become offensive over time or was registered before the coming into force of the Trade Marks Act 2002.

---

98 Commerce Select Committee, *supra* note 91, 11.
99 Ibid. 8.
100 Owen, *supra* note 86, 76.

The Maori Trade Marks Advisory Committee

In April 1999, the work of the Focus Group and subsequent consultations formed the basis of recommendations to Cabinet concerning measures to be included in the Trade Marks Act 2002. Amongst those was a recommerdation to establish a consultative group to advise the Commissioner. In September 1999, Cabinet agreed that the new Trade Marks Act should include a provision to establish what is now referred to as the Maori Trade Marks Advisory Committee ('the Committee').[101]

The Act requires the Commissioner to appoint an Advisory Committee in order to assist him determine whether a trade mark is offensive or not.[102] The key rationale for establishing the Committee was to minimise the risk that the Crown may inadvertently register as a trade mark Maori imagery and text, where registration or use of the trade mark was likely to cause offence to Maori.[103]

Accordingly, section 178 of the Act provides that the function of the Committee is to:

> Advise the Commissioner whether the proposed use or registration of a trade mark that is, or appears to be, derivative of a Maori sign, including text and imagery, is, or is likely to be, offensive to Maori.

The advice of the Committee is not binding on the Commissioner, who will consider it taking into account all relevant factors affecting registrabilty and may come to a determination on the eligibility of an application that is different from the advice of the Committee.[104]

Examination procedure First, all trade mark applications received by IPONZ are assessed to determine whether they contain a Maori sign, or are derived from a Maori sign.[105] An application containing a Maori sign will be forwarded to the Committee to determine whether the mark is likely to be offensive to Maori. Members of the Committee are required to advise the

---

[101] IPONZ Trade Mark Practice Guidelines, 'Sections 177–180 of the Trade Marks Act 2002', 2, available at www.iponz.govt.nz/pls/web/dbssiten.main

[102] Trade Marks Act 2002, s. 177(1).

[103] However, many expressed concerns that by requiring the establishment of a Maori Advisory Committee, s. 178 discriminates against other 'significant sections of the community'.

[104] See IPONZ Trade Mark Practice Guidelines, 'Sections 177–180', *supra* note 101.

[105] Where the examiner is not sure whether or not the trade mark applied for contains a Maori sign or is derived from a Maori sign, the application is forwarded to the Advisory Committee.

Commissioner within a set time-frame of the outcome of their preliminary considerations. If individual members consider that the registration of the trade mark will not cause offence to Maori, the application will then proceed through the usual process of trade mark examination. If, on the other hand, members of the Committee have concerns regarding the potential offensiveness of the trade mark, the Committee will meet to consider the application and determine whether the mark is either: (i) not offensive to Maori; (ii) not likely to be offensive to Maori; (iii) likely to be offensive to Maori, or (iv) offensive to Maori. Alternatively, the Committee may consider that further information is required before a determination can be made.[106] If the Committee advises the Commissioner that a trade mark is offensive, or likely to be offensive to Maori, the Commissioner may raise concerns that the mark is not registrable under section 17(1)(b)(ii) of the Act. Once the Committee has advised the Commissioner on a trade mark, the applicant will be sent a Compliance Report and will be invited to respond within 12 months to have his application in order for acceptance.[107]

Since the coming into force of the Trade Marks Act 2002, up until June 2008, the Advisory Committee has assessed a little over 1500 trade marks containing Maori imagery and text. Of these, the Committee found that 16 were likely to be offensive to Maori.[108]

Examples of offensive marks   Examples of trade marks containing Maori imagery that were registered in the past, but would be unlikely to be acceptable for registration today, include the image of a Maori head, with the words MAORI CHIEF in relation to butter (1893), the image of a *Tiki* (traditional ornament) with the words CODY'S PALE ALE and TIKI in relation to ale and stout (1914), the head of a Maori with the words NATIVE SAUCE and NATIVE BRAND in relation to Worcester sauce, pickles and chutney (1927),

---

[106]   In that case, the Committee will advise the Commissioner of the nature of the information required. The Commissioner will consider the Committee's advice, which is not binding, and determine whether to advise the applicant to obtain the additional information.

[107]   For more information on the examination process, see IPONZ Trade Mark Practice Guidelines, *supra* note 101, 3 and 10–12.

[108]   Statistics as of June 2008, provided by the Intellectual Property Office of New Zealand. Offensive marks included the use of a *koru* (a fern frond symbolising life) in relation to biological tissues and biotech processes, a reference to *tane*, the god of forests and humankind, and the concept of *mana* (meaning power, authority, prestige and honour) in relation to alcohol. See Report of the Sixth Session of the Intergovernmental Committee on Intellectual Property and Genetic Resources, Traditional Knowledge and Folklore, Geneva, 15 to 19 March 2004, Document WIPO/GRTKF/IC/6/14, 19.

Goods: "butter" (1893)

Goods: "ale and stout" (1914)

Goods: "Worcester sauce,
pickles and chutney" (1927)

Goods: "cigarettes" (1931)

*Figure 3.1   Examples of trade marks containing Maori imagery that would
now be considered offensive*

and Maori carving devices with the words LOYAL'S CIGARETTES in relation to cigarettes (1931).[109] Maori attribute special significance to certain
words, images and locations.[110] As a consequence, the association of the head
of a Maori chief with goods such as butter or Worcester sauce, pickles and
chutney, and the association of carving devices or a *tiki* with cigarettes or ale
and stout, could be considered culturally offensive and inappropriate to a
significant number of Maori.

---

[109]   See IPONZ Trade Mark Practice Guidelines, 'Section 17', *supra* note 95, 35.
[110]   This has to be understood in light of the concepts of *tapu* and *noa*. *Tapu*
(which can be interpreted as 'sacred') contains a strong imposition of rules and prohibitions. A person, object or place, which is *tapu*, may not be touched or come into
human contact. On the other hand, *noa* is the opposite of *tapu* and includes the concept
of common. Things that are *tapu* and things that are *noa* are to be separated because
the association of something which is *tapu*, such as a chief, or a carving, with something which is *noa*, such as food or cigarettes, can be considered offensive. Ibid.

3.6.4   Conclusion

The New Zealand Trade Marks Act 2002 represents a significant development for the protection of TCEs, both for New Zealand and the international community. It introduces important changes in the trade mark registration system that take into account cultural offensiveness, and sets an example internationally for the protection of TCEs.

The experience of New Zealand shows that it is possible to adapt traditional intellectual property rights in order to protect TCEs, or at least their commercially exploitable aspects. Indeed, the New Zealand Trade Marks Act 2002 does not aim to provide a general protection of Maori culture and heritage, but only practical measures to deal with cultural offensiveness. However, even though it is limited, the protection provided by the Act is in line with New Zealand's approach to the protection of traditional cultural expressions, which is to focus on the prevention of misappropriation. Also, it represents a step forward towards New Zealand's wider aim, which is to achieve the goals and aspirations of traditional knowledge holding communities and people.[111] It remains to be seen whether New Zealand's policy options, which have shown positive results, could be adopted by other states in order to form a basis for domestic policy.

3.7   THE UNITED STATES' EXPERIENCE

3.7.1   Introduction

Over the years, the use of Native American names and images in sports teams' names, mascots and logos has been a widespread practice in both professional and amateur sports arenas in the United States. Whereas amateur teams do not usually own trade marks on those names and images, most professional teams have registered them as trade marks, and it is estimated that the sale of professional team apparel and the licensing of merchandise is a multi-billion dollar industry. High profile examples of uses of Native American names and images in sports teams' names, mascots and logos include the team name of the Atlanta 'Braves' professional baseball organisation and the fan ritual called the 'Tomahawk Chop', the Cleveland 'Indians' professional baseball team name and 'Chief Wahoo' mascot, and perhaps the most controversial of all, the Washington 'Redskins' professional football team name. Over the past decades, Native Americans and other individuals have been campaigning to

---

[111]   Document WIPO/GRTKF/IC/6/14.

change this practice as they consider it to be disparaging, racially discrimina-tory and to perpetuate racial stereotypes.

This part will first set out the context of the Redskins cases by examining section 2(a) of the Lanham Trademark Act ('the Lanham Act'), which enables the United States Patent and Trademark Office (USPTO) to refuse to register trade marks which contain immoral, deceptive, scandalous or disparaging matter. In particular, it will focus on trade marks which consist of or comprise scandalous matter and those which may disparage persons, living or dead, institutions, beliefs or national symbols. It will then move on to examine the litigation involving the Washington Redskins trade marks and conclude by analysing the efficiency and usefulness of section 2(a) of the Lanham Act to protect TCEs, and the potential implications of the Redskins cases.

3.7.2 Section 2(a) of the Lanham Trademark Act

Unlike analogous sections in predecessor statutes, which only focused their attention on morality,[112] section 2(a) of the Lanham Act is also designed to discourage the commercial use of offensive subject matter that may not directly implicate principles of morality or virtue.

Section 2(a) of the Lanham Act[113] provides that no trade mark, by which the goods of the applicant may be distinguished from the goods of others, shall be refused registration on the principal register on account of its nature unless it consists of or comprises (1) immoral, (2) deceptive or (3) scandalous matter; or matter which may (4) disparage or (5) falsely suggest a connection with persons, living or dead, institutions, beliefs or national symbols, or (6) bring them into contempt or disrepute.

The language of the statute draws a distinction between scandalous, immoral and deceptive marks, on the one hand, and disparaging, contemptuous and false

---

[112]   The Trademark Acts of 1881 and 1882 did not expressly ban immoral subject matter from registration. The 1905 Trademark Act was the first federal statute to directly and explicitly forbid registration of scandalous and immoral trade marks. Section 5(a) of the 1905 Act provided 'that no mark by which the goods of the owner of the mark may be distinguished from other goods of the same class shall be refused registration as a trademark on account of the nature of such mark unless such mark: (a) Consists of or comprises immoral or scandalous matter'. In 1947, the Lanham Act extended its definition of offensive matter in section 2(a) to also forbid the registration of trade marks that consist of or comprise matter that may 'disparage' or bring into 'contempt' or 'disrepute' persons (living or dead), institutions, beliefs, or national symbols. See Stephen R. Baird, 'Moral Intervention in the Trademark Arena: Banning the Registration of Scandalous and Immoral Trademarks' (1993) 83 *TMR* 666–7.
[113]   Section 2(a) of the Lanham (Trademark) Act of 1946 (as amended) 15 USC § 1052(a) (1988).

connection trade marks on the other. While trade marks falling within the first grouping are refused registration when they consist of or comprise matter that actually *is* scandalous, immoral or deceptive, trade marks falling within the second grouping are refused registration when they consist of or comprise matter that *may* be disparaging, contemptuous or suggestive of a false connection. In other words, registration will be refused even where the nature of the mark cannot be proven with certainty.

Scandalous trade marks

Because of the paucity of legislative history to aid in interpreting the term 'scandalous' in section 2(a) of the Lanham Act, courts have found that they must 'give the word "scandalous" its ordinary and common meaning'.[114] In particular, courts have looked to dictionary definitions existing at the time of the enactment of the Trademark Act in 1946. According to those definitions, the term 'scandalous' means:

> Giving offence to the conscience or moral feelings; exciting reprobation, calling out condemnation ... Disgraceful to reputation ... shocking to the sense of truth, decency, or propriety; disgraceful, offensive; disreputable, as scandalous conduct.[115]

Academics have divided cases considering scandalous marks into two separate categories, depending on the approach taken by reviewing bodies:[116] (i) the 'rule of association' approach, and (ii) the 'anti-contextual approach' or the 'per se rule'.[117] The rule of association approach acknowledges that a mark is not scandalous on its face, but may become scandalous when placed in a certain context. Consequently, where the association between the mark and the goods is offensive, registration will be refused. Where, on the other hand, the resulting association is innocent, registration will be allowed. Under this approach, an innocent term may therefore be considered scandalous because of its context, and an otherwise offensive mark may be registered because of

---

[114]   *In re Riverbank Canning Co.*, 95 F.2d 327, 328; 37 USPQ 268.
[115]   *In re McGinley*, 660 F.2d 481, 486; 211 USPQ 673.
[116]   Trade mark decisions in the United States can be made either by an administrative body or by a Federal Court.
[117]   See Ethan G. Zlotchew, '"Scandalous" or "Disparaging"? It Should Make a Difference in Opposition and Cancellations Actions: Views on the Lanham Act's Section 2(a) Prohibitions Using the Example of Native American Symbolism in Athletics' (1998) 22 *Colum.-VLA JL and Arts* 226 and Justin G. Blankenship, 'The Cancellation of Redskins as a Disparaging Trademark: Is Federal Trademark Law an Appropriate Solution for Words that Offend?' (2001) 72 *U Colo. L Rev.* 431.

its innocent context.[118] On the other hand, under the anti-contextual approach or per se rule, a reviewing body need not examine the context of the mark. It will only look at whether the mark is scandalous on its face.[119] Consequently, decisions taken under the anti-contextual approach or per se rule, without the association between the marks and the goods, are more subjective and unpredictable than under the rule of association approach.

It emerges from a thorough analysis of section 2(a) case law interpreting the term 'scandalous', that there are seven distinct groupings of decisions: (i) decisions having in common marks with a religious nexus; (ii) decisions having in common marks that consist of or comprise racial slurs, insults or epithets; (iii) decisions having in common marks that consist of or comprise profane matter; (iv) decisions having in common marks consisting of or comprising vulgar matter; (v) decisions having in common marks that relate to sexuality; (vi) decisions having in common innuendo marks; and (vii) decisions having in common marks that suggest or promote illegal activity.[120]

The most relevant categories of decisions in the context of the protection of TCEs are those consisting of or comprising religious content, and most importantly those concerning marks that consist of or comprise racial slurs, insults or epithets.

Decisions with a religious content can be divided into three main categories:

- those identifying the name of the Supreme Being. In that situation, the scandal arises from the trivialisation and commercialisation of the name of the Supreme Being. This applies to the use of all names that designate the Supreme Being and to any religious group, including minority groups, such as indigenous communities;

---

[118]   For example, while the trade mark MADONNA is legitimate as a registration for a pop music star (US Trademark Reg. No. 1,473,554 (1988)), it may become scandalous when placed on a bottle of wine, because of the potential religious significance. See *In re Riverbank Canning Co.*, *supra* note 114, 328. Similarly, in *Ex parte Martha Maid Mfg. Co.*, 37 USPQ 156 (Comm'r Patents 1938), it was held that the mark 'Queen Mary', while innocent enough on its face, took on a scandalous meaning when associated with women's undergarments. See Blankenship, *supra* note 117, 431–3.

[119]   This approach was taken in the case *In re Tinseltown, Inc.*, 212 USPQ 863 (TTAB 1981) where the Board held that the trade mark BULLSHIT was scandalous per se and that its association with fashion accessories did not make it any more or less scandalous.

[120]   This analysis is based on decisions interpreting s. 2(a) of the Lanham Act as well as decisions interpreting the statutory sections that preceded s. 2(a) of the Lanham Act. See Baird, *supra* note 112, 704.

- those consisting of or comprising words or symbols of great religious significance. This is relevant for indigenous communities as words or symbols with religious or sacred significance have often been registered as trade marks by third parties, often causing great offence; and
- those that name or otherwise identify a known religious organisation or its members.

Cases involving trade marks that consist of or comprise racial slurs, insults or epithets are relevant for the protection of TCEs as the use of such trade marks can be deeply offensive to indigenous communities. It has been acknowledged that there is a public interest in protecting the sensibilities of those living in a minority status because the use of such matter perpetuates racial stereotypes against minority groups and degrades those individuals of the identified race.[121]

Finally, there is no need for a majority of the general public to be shocked or offended to trigger protection under section 2(a). In *Maverty Media Group Ltd*, it was established that whether the trade mark comprises scandalous matter is to be ascertained from the standpoint of not necessarily a majority, but a substantial composite of the general public, and in the context of contemporary attitudes.[122] Consequently, it is enough that a minority group, such as Native Americans, be shocked or offended for scandal to be raised.

Disparaging trade marks
There is relatively little published precedent or legislative history on the disparagement provision of section 2(a) of the Lanham Act. Section 2(a) of the Lanham Act precludes registration of trade marks which consist of or comprise matter that may disparage: (i) living or dead persons, (ii) institutions, (iii) beliefs, and (iv) national symbols. As with scandalousness, it is presumed that Congress intended to adopt the ordinary and common meaning of the term 'disparage'. According to dictionary definitions of 'disparage' which were contemporary to the Trademark Act of 1946, 'disparage' means 'to speak slightingly of; to undervalue; to discredit', 'to dishonour by bringing discredit or reproach upon ... depreciate, cheapen'.

---

[121]   See Baird, *supra* note 112, 714–15. Additional concerns related to the use of racial slurs, insults and epithets include the facts that they might provoke responsive violence, they deeply wound those at whom they are directed, and they have an insidious effect on social relations. Indeed, it is believed that they reinforce prejudice and contribute to unjust discrimination, generate resentment and undermine self-esteem among members of the group about whom the remarks are made. See Kent Greenawalt, 'Insults and Epithets: Are They Protected Speech?' (1990) 42 *Rutgers L Rev*. 287–309.

[122]   See *In re Maverty Media Group Ltd*, 33 F.3d 1367; 31 USPQ.2d 1923, 1925.

For the purpose of determining section 2(a) disparagement, the relevant public has been interpreted in most decisions[123] as consisting of those individuals who are described, identified or implicated in some meaningful way by the subject matter of the registration at issue. Therefore, in order to demonstrate that a mark is disparaging to a particular group, such as Native Americans, in cancellation proceedings, claimants must show that (i) the trade mark is reasonably understood to refer to the claimants, and (ii) the 'substantial composite' associated with the mark find it disparaging or scandalous. In that case, the 'substantial composite' refers to the reasonable member of the relevant racial group, and not to any reasonable person.[124]

In contrast, in *Greyhound Corp. v Both Worlds, Inc.,*[125] the Trademark Trial and Appeal Board (TTAB) held that the claimants must establish that (i) the trade mark must be 'reasonably understood' to refer to the claimant, and (ii) a 'reasonable person of ordinary sensibilities' must consider the trade mark offensive or objectionable. Therefore, the second part of the *Greyhound* test is an objective standard. A reasonable person in society must find the trade mark offensive or objectionable. According to one commentator, the TTAB in *Greyhound* omitted a critical qualification, namely that to be disparaging, the mark must be viewed as offensive by a reasonable person of ordinary sensibilities who faces circumstances identical to those faced by the person or group that the mark has identified.[126] To hold otherwise and to consider the perceptions of those who are not referred to, identified by or implicated in some meaningful manner by the mark, inappropriately dilutes the significance of the perceptions of those who are the intended beneficiaries of the disparagement part of section 2(a). Consequently, offensiveness is to be measured from the perspective of the reasonable person of ordinary sensibilities who is identified by the questioned mark.

---

[123]   Case law interpreting the disparagement provision of s. 2(a) makes clear that offensiveness is to be measured from the perspective of the potentially damaged group. See *In re Hines*, 31 USPQ.2d 1685, 1688 (TTAB 1994); *In re In Over Our Heads, Inc.*, 16 USPQ.2d 1653, 1654 (TTAB 1990); *In re Condas S.A.*, 188 USPQ 544 (TTAB 1975); *In re Anti-Communist World Freedom Congress, Inc.*, 161 USPQ 304, 305 (TTAB 1969); and *Doughboy Industries, Inc. v The Reese Chemical Company*, 88 USPQ 227, 228.

[124]   See *In re Hines, supra* note 123, 1688.

[125]   *Greyhound Corp. v Both Worlds, Inc.*, 6 USPQ.2d 1635 (TTAB 1988).

[126]   See Baird, *supra* note 112.

3.7.3   The Redskins Case: *Harjo v Pro-Football, Inc.*

> I am not a sports team mascot. With all due respect to the teams who want to honor me by having a Native American mascot. It is outdated. It's the wrong way.
>
> Billy Mills, Oglala Lakota US gold medal winner in the 10,000 metres at the 1964 Olympics (2005)

Introduction
Over the years, more than 2,600 high school, college or professional teams in the United States have used Native American names and images as mascots, logos and team names.[127] Whereas most high school and amateur teams do not own trade marks on those names and images, most professional teams and many college teams have registered them as trade marks. Since 1969, over 600 high school, college and minor league teams have eliminated these uses, most because of political pressures. The University of Oklahoma was the first major collegiate institution to eliminate a Native American symbol in 1970. Its 'Little Red' mascot had been a traditional part of the school's athletics since the 1940s. It was followed in 1972 by Stanford University and the University of Massachusetts.[128] However, the practice remains widespread and Native Americans and other individuals have been campaigning to stop American sports team names, mascots and logos containing references to Native American culture as they consider them to be disparaging, racially discriminatory, to create racially hostile environments and to perpetuate racial stereotypes.[129]

The controversy surrounding the use of Native American names and images in sports teams' names, mascots and logos has led to boycotts, protests and demonstrations by Native Americans and their supporters. National public debate on these issues intensified when on 4 April 1994, following intense protest over the Cleveland Indians' use of 'Chief Wahoo' as their mascot, President Bill Clinton declined to wear a cap featuring the controversial mascot, when invited to throw out the first pitch in the inaugural game at Jacob's Field. Instead, he wore an alternate cap embroidered with a large 'C'

---

127   See Behrendt, *supra* note 2, 396.

128   See 'American Indian Sports Team Mascots, Chronology: 30 Years of Effort Addressing the Use of American Indian Related Sports Team Mascots', at www.aistm.org/1chronologypage.html. Other teams that have changed their names include the Dartmouth 'Indians' in 1974, the Saint John's University 'Redmen' in 1994, the Miami of Ohio 'Redskins' in 1996, the Sioux City Iowa 'Soos' and the Marquette University 'Warriors'. See Rachel Clark Hughey, 'The Impact of *Pro-Football, Inc. v Harjo* on Trademark Protection of Other Marks' (2004) 14 *Fordham Intell. Prop. Media and Ent. LJ* 327–8.

129   See Brooke A. Masters, 'Creative Legal Tactics Used Against Teams with Indian-Themed Names', *Houston Chronicle*, 11 April 1999, 17.

rather than the 'Chief Wahoo' emblem.[130] On the one hand, supporters of maintaining registered trade marks that use objects of Native American culture as mascots and team names argue that (i) the original intent behind the selection of Native American mascots or team names was to honour Native Americans; (ii) Native American culture embodies the virtues of athletics that teams want to emulate; (iii) team names have been in place for a long time; and (iv) forcing athletic teams to change their name would destroy their ability to market merchandise. On the other hand, Native Americans and their supporters argue that trade marks containing Native American names and images, that are often sacred to their communities, are disparaging and should therefore be cancelled from the national register.[131]

In the United States, the sale of professional team apparel constitutes a multi-billion dollar industry and several major college teams earn millions each year in licensing agreements. In a *New York Times* article of 31 January 1993, it was pointed out that in 1992 alone, estimates suggested that Major League Baseball sold about US$2.4 billion in licensed merchandise, the National Football league sold about US$2.1 billion and the National Basketball Association sold about US$1.4 billion.[132] Similarly, many college and university teams rely on the licensing of their trade marks for revenue to enhance the visibility of their athletics programme and to produce additional merchandise sales. It was estimated that in 1992 college merchandising sales reached nearly US$1.5 billion. Florida State University, for example, was reported to earn as much as US$1.8 million each year selling merchandise with its team name and mascot.[133]

Some high profile examples of uses of Native American names and images as teams' names, mascots and logos in professional sports include the team name of the Atlanta 'Braves' professional baseball organisation and the fan ritual called the 'Tomahawk Chop', which was considered by Native American protestors to be offensive and to perpetuate negative stereotypes,[134]

---

[130]   See John B. Rhode, 'The Mascot Name Change Controversy: A Lesson in Hypersensitivity' (1994–95) 5 *Marq. Sports LJ* 141.
[131]   See Christian Dennie, 'Native American Mascots and Team Names: Throw Away the Key – the Lanham Act is Locked for Future Trademark Challenges' (2005) 15 *Seton Hall J Sports L* 201–2.
[132]   See Calvin Sims, 'It's Not Just How Well You Play the Game ...', *New York Times*, 31 January 1999, 5.
[133]   See Clark Hughey, *supra* note 128, 330.
[134]   See Behrendt, *supra* note 2, 393–4. Since the early 1990s, the 'Tomahawk chop' has been performed by the Atlanta Braves as a rallying cry, by moving their arms up and down in accordance with a rhythmic chant, to imitate the swinging of a tomahawk. Often, the cry is also performed by the fans with foam tomahawk toys. Tomahawks are a popular symbol of Indian culture. The cheer became a target of

the Cleveland 'Indians'' professional baseball team name and 'Chief Wahoo' mascot, which were strongly opposed because they were considered to be derogatory and racially offensive,[135] and the use of the word 'Redskins' by the Washington professional football team.[136]

The Redskins dispute

The Redskins dispute involves six trade marks owned by Pro-Football Inc., the corporate owner of the Washington football team, which include the word 'Redskin' and were all used in connection with goods and services related to the football team, including merchandise and entertainment services.[137] The oldest of these trade marks, 'The Redskins', which was written in a stylised

---

protest by Native Americans and other individuals, who argued that it belittled Indian people and their history. According to Clyde Bellecourt, a protest leader and executive director of the American Indian Movement, Indians should not be treated as mascots. He expressed his concerns about sports fans mocking Native American rituals by asking 'Why not name the team the "Atlanta Bishops" and hand out crucifixes to everyone who entered the stadium'. See '"Indians", "Braves" and "Redskins", A Performative Struggle for Control of an Image' (1999) 85 *Quarterly Journal of Speech* 188. Atlanta Braves fans, on the other hand, argue that their conduct is part of a celebration and that their performance is out of respect for the team. They feel that fan rituals are harmless and that the team name honours Native Americans. See Behrendt, *supra* note 2, 394.

[135]   See Behrendt, *supra* note 2, 395. Supporters of Chief Wahoo say that the mascot was not created to offend Native Americans, but to honour them since both the team name and Chief Wahoo pay homage to an early baseball player, Louis Sockalexis, who was one of the first Native Americans to play professional baseball. On the other hand, opponents of the Cleveland 'Indians' team name and especially of 'Chief Wahoo' perceive the team's moniker and Chief Wahoo logo, which depicts a red-faced, hooked-nosed, grinning caricature of a Native American, to be disparaging to Native American culture. Opposition escalated when on 10 April 1998, opening day for the Cleveland Indians baseball team, protestors burned an effigy of Chief Wahoo and were arrested by Cleveland police on charges of aggravated arson. Although the city did not prosecute the protestors, they sued the city, the arresting officers and their commanders for civil rights violations stemming from their allegedly baseless arrest and detention. Ultimately, the case went to the Supreme Court of Ohio, which decided that the right to free speech was not violated by arrest of the protestors after burning an effigy where the municipality's interest was to preserve public safety. See *Bellecourt v Cleveland*, 104 Ohio St.3d 439.

[136]   Other notorious examples include the Chicago 'Blackhawks' professional hockey organisation, the Cleveland 'Indians' professional baseball organisation, the Kansas City 'Chiefs' professional football organisation, the Florida State University 'Seminoles', the University of Illinois 'Fighting Illini' and the University of North Dakota 'Fighting Sioux'.

[137]   The Redskins football team was named in 1933 in honour of the team's head coach, 'Lone Star' Dietz, a Native American. It became the Washington Redskins after the team moved from Boston to Washington in 1937.

script, was registered in 1967. Three other trade marks were registered in 1974, another in 1978 and the sixth, the word 'Redskinettes' was registered in 1990.

In 1992, seven Native Americans[138] representing various tribes filed a complaint with the TTAB to cancel the registration of the six marks, claiming that they had disparaged Native Americans at the times of registration and had thus been registered in violation of section 2(a) of the Lanham Act. They asserted that the word 'redskin(s)':

> was and is a pejorative derogatory, denigrating, offensive, scandalous, contemptuous, disreputable, disparaging and racist designation for a Native American person.[139]

This complaint became the case of *Harjo v Pro-Football, Inc.*[140]

The Trademark Trial and Appeal Board's decision

The claimants argued that the 'Redskins' trade mark and other variations of that trade mark were void *ab initio* and that the word 'redskin(s)' is and has been a deeply offensive, humiliating and degrading racial slur. They contended that a substantial composite of the general public considered 'redskin(s)' to be offensive and that the inherent nature of the word 'redskin(s)' and the defendant's use of it perpetuated the devastating and harmful effects of negative ethnic stereotypes. Further, they contended that Native Americans have understood and still understand the word 'redskin(s)' to be a disparaging racial epithet that brings them into contempt, ridicule and disrepute.[141] In particular, the claimants argued that the TTAB must consider evidence regarding the historical setting in which the word 'redskin(s)' has been used, the present societal relations of Native American culture with other cultures, and the linguistic and written use of the word 'redskin(s)'.[142]

The defendant argued, among other things, that laches barred the Native Americans' claim. It contended that the claimant's evidence was biased and flawed and that it did not focus on either the appropriate time period or population and contained other specified inadequacies. The defendant denied that the term 'redskin(s)' was disparaging, offensive and derogatory. It contended that the initial use of the term 'redskin(s)', the modern context of the term and

---

[138] Suzan Shown Harjo, Raymond D. Apodaca, Vine Deloria, Jr, Norbert S. Hill, Jr, Mateo Romero, William A. Means and Manley A. Begay, Jr.

[139] See *Harjo v Pro-Football, Inc.*, 50 USPQ.2d 1705, 1708 (TTAB 1999).

[140] Ibid.

[141] Ibid. 1719.

[142] Ibid. 1719–20.

the spoken and written use of the term, in connection with a sports team name, were neutral designations that honoured Native Americans.[143]

Evidence included dictionary entries for 'redskin(s)', book and media excerpts from the late nineteenth century through the 1940s that used the term 'redskin(s)' and portrayed Native Americans in a pejorative manner, a study that found derogatory use of the term in Western-genre films from before 1980, the claimant's testimony about their views of the term, results from a 1996 survey of the general population and Native Americans that asked whether the various terms, including 'redskin(s)' were offensive, newspaper articles and game programme guides from the 1940s onward using Native American imagery in connection with Washington's football team, and testimony and documents relating to Native American protests.

The TTAB examined whether, at the time the defendant was issued each of the challenged registrations, the defendant's registered marks consisted of or comprised scandalous matter, or matter which may disparage Native American persons, or matter which may bring Native American persons into contempt or disrepute.

Scandalous matter   In deciding whether the trade mark 'Redskins' was scandalous, the board adopted the 'per se rule'. Thus, it looked at the mark in isolation, without taking into consideration the fact that 'Redskins' is attached to a football team.

On the basis of a dictionary definition of the word 'scandalous' contemporary to 1946, when the Lanham Act was adopted, the board looked at whether the mark was giving 'offence to the conscience or moral feelings; exciting reprobation, [or] calling out condemnation'.[144] The Board examined whether the mark was scandalous 'from the standpoint of not necessarily a majority, but a substantial composite of the public'. It carried out a two-step analysis to determine whether 'Redskins' was scandalous. First it looked at 'the likely meaning of the matter in question' and secondly, whether in view of the likely meaning, 'the matter is scandalous to a substantial composite of the general public'.[145]

The Board decided that the meaning of the matter in question, namely the word or root word 'redskin', clearly carried an allusion to Native Americans, and that this allusion was reinforced by the design elements in the registered marks incorporating the profile of a Native American person and a Native American spear. However, the Board found that the claimants had not estab-

---

143   Ibid. 1720–21.
144   Ibid. 1735.
145   Ibid. 1736.

lished by a preponderance of the evidence that the marks in the respondent's challenged registrations consisted of or comprised scandalous matter.[146]

Matter which may disparage   In order to determine whether the trade marks were disparaging, the Board focused on the ordinary and common meaning of the word 'disparage'. It described the applicable test as whether in relation to identified 'persons, living or dead, institutions, beliefs, or national symbols', such matter may dishonour, deprecate, degrade or affect or injure by unjust comparison.[147]

The Board based its analysis on a two-step process. First, it asked '[w]hat is the meaning of the matter in question, as it appears on the marks and as those marks are used in connection with the services identified in the registrations?'. In answering this question, the Board determined that 'redskin(s)' had acquired a secondary meaning as the name of a professional football team. However, it found that the trade marks also carried the allusion to Native Americans inherent in the original definition of that word.[148] Secondly, the Board asked whether the meaning was 'one that may disparage Native Americans'. In this respect, the Board considered whether the word 'redskin(s)' as well as the graphics of the spear and the Native American portrait may disparage Native Americans by reference to the perception of Native Americans. In doing so it followed *In re Hines* and reiterated the principle that the views of the referenced group were to determine whether a trade mark was disparaging. Consequently, it examined whether, at the relevant times, a substantial composite of Native Americans in the United States perceived this subject matter as disparaging. With respect to the spear design and the portrait of a Native American in profile, the Board noted that there was not enough evidence to conclude that these two logos may disparage Native Americans. With respect to the word 'redskin(s)' on the other hand, the Board concluded that:

> The word 'redskin(s)', as it appears in the defendant's marks in those registrations and as used in connection with the identified services, may disparage Native Americans, as perceived by a substantial composite of Native Americans.[149]

The Board reached this decision based on the cumulative effect of the entire record of evidence, and not on one single item of evidence or testimony alone.[150]

---

[146]   Ibid. 1748.
[147]   Ibid. 1738.
[148]   Ibid. 1741–42.
[149]   Ibid. 1743.
[150]   Evidence included a survey on how the public perceived the word 'redskin',

The Board ordered each of the registrations to be cancelled under section 2(a) on the grounds that the subject marks may disparage Native Americans and may bring them into contempt or disrepute. However, it denied cancellation on the ground that the subject marks consisted of or comprised scandalous matter.[151]

The District Court's decision

Following the TTAB's decision, Pro-Football filed suit in the US District Court for the District of Columbia,[152] seeking reinstatement of its six registrations on the grounds that: (i) laches barred the Native Americans' petition; (ii) the TTAB's finding of disparagement was unsupported by substantial evidence; and (iii) section 1052(a) of the Lanham Act violated the First and Fifth Amendments to the US Constitution both facially and as applied by the TTAB.[153] Without reaching conclusion on the constitutional issues, the District Court granted summary judgment to Pro-Football on 30 September 2003, reversing the Board's decision on the alternate grounds that laches barred the Native Americans' petition and that the TTAB's conclusion of disparagement was unsupported by substantial evidence.[154]

The lack of substantial evidence   The District Court found that the TTAB's decision that the marks at issue 'may disparage' Native Americans was not supported by substantial evidence, was logically flawed and failed to apply the correct legal standards to its own findings of facts.

In order to determine disparagement, the Board applied the *In re Hines* two-part test, according to which claimants must show that (i) the trade mark is reasonably understood to refer to the claimants, and (ii) the 'substantial composite' associated with the mark must find it disparaging.[155] The court did not challenge the standard articulated by the TTAB for evaluating a disparagement claim and confirmed that only the perception of persons in that identifiable group are relevant to determine if the designation is disparaging. Therefore, it stressed that the burden to prove that a substantial composite of

---

dictionary evidence on the connotation of the word 'redskin' and linguistic evidence about the pejorative meaning of the word 'redskin' throughout history. Ibid. 1743–47.

151   Ibid. 1749.

152   Although the Federal District Court for the District of Columbia is normally a court of first instance, in this instance, it was acting in an appellate capacity. The District Court determined that the appropriate standard for reviewing the Board's findings was that derived from the Administrative Procedure Act. Therefore it would reverse the Board's findings only if they were unsupported by substantial evidence.

153   *Pro-Football, Inc. v Harjo*, 284 F. Supp.2d 96, 102; 68 USPQ.2d 1225.

154   Ibid. 145.

155   Ibid. 128–9.

all Native American Indians regarded the term 'redskin(s)' as disparaging, as of the dates of the challenged registrations, rests with the claimant. In addition, the court emphasised that the issue was not whether there was evidence that the term 'redskin(s)' was a disparaging or derogatory term in the abstract, but rather whether it was disparaging when used as a trade mark in relation to a professional football team. The court observed that the board made relatively few findings of fact and simply presented the evidence of the parties in the form of summaries without making clear which of these facts formed the basis for its conclusion that the 'Redskins' marks were disparaging.[156]

The court found that the evidence brought forward was insufficient to conclude that the 'Redskin(s)' trade marks disparaged Native Americans or brought them into contempt or disrepute. Consequently, it decided that the TTAB's findings were based solely on the 'cumulative effect of the entire record' and granted summary judgment to Pro-Football.[157]

The laches defence   Laches is an equitable defence that prevents a trade mark holder from suing an alleged infringer after a long delay. Under this principle, the claimant has a duty to act promptly in seeking a preliminary injunction. Undue delay in seeking such relief once the claimant has, or should have, knowledge of the infringement might result in its denial.[158]

The court stated that the laches defence would apply:

> [I]f (1) the Native Americans delayed substantially before commencing their challenge to the 'Redskins' trademarks; (2) the Native Americans were aware of the trade marks during the period of delay; and (3) Pro-Football's ongoing development of goodwill during the period of delay engendered a reliance interest in the preservation of the trademarks.[159]

On the first prong of the test, the court found that the defendants substantially delayed in bringing their challenge to the marks. It pointed out that in the case of the first trade mark, the defendants waited over 25 years to bring their case.[160] On the second prong of the test, the court found that the defendants had actual and constructive notice of the trade marks as well as of the widespread

---

[156]   According to the District Court, the board made specific findings of fact in only two areas: (i) linguists testimony, and (ii) survey evidence.

[157]   *Pro-Football, Inc. v Harjo, supra* note 153, 135–6.

[158]   See Jerome Gilson, *Trade Mark Protection and Practice* (LexisNexis: Newark, 1974) § 14.04[1] (Rel.50 – 12/03).

[159]   *Pro-Football, Inc. v Harjo, supra* note 153, 136–7. The court articulated a general three-prong test for laches on the basis of the test that the Court of Appeal for the District of Columbia Circuit articulated in *NAACP v NAACP Legal Defense & Educational Fund, Inc.*, 753 F.2d 131, 137 (D.C. Cir. 1985).

[160]   *Pro-Football, Inc. v Harjo, supra* note 153, 139–40.

use of Pro-Football's trade marks. In addition, 25 years had passed since first notice of the mark and the defendants had failed to provide sufficient excuse for the delay.[161] Finally, on the third prong of the test, the court found that cancelling the trade marks would subject Pro-Football to undue economic prejudice.[162] It stressed that Pro-Football was entitled to rely on the security of the trade marks at issue and that the 25 year delay, where Pro-Football had heavily invested in the marks, would clearly result in economic prejudice.[163]

Although the District Court reversed the decision of the TTAB to cancel the trade marks, it based its analysis on the insufficiency of the evidence. It did not hold that any other mark using Native American terms could not be cancelled as disparaging. In other words, other marks may still be attacked.

The appeal

On 15 July 2005, the US Court of Appeals for the District of Columbia remanded the Redskins case to the District Court for further consideration of the issue of laches.[164] The Court of Appeals agreed with the Native Americans that the District Court mistakenly applied the doctrine of laches to one of the claimants, Mateo Romero, who was only one year old in 1967, when the District Court started the clock for laches. It ruled that, as to Romero, the District Court's approach ran counter to the 'well-established principle of equity that laches runs only from the time a party has reached his majority'.[165]

The court explained that laches is an equitable doctrine 'founded on the notion that equity aids the vigilant and not those who slumber on their rights'. It stressed out that this defence, which Pro-Football has the burden of proving 'requires the proof of (i) lack of diligence by the party against whom the defence is asserted, and (ii) prejudice to the party assessing the defence'.[166]

Pro-Football argued that a ruling in favour of the claimants would mean that trade mark owners 'could never have certainty, since a disparagement claim could be brought by an as yet unborn claimant for an unlimited time

---

161   Ibid. 140–1.

162   The court referred to *Hot Wax, Inc. v Turtle Wax, Inc.*, 191 F.3d 813, 824; 52 USPQ.2d, 1065 and pointed out that economic prejudice arose from investment in and development of the trade mark and that the continued use and economic promotion of a mark over a prolonged period added weight to the evidence of prejudice. In addition, it added that where the length of time was great in bringing the claim, prejudice would be more likely to have occurred and less proof of prejudice would be required. See *Pro-Football, Inc. v Harjo, supra* note 153.

163   Ibid. 144.

164   *Pro-Football, Inc. v Harjo*, 415 F.3d 44, 50; 75 USPQ.2d 1525.

165   Ibid. 48.

166   Ibid. 47.

after a mark is registered'.[167] The court, however, was not moved and pointed out that even if registrations of some marks would remain perpetually at risk, it was unclear why this fact authorised, let alone required, abandonment of equity's fundamental principle that laches only attach to parties who have unjustifiably delayed in bringing suit.[168] Romero had brought his own claim and there was no reason why the laches of others should be imputed to him.

While retaining jurisdiction over the case, the Court of Appeals decided to remand the record to the District Court for the purpose of evaluating whether laches barred Romero's claim. In particular, when assessing prejudice, the District Court was instructed to address both trial and economic prejudice.[169]

Record remanded to the District Court

Following remand of the record to the District Court, the parties each briefed renewed cross-motions for summary judgment. In reviewing the cross-motions, the District Court concluded that it lacked jurisdiction to revisit its previous factual findings and legal conclusions that were not directly implicated by its evaluation of Romero's laches. Furthermore, it pointed out that the Court of Appeals did not consider its conclusion that the TTAB's cancellation decision lacked substantial evidence or that the other defendants' claims were barred by laches, and did not provide any indication that it believed those conclusions to be in error. Therefore, it considered that there was no reason to revisit its prior findings.[170]

The District Court established that Romero had waited seven years and nine months after reaching the age of majority before petitioning to cancel the six trade marks in question and that this delay was unreasonable in light of the undisputed facts of the case. The court therefore found that Pro-Football had established a lack of diligence on Romero's part with respect to pursuing his

---

[167] Ibid. 49.

[168] 'Why should equity elevate Pro-Football's perpetual security in the unlawful registration of a trade mark over the interest of a Native American who challenged this registration without lack of diligence? Why should laches bar *all* Native Americans from challenging Pro-Football's "Redskins" trade mark registrations because *some* Native Americans may have slept on their rights?'. Ibid.

[169] As to trial prejudice, the court was directed to consider the extent to which Romero's post-majority delay resulted in a 'loss of evidence or witnesses supporting [Pro-Football's] position. As to economic prejudice on the other hand, the court was encouraged to take briefing on whether economic prejudice should be measured based on the owner's investment in the marks during the relevant years, on whether the owner would have taken a different course of action (e.g. abandoned the marks), had the claimant acted more diligently in seeking cancellation, or on some other measure.' Ibid. 50.

[170] *Pro-Football, Inc. v Harjo*, 567 F. Supp.2d 46, 52; 87 USPQ.2d 1891.

cancellation petition and that his claim was therefore barred by laches.[171] In addition, the court found that Romero's delay resulted in both trial prejudice and economic prejudice to Pro-Football, such that it would be inequitable to allow him to proceed with his cancellation petition. The court therefore granted Pro-Football's motion for summary judgment as to its laches defence.[172]

Conclusion

While in the latest case of the 17-year-old Redskins saga, the District Court decided in favour of Pro-Football, it reiterated, as it did in its 30 September 2003 Memorandum Opinion, that this 'opinion should not be read as ... making any statement on the appropriateness of Native American imagery for team names'.[173]

This case study demonstrates the potential of trade mark law, and in particular section 2(a) of the Lanham Act, to protect TCEs holders against offensive marks or offensive uses of their traditional verbal expressions. However, it should be pointed out that even if the outcome of the case had been positive for the applicants, revocation of the 'Redskins' trade marks would not have prevented the owners from continuing to use the name and logo. However, it would have ended the protected status and given the financial stakes, loss of trade mark registration could have potentially induced the owners to rename the team.

3.8   CONCLUSION: EFFICIENCY AND LIMITATIONS OF TRADE MARK LAW TO PROTECT TCES

As has been examined in this chapter, trade marks can provide both positive and defensive protection for TCEs and can offer a quick, practical and effective solution for their protection. There is no need for the creation of a new *sui generis* IP or IP related system, which would take a long time to establish, as trade mark laws can be used as such or with minor adaptations; and finally, once registered, trade marks can potentially be renewed perpetually, provided that the necessary steps are taken.

The trade mark system can help satisfy many of the concerns and policy objectives of TCEs holders. First, the registration of TCEs as trade marks may assist in preventing or controlling the unwanted commercial use of TCEs by

---

[171]   Ibid. 53–7.
[172]   Ibid. 62.
[173]   Ibid.

third parties and increase their commercial benefits, as the addition of a trade mark on a good adds to its value and increases consumer recognition of authentic indigenous goods. Secondly, when combined with an appropriate marketing strategy, the registration of TCEs as trade marks can assist in the promotion and dissemination of TCEs. Thirdly, the registration of a trade mark can be helpful in relation to the attribution and authentication of TCEs and help protect indigenous businesses and artists from imitations. Finally, trade marks can provide defensive protection against offensive and deceptive uses by taking into account cultural offensiveness in the absolute grounds for refusal to register a trade mark, or by creating new mechanisms by which the interests of TCEs holders are taken into account during the trade mark registration process.

However, despite positive results, there are some drawbacks in using trade mark laws to protect TCEs:

- trade mark laws will not prevent the offensive use of TCEs where the user does not seek to register a trade mark;[174]
- it is not possible for TCEs holders to obtain exclusive rights to trade marks based on TCEs where third parties have already registered such trade marks and the registration or use is not considered offensive;
- the requirement that trade marks must be used commercially means that trade marks are not an appropriate mechanism for many indigenous and traditional communities who do not want to see their words, designs and symbols used in that way. This can be the case for example with TCEs of a sacred nature;
- the trade mark system does not offer a comprehensive positive protection system, as it would be prohibitively expensive to register all existing traditional words, designs and symbols that indigenous communities may want to see protected as trade marks;
- there might be disagreement within an indigenous community as to whether a trade mark should be granted;[175]
- finally, trade mark laws leave aside the principle of prior authorisation, which is an important concern of TCEs holders.[176]

---

[174] Indeed, often, there is no intention by the company to register TCEs as trade marks. That was the case with the use of Maori names by Lego in its 'Bionicle' game and similarly, Canterbury of New Zealand expressed no intention to assert any claim of ownership over the text and imagery used.
[175] Examples include the opposition of the Baffin Regional Inuit Association to the Toonoonik Sahoonik's claim to the trade mark 'Nunavut Our Land' for clothing, which has not been registered. See Cassidy and Langford, *supra* note 1, 22.
[176] This principle is reflected in the Mataatua Declaration, which provides that

Trade mark law has not been a static phenomenon, but has developed in response to changes in socio-economic conditions. Rights have developed to cover new subject matter, such as sound marks, and cover new areas in terms of scope, such as trade mark dilution. Adapting trade mark laws to respond to the concerns and policy objectives of TCEs holders could provide an answer to today's socio-economic conditions in the context of TCEs, and offer practical and effective measures to deal with issues such as cultural offensiveness, as was shown in the New Zealand case study.

---

indigenous peoples of the world have a right to self-determination, and in exercising that right, they must be recognised as the exclusive owners of their cultural property. Also, it recognises that indigenous peoples are capable of managing their traditional knowledge themselves, but are willing to offer it to humanity, provided their fundamental rights to define and control this knowledge are protected. In the great majority of cases, Maori are not consulted in relation to the use of Maori imagery and text. However, there have been some examples where Maori were involved in the development of products using Maori imagery and text or where permission was sought. In 1998, New Zealand swimwear manufacturer Moontide launched a line of woman's swimwear made from material patterned with interlocking curvilinear *koru* designs. The line was developed in collaboration with a Maori entrepreneur, who acted on behalf of a local community, with direct responsibility to that group. According to Tony Hart, the firm's managing director, the use of the design was governed by the commercial viability of the product and cultural respect. Buddy Mikaere, a *kaumatua* (elder) in the local community, negotiated the use of the *koru* motif, in return for which part of the royalty from sales would go to the *Pirirakau hapu* (sub-tribe) of the Ngati Ranginui people. See Shand, *supra* note 73, 21.

4. The protection of traditional cultural expressions with certification marks and collective marks

4.1 INTRODUCTION

The first certification scheme to protect TCEs was established in Canada in 1958, when the Department of Indian and Northern Affairs developed the 'Igloo Tag' trade mark programme to certify the authenticity of Inuit art.[1] This pioneering scheme was soon followed by other initiatives in the United States (1961), and later in Australia (2000) and New Zealand (2002). In 2001, WIPO's fact-finding missions highlighted indigenous peoples' demand for the improved use of certification systems to protect TCEs.

This chapter evaluates the efficacy of a system based on certification or collective marks to protect TCEs. In doing so, it examines and compares the certification schemes that were set up in New Zealand, Australia and the United States, as well as wider development initiatives using certification systems in East and Southeast Asia, which have indirectly contributed to the protection of traditional handicrafts.

---

[1]   The 'Igloo Tag' is well-known in the Canadian marketplace for identifying authentic Inuit sculptures. Other examples of certification marks that have been registered in Canada by Aboriginal communities include the 'Irocraft' mark that was used by a Six Nations Company to market Iroquois crafts, books and cultural articrafts, and the three certification marks 'Cowichan', 'Genuine Cowichan' and 'Genuine Cowichan & Design', owned by the Cowichan Band Council of British Columbia and indicating that clothing products have been hand-knit in one piece according to traditional methods by members of the Coast Salish Nation using raw, unprocessed, undyed, hand-spun wool made and prepared in accordance with traditional methods. See WIPO, *Intellectual Property Needs and Expectations of Traditional Knowledge Holders*, WIPO Report on Fact-Finding Missions on Intellectual Property and Traditional Knowledge (1998–99), WIPO: Geneva, 2001, 123 and David Spratley, *Protecting Aboriginal Knowledge, Culture and Art under Canadian Intellectual Property Laws* (Davis & Company LLP: Vancouver, 2005) 19.

4.2   DEFINITIONAL CONSIDERATIONS

Certification and collective marks are special types of marks. They inform the public about certain characteristics of the products or services marketed under the mark. Article 7*bis* of the Paris Convention provides for mutual obligation of registration and protection of collective marks in the countries of the Union.[2] However, it leaves each country to be the judge of the particular conditions under which a collective mark will be protected and provides that it may refuse protection if the mark is contrary to the public interest. Even though the Paris Convention only refers to collective marks, it is generally understood that the term also includes certification marks.[3] Certification and collective marks can be indications of geographical origin. As such, they can be protected under the TRIPS Agreement. The TRIPS Agreement incorporates by reference a number of Articles of the Paris Convention, including Article 7*bis*. As a consequence, collective marks which belong to associations and are serving as geographical indications are protected under TRIPS.[4] This could be the case where traditional artists are organised into associations on the basis of their common geographical location, and when their artworks have attributes which are physically connected with the location.

The Community Trade Mark Regulation[5] allows for registration of Community collective marks, but not certification marks. It provides that a Community collective mark shall be a Community trade mark (CTM) if it is capable of distinguishing the goods or services of the members of the associ-

---

2   As originally established in Paris in 1883, the Paris Convention made no provision for the protection of collective marks. However, at the Washington Conference of 1911, Article 7*bis* was introduced in the Convention. It was later amended at the London Conference of 1934.

Article 7*bis* of the Paris Convention provides that: 'The countries of the Union undertake to accept for filing and to protect collective marks belonging to associations the existence of which is not contrary to the law of the country of origin, even if such associations do not possess an industrial or commercial establishment. Each country shall be the judge of the particular conditions under which a collective mark shall be protected and may refuse protection if the mark is contrary to the public interest. Nevertheless, the protection of these marks shall not be refused to any association the existence of which is not contrary to the law of the country of origin, on the ground that such association is not established in the country where protection is sought or is not constituted according to the law of the latter country.'

3   See Norma Dawson, *Certification Trade Marks, Law and Practice* (Intellectual Property Publishing Ltd: London, 1988) 13.

4   See Jeffrey Belson, *Certification Marks* (Sweet & Maxwell: London, 2002) 23. For a discussion of the protection of TCEs with geographical indications, see Chapter 6.

5   Council Regulation (EC) 40/94 on the Community Trade Mark.

ation which is the proprietor of the mark from those of other undertakings. Under the Community regime, associations of manufacturers, producers, suppliers of services or traders which, under the terms of the law governing them, have the capacity in their own name to have rights and obligations of all kinds, to make contracts or accomplish other legal acts and to sue and be sued, as well as legal persons governed by public law, may apply for Community collective marks.[6] Such an association can include an association of traditional artisans or indigenous groups of artists.

4.2.1 Certification Marks

A certification mark is a mark which indicates that the goods or services in connection with which it is used are certified by the proprietor of the mark in respect of geographical origin, material, mode of manufacture of goods or performance of services, quality, accuracy or other characteristics. In other words, they are indicia of conformity of goods or services to particular standards, stipulated by the proprietor of the mark.

Any person or entity that authorises traders to use a certification in relation to certain products or services may apply for a certification mark. However, the applicant must be considered competent to certify the products concerned. The owner of the certification mark is ultimately responsible for controlling its use and for ensuring that the mark is not used on non-compliant goods. The applicant must also supply a copy of the regulations governing the use of the certification mark, which must indicate who is authorised to use the mark, the characteristics to be certified by the mark, how the certifying body is to test those characteristics and supervise the use of the mark, the fees to be paid in connection with the administration of the certification scheme and the procedures for resolving disputes. Unlike collective marks, certification marks are not confined to any membership. They can be used by anybody who complies with the standards defined by the owner of the certification mark.

For example, TCEs holders can use certification marks to indicate that their product or services are produced by indigenous people, that they are produced according to traditional methods, that their products meet certain standards or that they consist of traditional indigenous designs.

4.2.2 Collective Marks

A collective mark is a mark which distinguishes the goods or services of members of an association which is the proprietor of the mark from those of

---

6   Ibid. Art. 64(1).

other undertakings, without any requirement for certification of the goods or services. In most jurisdictions, applicants are required to supply a copy of the regulations governing use of the collective mark. These generally indicate who is authorised to use the mark, the conditions of membership of the association, any conditions for use of the mark, as well as sanctions against misuse. The cost, duration and scope of protection applicable to collective marks are similar to those of ordinary trade marks. However, since the cost of registering a collective mark is divided between the members of the association, it becomes much cheaper for an individual member. This can be an attractive argument for indigenous groups of artists for whom the cost of registering an ordinary trade mark to market their products or services could be dissuasive.

An association of traditional artists can register a collective mark and authorise its members to use it in relation to their products or services. In that way, a collective mark can be used as a tool to help them obtain consumer recognition and customer loyalty and develop a joint marketing campaign for their products. Collective marks are often used to show membership in a union, association or other organisation. Membership as such may be an incentive to some customers to buy a product bearing the collective mark. In addition, a collective mark can also have the function to inform the public about certain features of a product associated with the mark. This is particularly relevant in the case of TCEs, which usually have characteristics that are specific to the producers of a particular region, linked to the historical, cultural or social conditions of the area. In such case, a collective mark can be a useful tool to communicate these features to prospective consumers, thereby benefiting all the members of the association.[7]

Unlike certification marks, the proprietor association of a collective mark does not have to set standards to be met by its members in order to be able to use the mark. However, it may do so if it wishes. Consequently, collective marks may also perform a certification function. This is particularly relevant in countries that do not provide for registration of certification marks.[8] Note that there is a certain level of confusion between certification and collective

---

[7]   See ITC and WIPO, *Marketing Crafts and Visual Arts: The Role of Intellectual Property – A Practical Guide* (ITC and WIPO: Geneva, 2003) 82–3.

[8]   As regards certification and collective marks, national laws for the registration of trade marks can be classified into three categories: (i) those which permit registration of certification marks only, in which case use of the marks is open to all who meet the standards; (ii) those which permit registration of collective marks only, in which case collective marks may also perform a certification function; however, because they are registered as collective marks, their use is only permitted to members of the proprietor association; and (iii) those which permit registration of both certification and collective marks. In this category also, collective marks may perform a certification function. See Dawson, *supra* note 3, 85.

marks. As Jeffrey Belson pointed out, during the first century of the registration system, there was confusion over the respective roles of certification and collective marks and this situation has not improved due to a proliferation and growing divergence of policy and law on certification and collective marks. For example, a mark may become a CTM collective mark and a national domestically-registered certification mark. Also, as there can be varying degrees of conflation, the usefulness and specificity of the information conveyed by a collective mark may at times be close to that of a traditional certification mark and at other times less so.[9]

A good example of how collective marks can be used to promote an artisanal industry is provided by the Marinha Grande Mglass collective mark.[10] Marinha Grande is a region in Portugal with a 250-year-old tradition in mouth-blown glass and crystal works of art. The Mglass collective mark was established in 2001 to promote and publicise the glass industry of the Marinha Grande region.[11]

Another example comes from the Andean region of Peru, where for centuries indigenous farmers have bred and selected traditional crop varieties, thus maintaining a high level of genetic diversity. The conservation of these varieties and the historical, cultural and social character of the landscape is extremely important to the Andean indigenous communities. In 1997, ANDES, the Quechua-Aymara Association for Sustainable Livelihoods and six communities of the Pisac area began working on the idea and implementation of a 'Potato Park' as a 'Community Conserved Area'.[12] The Park was opened in early 2000. The running of the Park is entrusted to the Association of Communities of the Potato Park, which was granted a collective mark by the Peruvian Patent Office, to be used to market potatoes and other products from the Potato Park. The logo is expected to guarantee that products are grown in the Park and are of high quality, and to enable the communities to highlight both the collective nature of their enterprise and the cultural characteristics of the association.[13]

---

[9]   See Belson, *supra* note 4, 42–3.

[10]   Portuguese collective mark No. 343.636. The MGlass collective mark is owned by the Comissão Regional de Cristalaris.

[11]   See ITC/WIPO, *supra* note 7, 129. See also www.vitrocristal.pt

[12]   Community Conserved Areas are natural and/or modified ecosystems containing significant biodiversity values, ecological services and cultural values, voluntarily conserved by indigenous, mobile and local communities through customary laws or other effective means. See International Institute for Environment and Development (IIED), *Traditional Resources Rights and Indigenous People in the Andes* (IIED, 2005) 7.

[13]   Ibid. 2 and 6–7.

4.3   THE 'ORIGIN RELATED' ELEMENT

A collective mark denotes the common origin of the products and services from those individual producers or enterprises that use it. It is often used to show membership in an association. A collective mark can be used by an association of traditional artists in relation to their products and services.

A certification mark can be used to guarante: (i) the geographical origin of the goods or services, for example, that craftworks have been produced by an indigenous community of a specific region; and/or (ii) the material, mode of manufacture or quality of goods or services, for example, that craftworks have been manufactured by a specific indigenous group, often using raw material and according to traditional methods of manufacture.

4.4   THE TOI IHO™ CERTIFICATION MARK FOR MAORI ARTS AND CRAFTS

4.4.1   Introduction

Toi iho™ is a registered trade mark[14] used to promote and sell authentic, quality Maori arts and crafts. It was developed and implemented by Te Waka Toi,[15] the Maori arts board of the Arts Council of New Zealand Toi Aotearoa (Creative New Zealand)[16] in 2002, in response to calls from Maori to assist them retain ownership and control of their *taonga* (Maori knowledge, imagery and design) and maintain the integrity of their art culture in an increasingly commercialised world. The toi iho™ mark is a promotional initiative recognising Maori art and artists. It involves a registered trade mark used to promote and sell authentic, quality Maori arts and crafts and to authenticate exhibitions and performances of Maori arts and artists. It is intended to certify that the arts and crafts are made by a person of Maori descent and to provide a mark of quality.

---

14   'Toi iho' means the essence of creation.
15   Te Waka Toi is a seven-member board that allocates project grants and develops initiatives. It is the guardian and administrator of the toi iho™ marks. It aims at maintaining the integrity of Maori art culture and promotes Maori art and artists nationally and internationally.
16   The Arts Council of New Zealand Toi Aotearoa (Creative New Zealand) is a government organisation responsible for developing the arts in New Zealand. It was established as a Crown entity under s. 6 of the Arts Council New Zealand Toi Aotearoa Act 1994.

4.4.2 The Toi Iho™ Mark

There are four categories of toi iho™ marks:

- the **toi iho™ Maori Made mark**, which is exclusively intended for individuals and groups of artists who are of Maori descent;
- the **toi iho™ Mainly Maori mark**, which is for groups of artists, most of whom are of Maori descent, who work together to produce, present or perform works across artforms;
- the **toi iho™ Maori Co-Production mark**, which is for Maori and non-Maori artists and businesses working collaboratively to produce, present or perform works across artforms; and
- the **toi iho™ Licensed Stockist mark**, which is for art and craft retailers and galleries who stock the work of licensed mark users.

The toi iho™ Mainly Maori and the toi iho™ Maori Co-Production marks, also known as the companion marks, acknowledge the growth of innovative, collaborative ventures between Maori and non-Maori, and their commercial benefits are undeniable. They are a useful tool for the integration of Maori artists within the broader society and can help them gain a wider exposure in the arts and crafts market. According to Elizabeth Ellis, Chair of the Te Waka Toi board:

Figure 4.1   Toi iho™ marks

Contemporary Maori art is open to all sorts of influences. These companion marks recognise cross-cultural influences, and the innovation and cutting-edge work that often results from such collaborations ... A manufacturer, for instance, might collaborate with a Maori designer to produce fashion wear on a large scale while still maintaining the design's artistic integrity. The Maori designer would have to meet the mark's authenticity and quality requirements.[17]

4.4.3   Aims

The aims of the toi iho[TM] mark are to:

- distinguish Maori arts and crafts from other arts and crafts;
- promote Maori arts and artists nationally and internationally;
- assist Maori to retain ownership and control of their knowledge, imagery and designs;
- maintain the integrity of the Maori art culture.[18]

4.4.4   Criteria and Procedure

In order to become a licensed user of a toi iho[TM] mark, Maori artists, individuals or groups have to (i) verify their Maori descent, and (ii) prove their ability to create quality works. According to Elizabeth Ellis, the mark should be associated 'not just with ethnicity but also with the idea of quality and high quality work, so the two things go together'.[19]

Maori descent
According to article 1.2 of the rules governing the use by artists of the toi iho[TM] Maori Made mark,[20] the toi iho[TM] Mainly Maori mark[21] and the toi iho[TM] Maori Co-Production mark,[22] a person is of Maori descent if:

---

[17]   Toi Iho Maori Made Mark Launch, Press Release of Creative New Zealand, available at www.scoop.co.nz/mason/stories/CU0202/S00022.htm
[18]   See www.toiiho.com/aboutus/guide.html
[19]   Ibid.
[20]   Arts Council of New Zealand Toi Aotearoa, Rules Governing the Use by Artists of the Toi Iho[TM] Maori Made Mark, www.toiiho.com/pdfs/Rules%20 maorimade%20book.pdf
[21]   Arts Council of New Zealand Toi Aotearoa, Rules Governing the Use by Artists of the Toi Iho[TM] Mainly Maori Mark, www.toiiho.com/pdfs/Rules% 20mainly%20maori.pdf
[22]   Arts Council of New Zealand Toi Aotearoa, Rules Governing the Use by Artists of the Toi Iho[TM] Maori Co-Production Mark, www.toiiho.com/pdfs/ rules%20co%20productions.pdf

(a) such descent is verified to Creative New Zealand in writing by:
     [...]
     (iii) A kaumātua [elder] or kuia [grandmother] of a person's Iwi [tribe];
     (iv)   A representative of a person's Iwi, Rūnanga [tribal assembly] or Trust Board;
     (v)   A representative of an Urban Maori Authority; or
     (vi)   A person recognised by Creative New Zealand as a highly regarded person in the Maori community; or
(b) Creative New Zealand, after having considered such evidence as it deems appropriate, determines that the person is of Maori descent.

Note that contrary to other legislations, which often define members of indigenous groups narrowly, with the consequence that some individuals might be excluded from the scope of the definition,[23] the rules governing the use by artists of the toi iho™ marks make it possible for a variety of persons, within the artist's *iwi* (tribe), to verify his or her Maori descent. In addition, the fact that the certification is not at the sole discretion of the artist's *iwi*, but can also be granted by a representative of an Urban Maori Authority, or a person recognised by Creative New Zealand as a highly regarded person in the Maori community, helps avoid situations where an *iwi* would arbitrarily decide not to certify someone.

---

[23] The issue of how to determine indigenous descent raises questions of self-determination which are interpreted differently by different indigenous groups. The Indian Arts and Crafts Act of 1990 (IACA), for example, has been criticised for the exclusion of some Indian people under the Act's narrow definition of 'Indian'. According to the Indian Arts and Crafts Act, the term 'Indian' means any individual who is a member of an Indian tribe, or who is certified as an Indian artisan by an Indian tribe. The term 'Indian tribe', in turn, means any Indian tribe, band, nation, Alaska Native village, or other organised group or community which is recognised as eligible for the special programmes and services provided by the United States to Indians because of their status as Indians, or any Indian group that has been formally recognised as an Indian tribe by an organisation legislatively vested with state tribal recognition authority. Many Native Americans, however, are excluded from the protection of IACA because proving the requisite Indian ancestry can sometimes be difficult. Indeed, persons who were adopted, have lost their records or whose ancestors did not sign the tribal rolls would be excluded from tribal membership. In addition, members of tribes with matrilineal or patrilineal systems of enrolment, or members of tribes requiring blood quantum limits, could be ineligible for enrolment in the tribe. Also, many tribes may not be recognised by the government following its policy to assimilate tribes into the white culture in the 1950s, by terminating their tribal status. The consequence of the narrow definition of 'Indian' in IACA is therefore that it prohibits some people of the Indian race from claiming to be Indian. For more information, see Jon Keith Parsley, 'Regulation of Counterfeit Indian Arts and Crafts: An Analysis of the Indian Arts and Crafts Act of 1990' (1993) 18 *American Indian Law Review* 497–503.

Quality

In order to prove their ability to create quality works, applicants must provide examples of works they have recently produced. The quality of these works is assessed by a panel of specialists in Maori artforms. The panel examines the Maori components of the work, the design and media, the process and technique used, the level of skill and expertise required to produce the work, and the aesthetics of the work. If the Panel is satisfied that the work is distinguishable as a work of Maori art or craft, being a work which comprises an implicit or explicit reference to something Maori, and if it is a work of quality, a licence will be granted.[24]

Rights granted

Once a licence is granted, the applicant is entitled to use respectively the words 'toi iho[TM] Maori Made mark', 'toi iho[TM] Mainly Maori mark', 'toi iho[TM] Maori Co-Production mark' or 'toi iho[TM] Licensed Stockist mark', in association with the relevant logo for a one-year period. The toi iho[TM] mark, which has been registered for a wide range of classes of goods and services, may be used in the form of labels, stickers or swing-tags attached to works for sale, or banners to promote and advertise exhibitions and performances of Maori artists.

4.4.5   Results to Date

After its first licensing meeting in June 2002, approximately 50 artists and six retailers were successful in registering with the toi iho[TM] mark. As of June 2008, 225 individual artists have been granted a licence and 14 retailers have been approved.[25]

According to Creative New Zealand, around 75 per cent of applications are approved and successful applicants are granted the right to use the toi iho[TM] mark alongside their artworks. To date, all applicants that have not been awarded the right to use the toi iho[TM] certification mark have been asked to reapply after some professional development or after further examples of their work are supplied.[26]

In August 2003, Creative New Zealand surveyed a sample of artists registered with the toi iho[TM] mark. The survey identified that there were business

---

[24]   Rules Governing the Use by Artists of the Toi Iho[TM] Maori Made Mark, as well as those Governing the Toi Iho[TM] Mainly Maori Mark and the Toi Iho[TM] Co-Production Mark, art. 3.1.

[25]   See Arts Council of New Zealand Toi Aotearoa, *Annual Report for the Year Ended 30 June 2008* (Creative New Zealand: Wellington, 2008) 30.

[26]   Ibid.

development issues for many artists. While all artists believed that the mark added value to their work, many were unsure how to capitalise on this, other than to raise their prices. On the other hand, artists with marketing knowledge had a higher level of long-term supply success because they were able to identify ways in which they could leverage off the toi iho™ advertising, using the toi iho™ logo on their website, business cards, etc.[27]

Overall, the introduction of the toi iho™ mark is expected to benefit both artists and consumers and to make a major contribution to the New Zealand economy. Maori art generates important foreign exchange, and the toi iho™ mark is anticipated to be a selling point for New Zealand. According to the Ministry of Maori Development, with the toi iho™ mark, 'customers will be assured that when they purchase what they think is Maori art, it actually is the real thing and not an import that's been mass-produced in Southeast Asia'.

The toi iho™ mark is currently administered by Te Waka Toi. However, a future goal is for the mark to be transferred to an autonomous Maori entity once it is well-established.[28]

4.5   ALASKA'S SILVER HAND PROGRAMME

4.5.1   Introduction

In the United States, the Department of Commerce last surveyed the Native American arts and crafts industry in 1985 and estimated sales of US$800 million. However, the sky-rocketing market since then has experts guessing that sales now far exceed US$1 billion.[29] Art productions are providing primary and secondary sources of income for a large percentage of Indian families. Alaska Native art alone is a multi-million dollar industry and locally produced art is an important supplement to income for many of Alaska's 100,000 indigenous people. Moreover, it is one of the few sources of income that is not associated with government jobs or payments.[30]

The Alaska Department of Commerce estimates that 75–80 per cent of what is displayed as Native artwork is not made by Alaska Natives at all. Instead, shops are full of imported and imitation Native style art, that are sold for one-half to one-fifth of the price of their Native-made counterparts. Labels bearing

---

[27]   Ibid.

[28]   See http://creativenz.govt.nz/what/maori/mark_facts.html

[29]   Scott S. Smith, 'The Scandal of Fake Indian Crafts', *Cowboys and Indians Magazine*, September 1998.

[30]   Julie Hollowell-Zimmer, 'Intellectual Property Protection for Alaska Native Arts' (2001) 24.4 *Cultural Survival Quarterly* 30.

the words 'authentic' or 'authentic reproduction' are often found on suppos-edly Native art work, but actually refer to something executed in a Native style rather than something that is Native-made or to a design whose copyright was purchased from an indigenous artist.[31]

Over the years, public education campaigns have included initiatives to prevent imitation Alaska arts and crafts from being sold as genuine. These include, for example, the distribution of brochures and postcards[32] in Alaska communities, gift shops, art galleries and on cruise ships to help visitors tell the difference between genuine Alaska Native arts and crafts and imitations.[33] However, the most successful initiative to date has been Alaska's Silver Hand programme to combat misrepresentation and misappropriation of Alaska Native arts and crafts.

4.5.2   Alaska's Silver Hand Programme

Alaska's Silver Hand programme[34] was established in 1961. It has been administered by the Alaska State Council on the Arts[35] since 1998. The Silver Hand programme uses a hand-shaped logo on a tag or sticker to identify Alaska Native art as authentic and to protect the work of Alaska Native artists, while at the same time guaranteeing consumers that items bearing the Silver Hand identification seal were hand-crafted in Alaska by an Alaska Eskimo, Aleut or Indian craftsperson or artist and made wholly or in significant part of natural materials.[36] While the Silver Hand programme was originally designed

---

31   Ibid.

32   These can be viewed on the Federal Trade Commission website at www.ftc.gov/alaska

33   The education campaign, which was a joint initiative from the Federal Trade Commission and the Alaska State Council on the Arts, started in 2002 and is still ongo-ing. It involved some 950,000 brochures being distributed at a cost of US$46,000. The campaign spurred reports from consumers who believed they may have been duped into buying counterfeit Alaska Native-made arts or crafts, as well as reports from former employees of Alaska gift shops reporting their ex-employers. See 'FTC Takes Action Against Fake Native Artwork', Kenai Peninsula Online, 8 October 2002, avail-able at http://peninsulaclarion.com/stories.100802/ala_100802alapm0010001.shtml. See also the Alaska State Council on the Arts on the 'Native Arts Program' at www.eed.state.ak.us/aksca/native2.htm

34   AS 45.65.010-.070.

35   The Alaska State Council on the Arts was formed in 1966. It forms part of the Department of Education and Early Development. Its mission is to enhance cultural development in Alaska by ensuring that art of the highest quality is accessible to all Alaskans. See www.eed.state.ak.us/aksca/

36   See Alaska State Council on the Arts, Silver Hand Permit Application, avail-able at www.eed.state.ak.us/aksca/forms/individuals/sh.pdf

Figure 4.2   Alaska's Silver Hand logo

to minimise the economic impact of Native-style imports that began to flood the tourist market after the Second World War,[37] its intent was later extended to protecting consumers and improving the economic position of the Alaska Native artists.

The Silver Hand programme is part of a wider initiative which also includes the 'Made in Alaska' programme. This parallel programme is designed to

---

[37]   See Hollowell-Zimmer, *supra* note 30.

promote products made or manufactured in Alaska and handicrafts produced by both Native and non-Native craftspersons. Its design depicts a mother bear and her cub with the words 'Made in Alaska' underneath.[38]

4.5.3   Criteria and Procedure

Under the Silver Hand statutory scheme, a person who makes an authentic Native handicraft within Alaska may, under certain conditions, obtain the authorisation to affix a state-administered identification seal, the Silver Hand symbol, attesting the origin and authenticity of the article.[39] The Silver Hand symbol must bear the words 'Authentic Native Handicraft from Alaska' and include a blank line for the artist's name and the place of origin of the article.[40]

In order to be issued a permit to use Silver Hand identification, an Alaskan Native must:

- be 18 years of age and a full-time resident of Alaska;
- submit a complete application form and supporting documents to the Alaska State Council of the Arts, along with a US$20 handling charge;[41]
- document that they are an Alaskan Native with a blood quantum of one-fourth or greater, either through possession of a 'Certificate of Indian Blood' from the Bureau of Indian Affairs of the United States Department of Interior, an official letter from a village or regional corporation established under the Alaska Native Claims Settlement Act of 1971, or an official letter from a village council or tribe in which the applicant is a member, together with a copy of a photo identification, such as a state identification card or driver's licence;[42] and
- certify on the application that they will affix the Silver Hand identification only on a handicraft that was or will be made: (a) entirely by the applicant; (b) within Alaska; and (c) in whole or in significant part of natural materials.[43] This means that works made jointly by an Alaska Native and any other person who is not also a separate permit holder in their own right are precluded.[44]

---

[38]   3 AAC 58.040.
[39]   AS 45.65.010.
[40]   AS 45.65.030.
[41]   See Silver Hand Permit Application, *supra* note 36.
[42]   3 AAC 58.020(c)(2).
[43]   3 AAC 58.020(c)(3).
[44]   See Nancy Kremers, 'Speaking with a Forked Tongue in the Global Debate on Traditional Knowledge and Genetic Resources: Is U.S. Intellectual Property Law and Policy Really Aimed at Meaningful Protection for Native American Cultures?' (2004) 15 *Fordham Intell. Prop. Media and Ent. LJ* 82. It is interesting to note that

Applications are reviewed within 30 days from the date of receipt. If the applicant is eligible, a non-transferable permit and Silver Hand tags will be issued.[45] The permit is valid for two years from the date it is issued and may be renewed within 30 days of the end of the two-year period.[46] A permit number is assigned to each holder for life, whether or not they continuously use it.[47] Permit holders may use the representation of the Silver Hand identification on catalogues, letterheads, business cards, in-store and for other advertising purposes.[48] Finally, the Silver Hand seal or a representation of that seal may not be used in a manner that is false or misleading, be modified, be incorporated into a business, company, or product logo or label, or be sold as art or as a dominant feature of a handicraft unless approved by the Alaska State Council on the Arts Chair in writing.[49]

The Alaska State Council on the Arts is responsible for the administration of the design, method of affixing, preparation, issuance and control of the identification seals. It is also responsible for the issuance of permits to agents who can distribute the seals to persons creating qualifying handicrafts and for the supervision of the use of the seals. Finally, the Alaska State Council on the Arts enforces the associated laws and rules in relation to the Silver Hand programme.[50]

Criminal penalties attach to violations of the statutory provisions. Hence, persons who knowingly or wilfully:

- affix or attach the identification seal to an article knowing that it is not an authentic Native handicraft;[51]
- sell or offer for sale an article with the seal affixed or attached, knowing that the article is not an authentic Native handicraft;[52]
- alter, change or counterfeit an identification seal or emblem;[53]
- sell or offer for sale an article that is not made in Alaska but that bears the emblem;[54]

---

unlike the Silver Hand programme, the toi iho™ certification mark for Maori arts and crafts allows the participation of non-Maori artists and entrepreneurs through the toi iho™ Mainly Maori Mark and the toi iho™ Maori Co-Production Mark.

[45]   See Silver Hand Permit Application, *supra* note 36.
[46]   3 AAC 58.020(d).
[47]   See Kremers, *supra* note 44, 82.
[48]   3 AAC 58.025(a).
[49]   3 AAC 58.025(b)–(e).
[50]   AS 45.65.020(b).
[51]   AS 45.65.060(a).
[52]   AS 45.65.060(b).
[53]   AS 45.65.060(c).
[54]   AS 45.65.060(d).

- use the emblem for an article that is not made in Alaska;[55]

are guilty of a class B misdemeanour.

Although it is not a statutory requirement, the Alaska State Council on the Arts maintains a central registry of all permit holders who are qualified to use the seal on their handicrafts.[56]

4.5.4   Results to Date

In recent years, the Silver Hand programme has grown in popularity among Alaska Native artisans. Whereas in 1995, 334 Alaska Natives were registered Silver Hand artisans, there were 925 in 1999,[57] 1,220 in 2006, and as of 1 January 2009, there were 1,580 registered permit holders.[58]

However, notwithstanding the growing use of the Silver Hand seal, many retailers are wary of the Silver Hand programme. They fear that shoppers might regard everything that doesn't bear the Silver Hand symbol as being an imitation product, and hence often prefer to remove the Silver Hand symbols[59] or to blur distinctions between Native and non-Native artworks, in order to be able to sell similar but less expensive items.[60] These concerns are also shared by some Native artisans who do not participate in the programme and who worry that tourists will wrongly assume that anything without a Silver Hand seal is not Native-made. In addition, there have been complaints that some people abuse the programme by sharing tags with unregistered friends or non-Native spouses. Finally, some Native artists have expressed concerns that labelling their work as 'Native' might limit the way it is perceived within the wider art community and that the narrow definition of 'authentic' discourages Native artists from using non-traditional materials or contemporary designs.[61]

Despite those criticisms, Alaska's Silver Hand programme is considered to be one of the best Native arts authentication programmes in use in the United States. It has the advantage of providing an efficient and reliable system,

---

[55]   AS 45.65.060(e).
[56]   See Kremers, *supra* note 44, 82–3.
[57]   See Hollowell-Zimmer, *supra* note 30.
[58]   Information provided by the Alaska State Council on the Arts in January 2009. Note that these numbers represent both active and dormant permit holders. Dormant permit holders details are retained as they often still have work available in the public market after their permit expires. Keeping their files allows the Alaska State Council on the Arts to provide information to the public, state agencies and Alaska Native Art patrons and legislators.
[59]   See 'FTC Takes Action Against Fake Native Artwork', *supra* note 33.
[60]   See Hollowell-Zimmer, *supra* note 30.
[61]   Ibid.

which protects both buyers and artists from works of questionable origin. The programme, which functions in a similar manner to a certification mark,[62] has the advantage that both state and federal agencies may have concurrent jurisdiction, which provides for a better enforcement of the statutory provisions. Indeed, it has been reported that complaints arising in connection with the Silver Hand programme have been, from time to time, investigated by the State Attorney General's office, the Federal Trade Commission, the Department of Justice, and the US Customs Service.[63] Furthermore, the state-run programme operates at minimal cost for Native Alaska artists. This has the advantage of sparing scarce financial tribal resources from operational expenses and trade mark registration and attorney fees.[64]

Following the positive results of the Silver Hand programme, which was the first of its kind in the United States, there have been other initiatives to set up a locally run government certification programme for the protection of Native arts and crafts, such as the New Mexico Certification Mark for Native American Arts and Crafts.[65]

---

[62]   The Silver Hand programme is not referred to in state statutory or administrative materials as a certification mark. However, the programme's legal requirements and regulatory support are similar to those in place for establishing and regulating a certification mark in the United States federal trade mark system. See Kremers, *supra* note 44, 84–5.

[63]   Ibid. 85.

[64]   Ibid.

[65]   In 2006, a proposal for a new Bill was introduced in New Mexico, to set aside funding for the state Regulation and Licensing Department to research and propose legislation to establish a New Mexico certification mark which would identify Native American arts and crafts produced in New Mexico under certain standards and criteria. See House Bill 48, Native American Arts Certification Mark, available at http://legis.state.nm.us/Sessions/06%20Regular/bills/house/HB0048.html. The New Mexico initiative stems from complaints about imitation art being sold in Santa Fe and Gallup, which is known as a hub for collectible jewellery produced by artists from the nearby Zuni Pueblo, the Navajo Nation and the Hopi reservation in eastern Arizona. See Susan Montoya Bryan, 'New Mexico Democrats Hope to Separate Real, Fake Artwork', *Daily Herald*, 11 February 2006, D2. According to the Indian Affairs Department, a certification mark would be beneficial for (1) the development of Indian arts and crafts to improve the economic status of members of Indian tribes and pueblos; (2) the development and expansion of marketing opportunities for arts and crafts produced by members of Indian tribes and pueblos; and (3) the protection of Indian artists and craftspeople, Indian tribes, Indian-owned businesses and consumers from the marketing of products as 'Indian made' when the products are not made by Indians. See Fiscal Impact Report on House Bill 48, *Native American Arts Certification Mark*, available at http://legis.state.nm.us/Sessions/06%20Regular/firs/HB0048.html. In addition, the fact that unemployment among the leading Southwestern arts tribes (Zuni, Navajo and Hopi), whose styles account for 90 per cent of the market, has reached over 70 per cent in the past two decades was also put forward as an incentive for the creation

4.6 THE INDIGENOUS ARTS CERTIFICATION SYSTEM

4.6.1 Introduction

Australian indigenous art is one of the oldest continuous traditions of art in the world, dating back at least 50 millennia. However, it is not until the second half of the twentieth century that Aboriginal artists began to receive widespread recognition in the West and that Aboriginal art has come to the forefront of Australia's national identity. Today, it is estimated that the indigenous arts industry in Australia is worth around AUS$200 million a year.[66] Despite this impressive figure, studies indicate that indigenous people are often not the first ones to benefit from this success, and the percentage of returns to indigenous people remains marginal. In 1989, it was estimated that indigenous people received just over AUS$7 million per year from the sale of arts and crafts, while this figure improved to approximately AUS$50 million in 1997.[67]

With the growing popularity of Aboriginal and Torres Strait Islander art, there has been a flooding of imitation products onto the indigenous arts market. This has raised concerns over three sets of questionable practices:

- the copying of indigenous styles by non-indigenous artists and passing off of these works as 'indigenous';[68]
- the use of misleading labels such as 'Authentic Aboriginal', 'Designed by Aboriginals' and 'Royalties paid to Aboriginal artists and communities' on products to indicate that they are of indigenous origin or have obtained the approval of indigenous people; and
- the appropriation of indigenous art styles, stories and themes by indigenous artists not associated with the particular style of dreaming stories they have depicted in their artwork.[69]

---

of the certification mark. The proposal is currently being considered by the New Mexico Legislature. See also Smith, *supra* note 29.

[66]   See Australian Government, Culture and Recreation Portal, www.culture andrecreation.gov.au/articles/indigenousart/

[67]   See Department of Aboriginal Affairs, *The Aboriginal Arts and Crafts Industry, Report of the Review Committee* (AGPS: Canberra, 1989) note 69; Aboriginal and Torres Strait Islander Commission (ATSIC) and Office of National Tourism, *National Aboriginal and Torres Strait Islander Tourism Industry Strategy* (1997) 5; and Terri Janke, *Our Culture: Our Future, Report on Australian Indigenous Cultural and Intellectual Property Rights* (report prepared for the Australian Institute of Aboriginal and Torres Strait Islander Studies and the Aboriginal and Torres Strait Islander Commission, 1998) 2.

[68]   See the example of non-indigenous painter Elizabeth Durack, who painted under the name and identity of Eddie Burrup, a male Aboriginal artist.

[69]   See Janke, *supra* note 67, 3.

A first proposal to develop a national indigenous 'authenticity trade mark' was raised in the 1980s, but the project was not taken forward at that time because of a lack of political support. In the 1990s, the National Indigenous Arts Advocacy Association (NIAAA)[70] developed the Indigenous Arts Certification System and advocated for the Australian government to implement the scheme in time for the Year of the Dreaming in 1997, and the Cultural Olympiad to follow. In 1999, the Australian government endorsed the proposal to use a system of certification trade marks and provided funding to the NIAAA to establish a national authenticity label through the Aboriginal and Torres Strait Islander Commission (ATSIC)[71] and the Australia Council for the Arts ('Australia Council').[72] The Indigenous Arts Certification System was launched in November 1999.

4.6.2   The Indigenous Arts Certification System

The Indigenous Arts Certification system is a two-tiered system consisting of the Label of Authenticity and the Collaboration Mark.[73] The Label of

---

[70]   The NIAAA is a non-profit organisation dedicated to protecting indigenous peoples' rights, culture, cultural respect, protocols and values through the promotion and protection of Aboriginal and Torres Strait Islander arts and crafts. Label of Authenticity Rules, rule 1, available at www.wipo.org/tk/en/studies/cultural/minding-culture/studies/indigenousarts.pdf

The NIAAA advocates for the continued and increased recognition and protection of the rights of indigenous artists. It provides advice, information, referrals and support services to indigenous artists and organisations. See www.culture.com.au/exhibition/niaaa/about.htm. Over the years, the NIAAA has been involved in high profile cases. In particular, it has played a significant role in a number of copyright cases, including *Milpurrurru and Ors v Indofurn Pty Ltd and Ors* (1994–95) 30 IPR 209 and *Bulun Bulun and Anor v R & T Textiles Pty Ltd and Anor* (1998) 41 IPR 513.

[71]   ATSIC was established by the Aboriginal and Torres Strait Islander Commission Act 1989 and began operations on 5 March 1990 as a means to involve indigenous people in the processes of government affecting their lives. However, on 16 March 2005, ATSIC was abolished by the Parliament. The ATSIC website has been archived at http://pandora.nla.gov.au/pan/41033/20060106/ATSIC/about_atsic/default.html

[72]   The Australia Council is the principal arts funding and advisory body in Australia. See www.ozco.gov.au

[73]   Respectively Certification Marks 772564 and 772566. NIAAA first sought to register the Label of Authenticity and Collaboration Mark as normal trade marks and then as certification marks. NIAAA experienced delays in obtaining the registration of the trade marks because at the examination phase, the Trade Mark Office considered that there were grounds that might preclude the application from being registered, one of them being that the trade mark for the Label of Authenticity was considered to be substantially identical with, or deceptively similar to, that of Nike (see Figure 4.3). Consequently, the Registrar of Trade Marks accepted the Label of Authenticity for

LABEL OF
AUTHENTICITY

Figure 4.3   Label of authenticity logo

Authenticity can only be used in relation to a work or service which is created, authored or produced wholly by an indigenous person. The Collaboration Mark, on the other hand, can be used where the work or service is authored, created or produced by an indigenous person with the assistance or input of a non-indigenous person, or where a product or service incorporates the work of an indigenous person and the product or service is to be commercially exploited under a written agreement on fair trading terms.[74] Both marks were registered in respect of a number of classes, mainly dealing with art and craft.

---

registration with an endorsement on the use of the mark which limited its use to 'the colors black, red and yellow with a black border surrounding the triangular device, which border is in turn surrounded by a black border'. See Matthew Rimmer, 'Australian Icons: Authenticity Marks and Identity Politics' (2004) 3 *Indigenous Law Journal* 154.

[74]   Label of Authenticity Rules, rule 1. The Collaboration Mark is regulated by the Collaboration Mark Rules. The indigenous artist and the producer or manufacturer must jointly apply to use the Collaboration Mark for manufactured products incorporating the work or contribution of the indigenous artist. They must enter into a written agreement for licensed use of the copyright in a particular work or works of the artist and show that the goods are to be commercialised pursuant to a written agreement on fair trading terms. Once approved, the licensee must enter into a written Agreement with NIAAA to use the Collaboration Mark in relation to the licensed goods and services on set terms and conditions. One of those is that the Collaboration Mark must be used as part of the labelling and packaging of licensed goods and must be accompanied by information as to the identity of the indigenous artist and the indigenous community, language group and land to which the artist belongs. The Collaboration Mark can be used against payment of a fee, which varies from AUS$50 to AUS$250 depending on the number of labels required. See Terri Janke, *Minding Culture: Case Studies on Intellectual Property and Traditional Cultural Expressions* (WIPO: Geneva, 2003) 8.

The system also comprises the Notice for Use by Indigenous Arts Retailers, which reproduces the Label of Authenticity and the Collaboration Mark in the form of a sticker to be affixed onto shop windows or doors.[75]

As the owner of the Label of Authenticity and the Collaboration Mark, NIAAA has the exclusive right to use and to allow other persons, known as approved users, to use the labels in respect of the goods and services for which they have been registered. In other words, NIAAA is responsible for the promotion, marketing, policing and enforcement of the labels. Due to cessation of funding, however, NIAAA closed its office in 2002 and the future of the Indigenous Arts Certification System is uncertain. This case study will therefore focus on the rationale for establishing the certification system, its implementation and its registration and operational modalities. Also, it will provide an interesting element of comparison with the toi iho™ Certification Mark for Maori Arts and Crafts and the Alaska Silver Hand programme.

4.6.3   Aims

The aims behind the creation of the Indigenous Arts Certification System were:

- to maintain the cultural integrity of Aboriginal and Torres Strait Islander art;
- to ensure a fair and equitable return to Aboriginal and Torres Strait Islander communities and artists for their cultural produce;
- to maximise consumer certainty as to the authenticity of Aboriginal and Torres Strait Islander-derived works/products;
- to maximise the multiplicity and diversity of Aboriginal and Torres Strait Islander art; and
- to promote an understanding both nationally and internationally of Aboriginal and Torres Strait Islander cultural heritage and art.[76]

However, one of the main concerns of the government initiative was to provide stronger protection for consumers of indigenous art and culture and to

---

75   The Notice for Use by Indigenous Art Retailers indicates to consumers that the retailer supports users of the Label of Authenticity and the Collaboration Mark. It recognises retailers and point of sale outlets as traders in indigenous works or goods that have been created by certified indigenous creators under the Label of Authenticity and the Collaboration Mark. In order to be able to use the Notice on their premises, retailers must be approved and pay AUS$250 per shop for a 12-month period. See Janke, *supra* note 74, 11.

76   See Marianna Annas, 'The Label of Authenticity: A Certification Trade Mark for Goods and Services of Indigenous Origin' (1997) 3 *Aboriginal Law Bulletin* 4–6.

relieve the anxiety of consumers, and more particularly of international tourists visiting Australia for the Sydney Olympic Games in 2000. It was argued that this new policy initiative represented a shift in emphasis from the protection of indigenous creators under copyright law to the protection of consumers under trade mark law.[77]

4.6.4   Criteria and Procedure

Indigenous artists who want to use the Label of Authenticity must submit an application to the NIAAA using the prescribed form together with a fee of AUS\$30, renewable every year.

Applicants must:

- show that the products or services are derived from a work of art created by, and reproduced or produced and manufactured by, Aboriginal or Torres Strait Islander people;
- satisfy the definition of authenticity.

An interesting feature of the Label of Authenticity is that applicants must specify in the application the goods and/or services in respect of which they intend to use the Label of Authenticity and from time to time inform NIAAA of any expansion of those goods or services.

Indigenous identity
The first criterion that needs to be satisfied is that applicants must show that they identify as an Aboriginal or Torres Strait Islander and have permission from the relevant community to make the artwork. For that purpose, applicants are required to obtain a form from an Aboriginal Corporation certifying that they are an indigenous person.[78]

When defining who is an 'Aboriginal or Torres Strait Islander person', the NIAAA has adopted a three-pronged approach, which takes into account:

---

[77]   This was also due to the fact that in response to recent copyright actions in Australia involving indigenous art, pirates have shifted their attention away from the copying of individual works to the reproduction of styles of work, a matter which is particularly well-suited to certification marks. See Rimmer, *supra* note 73, 142 and 153 and Leanne Wiseman, 'The Protection of Indigenous Art and Culture in Australia: The Labels of Authenticity' (2001) 23 *EIPR* 14.

[78]   Either an ATSIC Confirmation of Aboriginality or Torres Strait Islander Descent form, or a Label of Authenticity Confirmation of Aboriginality or Torres Strait Islander Descent form. See Label of Authenticity Rules, rule 3.2. On the issue of self-determination, see also *supra* para. 4.4.4 on the determination of Maori descent and *infra* para. 7.5.4 on the determination of Indian descent.

(i) whether the applicant is a person of Aboriginal or Torres Strait Islander descent; (ii) identifies as an Aboriginal or Torres Strait Islander; and (iii) is accepted as such in the indigenous community in which they live, or come from, or with which they identify.[79] In addition, applicants may trace their descent from a different indigenous community from the indigenous community with which they identify or in which they are accepted as indigenous.[80] Once approved, artists can purchase labels and affix them to their art and cultural products.

Authenticity

The definition of 'authenticity' that should be operative in the certification scheme has raised concerns amongst the different stakeholders. The NIAAA stressed that it would not determine who is an Aboriginal or Torres Strait Islander person, as it considered it would be both culturally and legally unacceptable. Instead, it stated that it would be up to the individual applicant to prove whether they were of Aboriginal or Torres Strait Islander descent.[81] As a consequence, during the research phase for the Label, indigenous producers were consulted as to what 'authorship' and 'origin' meant to them and their works of art, with a view to reaching a definition of 'authenticity'. The following definition came out of the consultation phase:

> [Authenticity is] a declaration by indigenous Australian artists of identity with, belonging to, knowledge about, respect for and responsibility towards the works of art they create. 'Identity' is defined in relation to upbringing, beliefs, stories, cultural ways of living and thinking, and knowing what it is to be Aboriginal or Torres Strait Islander. 'Belonging' means to be either connected with stories about country or connected with the experience of history in being indigenous in Australia. 'Knowledge' is about the familiarity gained from actual experience and also having a clear and certain individual perception of expression. 'Respect and responsibility' is about having regard for and looking after culture. It is about acting in a way which is sensitive to others and which does not exploit other peoples' identity, knowledge and belonging.[82]

However, the definition of 'authenticity' has raised some issues and concerns. Firstly, there were concerns that the label confused the issue of indigenous authorship with that of authenticity and erroneously suggested a 'pan-Aboriginal' identity.[83] Some indigenous groups considered that some specific works belonged to particular areas, and that to be considered truly authentic,

---

79   See Label of Authenticity Rules, rule 3.3.
80   See ibid.
81   See Rimmer, *supra* note 73, 157.
82   See Annas, *supra* note 76.
83   See Rimmer, *supra* note 73, 158.

they needed to be produced in those regions, by an indigenous person who has the authority of that community. Examples included the didgeridoo, which is characteristic of the Kimberly region, and the dot painting style, which comes from central Australia and the Western Desert region.[84]

In a similar way, it was argued that there were no safeguards in the certification system against the appropriation of region-specific art styles. It was argued that the scheme was flawed because it implied that Aboriginality guarantees authenticity when the work of one indigenous group can be copied by another. As a consequence it would be possible for an indigenous artist to produce an item that is not authentic.[85]

It was suggested that the label was initially aimed at tourist art rather than fine art and that the scheme failed to distinguish fine art from manufactured tourist art.[86] Consequently, those operating in the fine art arena have been reluctant to apply for the Label of Authenticity, believing that their own signature, label or document of authenticity would be enough to verify the authenticity of their work in the national or international arts arena.[87]

One commentator argued that it was not clear whether in order to satisfy the definition of authenticity, indigenous artists needed to comply with customary law. Consequently, given the impact that customary law potentially has on indigenous art and culture, it would be preferable if artists were only able to use the Label of Authenticity on their works where they could demonstrate that customary law had been complied with.[88] In this perspective, it was

---

[84]   See Wiseman, *supra* note 77, 21.

[85]   See Rimmer, *supra* note 73, 159, citing Norman Wilson, *Submission to the Contemporary Visual Arts and Crafts Inquiry* (Department of Communications, Information Technology, and the Arts: Canberra, 2001) 8.

[86]   Indeed, while there is a wide range of products of Aboriginal art, it has been suggested that they can be reduced to two broad categories: fine art and tourist art, the ultimate buyers being collectors and tourists or casual buyers. While collectors will look for ethnographic authenticity, aesthetic appeal and rarity, casual buyers will want something relatively inexpensive, but with a distinctively Aboriginal flavour. It was suggested that the main focus of the Label of Authenticity and the Collaboration Mark would be the souvenir products market rather than the fine art one. See Rimmer, *supra* note 73, 158 and Wiseman, *supra* note 77, 15 and 20.

[87]   See Rimmer, *supra* note 73, 158.

[88]   The issue arises from the fact that the right to reproduce pre-existing designs, themes or stories is vested in traditional custodians and the rights to this knowledge and the authority to disclose it to others are governed by a complex social system based on a series of qualifications. The Aboriginal author of a work based on a traditional pre-existing design, theme or story holds the knowledge embodied in a work in trust for the rest of the clan. In that way, the knowledge is collectively owned by the clan. The author of the work must be careful not to distort or misuse the knowledge and cannot authorise reproduction of the work without observing Aboriginal customary law. See Wiseman, *supra* note 77, 20 citing Terri Janke, 'Protecting Australian Indigenous Arts

suggested that one way the elders of an indigenous community could ensure customary law was upheld would be to address this issue when indicating that the artist is someone who belongs to and is accepted by that indigenous community.[89]

Finally, there were concerns that the authenticity scheme would serve to typecast indigenous artists in a narrow and rigid fashion or 'pigeon-hole' them as indigenous artists, thereby reducing the range of their art. Indeed, it was argued that the notion of authenticity only seemed to relate to 'traditional' indigenous art, which employed traditional techniques, materials and imagery, such as the well-known dot painting, and it was argued that such a conception of indigenous art would do many artists a disservice and would reinforce public misconceptions about indigenous art. It was feared that seeing indigenous art in those terms may exclude urban and non-traditional Aboriginal artists, whose work might not be considered 'real' or 'authentic'.[90]

Use of the certification mark

The Label of Authenticity Rules incorporate rules for complying with indigenous customary law. They provide that in the case of works or services which purport to encode, depict or reflect the ceremony, law, knowledge, customs, stories, dreaming or ritual of the traditional indigenous owners, the Label of Authenticity should only be used in connection with those works or services if they were produced in accordance with any customs or law of the relevant traditional indigenous owners of the land in question and where permission of the traditional owners has been given for the creation of the work.[91] The aim of this provision was to alleviate the problem of indigenous artists painting other styles that they have no claim or belonging to.[92]

4.6.5   Results to Date

Because of a strict registration process – to register successfully, the applicant's Aboriginality had to be supported in writing under the common seal of two indigenous organisations – more than 75 per cent of applications were not supported with sufficient documentation. In July 2000, out of 200 applicants, 150 had not met the minimum criteria.[93] In total, approximately 160 artists have used the Label of Authenticity since it was launched in 2000, despite

---

and Cultural Expressions: A Matter of Legislative Reform or Cultural Policy?' (1996) 7 *Culture and Policy* 14.

[89]   See Rule 4.1.
[90]   See Rimmer, *supra* note 73, 159–60 and Wiseman, *supra* note 77, 20.
[91]   See Label of Authenticity Rules, rule 4.1.
[92]   See Janke, *supra* note 74, 9.
[93]   See Rimmer, *supra* note 73, 156.

there being from 7,000 to 20,000 Aboriginal people earning a living from art in Australia. However, the Label of Authenticity has failed to gain wide support at the primary production level, particularly among Aboriginal Arts and Crafts Centres, which are the major producers of Aboriginal art. Instead, the majority of persons sought permission from NIAAA to use the Collaboration Mark.[94]

4.6.6 Future of the Indigenous Arts Certification System

In December 2002, the Indigenous Arts Certification System stopped operating due to cessation of its federal funding of more than AUS$500,000. The Australia Council, which paid NIAAA AUS$1 million over three years, and the ATSIC which had given NIAAA more than AUS$1.2 million over eight years, both halted their payments because they said that NIAAA had failed to be accountable.[95] While both the Label of Authenticity and the Collaboration Mark remain registered, there is presently no office to administer and implement the Indigenous Arts Certification System.

Following this announcement, the Aboriginal and Torres Strait Islander Arts Board of the Australia Council commissioned a review of the NIAAA. The report of the Australia Council, which relied upon several sources, including information held by the Australia Council, public information produced by the NIAAA, consultations with stakeholders, and a questionnaire sent to 150 industry organisations and art and craft associations, was very critical of the governance and management of the NIAAA, the implementation of the national certification scheme and the NIAAA's wider advocacy role.[96]

In particular, the report claimed that:

- the leadership of the organisation was volatile and unstable and that in many instances there had been changes of Board members and key staff, following which the NIAAA would undergo periods of inactivity;
- there had been complaints by some stakeholders that the organisation was focused on Sydney and was not representative of all regions of Australia; they ascertained the need for a process whereby the NIAAA's governing committee would be composed of representatives from various regions;

---

94   See Janke, *supra* note 74, 1.
95   See Debra Jopson, 'Aboriginal Seal of Approval Loses its Seal of Approval', *Sydney Morning Herald*, 14–15 December 2002, 7.
96   See Australia Council, *Final Report of the Review of the National Indigenous Arts Advocacy Association* (Australia Council: Sydney, 2002) as detailed in Rimmer, *supra* note 73, 161.

- there were concerns about the scheme's definition of 'authenticity';
- there were practical problems with the implementation of the system;
- the NIAAA had failed to win stakeholders' support, including creative artists, indigenous communities and regional art centres, and there was resistance to the use of the authenticity marks amongst arts and crafts centres;
- the authenticity mark lacked support in urban galleries;
- there were concerns about the failure of the NIAAA to meet deadlines to implement the authentication system, especially its failure to implement the scheme in time for the 2000 Olympic Games;
- the report claimed that the NIAAA had undertaken few of the core functions of an intellectual property and promotion agency at the national level, had few links with other non-profit organisations and undertook little advocacy work with government agencies; in addition, the inquiry had sought feedback from art and craft centres, other organisations and government agencies, which all reported that they had little or no contact with the NIAAA for the last two or three years;
- finally, the report claimed that the funding agencies, the Australia Council and the ATSIC, had failed to properly supervise the authenticity marks scheme and that the federal government was ultimately to blame because it should have entrusted the implementation of the Indigenous Arts Certification System to a government agency instead of the NIAAA. The report recommended that the Australia Council, the Department of Communications, Information Technology and the Arts, and the National Arts Policy Centre of ATSIC, should consider the development of a national authenticity policy.[97]

4.6.7 Regional Certification Marks

Since the cessation of the NIAAA's funding, there have been a growing number of regional arts centres registering trade marks, allowing for each region to authenticate and promote their own works rather than have their works authenticated by a national body. Indeed, it was suggested by some commentators[98] that the implementation of the authenticity marks scheme did not appear to have the support of local communities and remote artists and that instead of concentrating on a national label of authenticity, it might be more productive to develop regional and local trade marks for indigenous artistic centres and communities, which might help empower local communities.

---

[97]   Ibid. 161–4.
[98]   See Rimmer, *supra* note 73, 165, citing Wilson, *supra* note 85, 8.

In 2000, regional organisations, such as the Association of Northern Kimberley and Arnhem Aboriginal Artists (ANKAAA)[99] and Desart developed regional labelling systems. Desart is an Association of the Central Australian Aboriginal Art and Craft Centres, located in Alice Springs in the Northern Territory. It was incorporated in 1992 and represents 33 art centres. It is funded by ATSIC. Its mission is to provide support services to central Australian Aboriginal art centres and, in doing so, to foster and support their aims for community development, cultural maintenance and economic growth. Desart acts as an advocate for the rights and welfare of Central Australian Aboriginal artists and as a voice for remote Aboriginal art centres.[100]

Art centres are usually non-profit organisations which are owned and governed by Aboriginals. They encourage the production of art by local Aboriginal artists and assist them with the selling, promoting, collecting, documenting, exhibiting and marketing of their artwork. In most communities, arts centres provide the only source of self-generated income for Aboriginal people. Hence, they play an important role in the financial well-being of communities, while at the same time providing an important platform for cultural maintenance and education.[101]

In 2000, Desart registered a certification mark, the Desart mark,[102] in a number of classes in relation to the sale of indigenous arts. The Desart certification mark was developed to enhance the marketing of artistic works and to develop their licensing potential. It certifies the provenance, authenticity and quality of the artworks to which it is applied. Since its registration, it has been used on licensing merchandise, thereby offering potential for art centres to generate funds independently of government subsidies.[103] In addition, it has also been used on exhibition catalogues, books and other publications.

According to Desart, since its registration, the Desart mark has been effective in advancing the reputation and status of Desart as a collective organisation representing the rights of artists. In addition, the use of the Desart mark has been a valuable help to unify the industry.[104]

In addition to regional organisations, since 2000, there has been a growing number of regional art centres registering and using their own distinctive labelling systems, thereby allowing each region to authenticate and promote

---

99   See ANKAAA website, www.ankaaa.org.au/
100 See Desart website, www.desart.com.au/index.htm
101 See Janke, *supra* note 74, 119.
102 Certification mark 783368.
103 Art centres are normally funded by ATSIC but are continually under threat of having their subsidies withdrawn. See Janke, *supra* note 74, 123.
104 Ibid. 123.

their own works rather than having their works authenticated by a national body.[105] However, this practice, which is said to be gaining market recognition, raises questions as to the level of consumer trust and recognition that such marks or labels can obtain.[106]

One of the questions that arise, when having a dual system where there is a national Label of Authenticity alongside trade marks or labels of regional organisations, is to what extent indigenous artists who already use a trade mark or label to distinguish their goods and services would be interested in also adopting the Label of Authenticity.

In a 1997 discussion paper,[107] which put forward proposals for the improved recognition and protection of indigenous cultural and intellectual property, indigenous groups[108] were consulted about the idea of a national label of authenticity. Most submissions favoured the establishment of a central administering body that could authorise creators across Australia to use the mark in accordance with the rules for its use. Some submissions, however, favoured state-based labels. The Tasmanian Aboriginal Land Council, for example, suggested that the mark should be controlled by appropriate groups recognised at the state level. It reported that Tasmanian Aboriginals would most likely prefer to have their own certification mark.[109]

In response to these concerns, the NIAAA had suggested that since there were already a number of registered trade marks for indigenous products at the time of the launch of the authenticity marks scheme, there should be a dual labelling system with respect to indigenous goods and services. In other words, in addition to the Label of Authenticity or the Collaboration Mark, indigenous goods or services could have a second label attached to them, such as a trade or business name, or a trade mark, which would indicate the product's source and authenticity.[110]

---

[105]   Ibid. 148.

[106]   Art centres also use other means of authenticating artworks. These include maintaining complete records of the production of artists in the centre, providing documentation to purchasers at the time of sale, including the story of the artwork, its history and creation, and details of the artist, including age, traditional area, tribal grouping and language, as well as a photo of the artist with the artwork.

[107]   See Janke, *supra* note 67.

[108]   In 1996, ATSIC established an Indigenous Reference Group to find out what indigenous people consider should be protected, and how problems in this area could best be solved. The Indigenous Reference Group consisted of indigenous people who had expertise and experience in various areas of culture and intellectual property. Ibid. 278.

[109]   Ibid. 204.

[110]   See Wiseman, *supra* note 77, citing the National Indigenous Arts Advocacy Association Inc., *Discussion Paper on the Proposed Label of Authenticity* (August 1997) 4.

One other way to answer these concerns would be to set up an integrated multi-level labelling system that would make use of state, regional and local indigenous structures whereby a central state body would be the registered owner of the certification mark and would grant other state or regional bodies a licence to use or the power to authorise use of the national certification mark. These would in turn be allowed to grant local bodies, such as indigenous art centres, a licence to use the certification mark or the power to authorise indigenous artists to use it.

4.7   INITIATIVES IN EAST AND SOUTHEAST ASIA

In recent years, initiatives using labelling schemes that were aimed at improving incomes in rural communities and alleviating poverty have emerged in various countries of East and Southeast Asia. Although these initiatives were not aimed specifically at protecting TCEs, in an effort to promote indigenous industries they have indirectly contributed to the protection of traditional handicrafts.

4.7.1   The One Village One Product Initiative in Oita

One Village One Product (OVOP) is a strategic movement designed for regional development, which encourages and empowers local citizens to develop indigenous industries with a global outlook. OVOP requires people to take up a product or industry distinctive to their region and cultivate it into a nationally and globally accepted one, which reflects pride in the local culture.

The movement was initiated in 1979 in the Oita Prefecture of the Kyushu Island of Japan by its former governor, Morihiko Hiramatsu. At the time, the Oita Prefecture had the lowest average income rate in Kyushu, suffered from isolation due to its remote geographical location in a mountainous rural part of the island, was facing depopulation amongst the younger generations and a decrease in the productivity of its indigenous industries.[111] In an effort to remedy this situation and revitalise the local economy, Hiramatsu suggested that local people should explore the local resources available to them and develop indigenous industries under the guidance of the local administration, thus encouraging each community to develop one marketable product and commercialise it under the One Village One Product brand.

---

[111]   See Kunio Iguza, 'Revitalization in Asia and Local Revitalization Efforts: A View from One Village One Product (OVOP) Movement in Oita', http://ideaix03. ide.go.jp/English/Ideas/School/pdf/igusa.pdf, 8.

The aims behind the movement were: (i) to prevent depopulation and loss of energy in the Oita Prefecture; (ii) to find and nurture products and industries that could best reflect and benefit each region; and (iii) to eradicate heavy dependency on government, and promote autonomy and willingness amongst regional people.[112]

In doing so, the OVOP movement relied on three basic principles: the 'local yet global' principle, according to which the OVOP movement should aim towards the creation of globally accepted products that reflect pride in the local culture; the 'self-reliance and creativity' principle, according to which the OVOP movement should be realised through independent action, utilising the potential of the region without government subsidies; and the 'human resource development' principle, according to which the OVOP movement should foster global-minded, challenging leaders, with the capacity to drive OVOP into further success.[113]

Since its inception, the movement has been widely adopted by local governments in Japan to promote local industries.[114] During the 1980–2002 period, OVOP was introduced into 58 cities, towns and villages of the Oita Prefecture in relation to over 300 products, which include both tangible and intangible products. In 2002, OVOP products comprised 338 local specialties, which amounted to 141 billion yen in sales, representing a huge increase in the number of products and amount of sales since the movement was introduced in 1980 (see Table 4.1).

4.7.2   Expansion of the OVOP Initiative

The OVOP movement has often been presented as a new paradigm for development, applicable to issues of regional development throughout Asia and offering potential for sustainable social change and improvement. The principles which underlie it, together with the efforts of the local citizens which sustain it, have attracted attention both domestically and in many countries of East and Southeast Asia, including China, Thailand and Malaysia, where similar initiatives have been implemented.[115]

---

[112]   See www.ovop.jp

[113]   Ibid.

[114]   Other areas of Japan which have implemented movements based on the OVOP model include the Hokkaido One Village One Product Movement in the prefecture of Hokkaido; the Home Town Products Promotion Scheme in the prefecture of Iwate; the One Region, One Production Centre Project in the prefecture of Yamagata; the Fukushima Home Town Products Promotion of the prefecture of Fukushima; the Indigenous Products Kingdom Project of the prefecture of Toyama; and the Pilot Project for Local Development of the prefecture of Nagano.

[115]   See Iguza, *supra* note 111, 1.

Table 4.1 Growth in product types and in sales of OVOP products (1980–2002)

Year	1980	1985	1990	1995	1997	1998	1999	2000	2002
Sales (billion yen)	35.9	73.4	111.7	129.4	137.3	136.3	139.8	140.2	141
% growth from 1980	100	204	328	360	382	380	389	391	393
Number of products (local specialties)*	143	247	272	289	306	312	318	329	336

Note: * In addition to specialties, OVOP products also comprise facilities, cultural items and items related to the environment.

Source: Oita Prefecture One Village One Product Promotion Division

In the 1980s, some Asian countries started launching projects inspired by the OVOP movement which involved regional development policies and were aimed at promoting the development of local industries. In China, Shanghai and Wuhan were the first cities to initiate a movement with respectively the One Hamlet, One Product and One Village, One Treasure campaigns, to encourage the development of local industries to process goods produced in their surrounding rural areas.

In Southeast Asia, similar projects developed, following the pattern set by OVOP in Oita. The Philippines started a One Barangay, One Product project, while in Malaysia, the state of Kedah developed the Satu Kampung, Satu Produk initiative. By the 1990s, the East Java region in Indonesia began the Back to Village campaign to encourage citizens to return to rural areas. Finally, in 2001, Thailand embarked on the nationwide One Tambon, One Product initiative, and soon after, Cambodia and Laos started similar projects of regional development on a national scale.

In September 2004, the first OVOP Summit Forum was held in Thailand. The second OVOP Summit Meeting took place in China in November 2005 and was attended by representatives of 19 countries. In 2008, 11 countries including Chinese Taipei, Chile, Indonesia, Japan, Malaysia, Mexico, Papua New Guinea, Peru, the Philippines, Thailand and Vietnam, teamed up under the auspices of the Asia-Pacific Economic Cooperation Forum (APEC): (i) to build a web platform for integrating information on products and enterprises; (ii) to facilitate the ongoing promotion of local industry product display, information exchange, and the accumulation and sharing of knowledge; and (iii) to help develop business opportunities in overseas markets.[116]

---

[116] See www.apecovop.org/

4.7.3   The One Tambon One Product Project in Thailand

In 2001, the Thai Government initiated the One Tambon One Product (OTOP) project aimed at improving incomes in village communities to help alleviate rural poverty. Like the OVOP initiative, the project focused on the ability of the local communities to generate sustained income from effective commercialisation of unique products and handicrafts made from locally available materials, utilising local wisdom and skills handed down from generation to generation.[117]

The movement was implemented on a national scale, involving all 50,000 tambons (village sub-districts) across Thailand, which received government support to promote local capacity building in the form of advice, encouragement, facilitation mechanisms, logistical support and financial aid.[118] In addition, tambons also received special loans and grants to implement projects relating to the movement.

While the OVOP movement largely focuses on agricultural based products,[119] the Thai initiative is also greatly concerned with traditional handicraft products made in village communities, each 'lovingly crafted with the inimitable flavour and style of their localities'.[120] Such handicraft products typically consist of cotton and silk garments, artistry items, pottery, fashion accessories, gifts, household and decorative items, and many other articles indigenous to each community, which also fall within the subject matter of TCEs.

Products are selected for promotion within the OTOP scheme because of their quality and export potential. Once approved, producers are able to utilise the specially designed OTOP label, which guarantees that the products were produced within the OTOP scheme.

Although the OTOP initiative is not directly concerned with the protection of TCEs, it provides a valuable platform for their protection, which is in line with other national initiatives for the protection of TCEs through certification marks and labels of authenticity.

---

[117]   See Thai Ministry of Foreign Affairs, One Tambon One Product Project (OTOP), http://yuwathut.mfa.go.th/web/1146.php

[118]   The Thai Government supported the OTOP initiative by helping tambons identify potential OTOP products, providing advice on production, quality control and packaging and designs that would make them attractive to domestic and export markets. In addition, the OTOP production cycle comes under the supervision of a National OTOP Committee, with regional and provincial level committees to assist in identifying, developing and grading OTOP products. See John Leicester, 'Hand-Crafted Products of Thailand's Village Communities', Tourism Authority of Thailand News Room e-Magazine, www.tatnews.org/emagazine/2178.asp

[119]   See Iguza, *supra* note 111, 2.

[120]   See Leicester, *supra* note 118.

4.8   CONCLUSION: EFFICIENCY AND LIMITATIONS OF CERTIFICATION MARKS TO PROTECT TCES

A successful certification scheme to protect TCEs could bring a number of benefits to TCEs holders. Certification marks are potentially unlimited in time and allow for collective use. They do not confer a monopoly right but limit the class of people who can use a certain symbol. They reward the goodwill accumulated over time and provide an objective guarantee as to the characteristics of a product or service. For example, they can provide a guarantee that craftworks have been produced by indigenous communities, in that way protecting both the consumers and the indigenous artists from imitation products.

However, the effectiveness of a certification scheme and its ability to meet the concerns and policy objectives of TCEs holders depend on the way in which it is set up, implemented and policed. A comparative analysis of the toi iho™ Certification Mark, Alaska's Silver Hand programme and the Indigenous Arts Certification System is helpful to reveal important characteristics of a successful certification scheme to protect TCEs (see Table 4.2).

4.8.1   Aims of Certification Schemes

There are three sets of possible objectives for a certification scheme to protect TCEs: (i) objectives relating to the TCEs themselves, i.e. assisting TCEs holders to retain ownership and control of their TCEs, to promote and diversify their TCEs and to maintain the integrity of their TCEs; (ii) economic objectives, i.e. improving the economic position of TCEs holders and ensuring that they get fair and equitable returns; and (iii) objectives of consumer protection, i.e. maximising consumer certainty as to the authenticity of the TCEs. A successful certification scheme should encompass all three sets of objectives and not be too narrowly focused on regulating art and craft products for the tourist market. In that way, the certification scheme would be a more valuable tool for TCEs holders as it would help them fulfil some of their wider protection objectives, such as using TCEs to support their economic development, as well as gaining protection against misappropriation and false claims to authenticity.

4.8.2   Nature of Administrative Body and Funding

Whereas the administrative body of the Indigenous Arts Certification System was a non-profit organisation, the toi iho™ Certification Mark and Alaska's Silver Hand programme are administered by government agencies. The failure of the Indigenous Arts Certification System has shown the difficulty in administering a certification scheme at a national level, and it has been argued that the NIAAA failed in part for lack of proper supervision and assistance.[121] It was suggested that an effective certification scheme to protect TCEs would need significant government support and legal expertise. Indeed, in order to ensure the viability of a certification scheme, governments would need to show commitment and responsibility and retain control over the administration of the scheme.[122] In addition to the administrative aspect, sufficient funds need to be allocated to the functioning of the certification scheme with a clear mandate to develop a comprehensive and workable scheme, and funding agencies need to supervise and monitor the operation of the project.

4.8.3 Oversight of Quality

There needs to be an oversight of the quality of the products or services for which TCEs holders seek accreditation. While Alaska's Silver Hand programme and the Indigenous Arts Certification System do not have quality requirements in order to be allowed to use the certification mark, one of the distinctive features of the toi iho™ Certification Mark is that it is a quality mark. In order to be allowed to use the toi iho™ mark, indigenous artists need to have their work accredited as being of a certain standard by a panel of indigenous experts.

4.8.4 Support of Stakeholders

A successful certification scheme needs to gain the support of the stakeholders, that is, the TCEs holders. In New Zealand, indigenous artists have been positive about the introduction of the toi iho™ marks, which were adopted following a series of consultations with Maori artists from around the country. They were involved in the key decision-making around the words and designs used in the toi iho™ marks. Since then, the toi iho™ marks have been well-administered and have obtained wide community support. Similarly, Alaska's Silver Hand programme has also gained support over the years and is widely used by Alaska Native artists and craftsmen.

Finally, in order for a certification scheme to be successful, the owner of the marks will need to engage in public education campaigns for the acceptance

---

[121] See Rimmer, *supra* note 73, 176.
[122] See Peter Drahos, 'Towards an International Framework for the Protection of Traditional Group Knowledge and Practice', paper presented at UNCTAD-Commonwealth Secretariat Workshop on Elements of National *Sui Generis* Systems for the Preservation, Protection and Promotion of Traditional Knowledge, Innovations and Practices and Options for an International Framework, Geneva, 4–6 February 2004, 33 and Rimmer, *supra* note 73, 176.

of the mark, so that the public, the relevant industry bodies and consumers become familiar with the characteristics that the certification scheme represents.[123]

This chapter examined the certification schemes that were set up in New Zealand, the United States and Australia to protect TCEs, as well as some more recent development initiatives in East and Southeast Asia that rely on labelling systems and provide some indirect protection for TCEs. While the toi iho™ Certification Mark and Alaska's Silver Hand programme have been successfully implemented and the development initiatives show some promising prospects, the Indigenous Arts Certification Mark is no longer in operation. Nonetheless, the data collected in relation to all of these certification schemes was useful, when compared, in revealing important characteristics of a successful certification scheme.

Certification marks are valuable tools for the protection of TCEs as they help control the trade in non-authentic indigenous art and strengthen the position of indigenous artists by increasing consumer confidence in indigenous art and culture, while providing them with fair and equitable economic returns. Also, certification marks protect consumers by raising public awareness and maximising consumer certainty as to the authenticity of the TCEs. Ultimately, however, the success of a certification scheme to protect TCEs will depend on the way it is set up, implemented and policed.

---

[123]   See Wiseman, *supra* note 77, 23.

Table 4.2   Comparative analysis of the certification systems

	Toi iho™ certification mark	Alaska's Silver Hand programme	Indigenous arts certification mark
Operating since	2002	1961	2000
Still in operation	Yes	Yes	No (since 2002)
Name of administrative body	The Arts Council of New Zealand Toi Aotearoa (Creative New Zealand)	The Alaska State Council on the Arts	The National Indigenous Arts Advocacy Association (NIAAA)
Nature of administrative body	Government organisation	Government body (part of the Department of Education and Early Development of the State of Alaska)	The NIAAA is a non-profit organisation. It is a representative body for indigenous artists
Rules/Laws governing the certification scheme	Rules Governing the Use by Artists of the Toi Iho™ Maori Made Mark (2002)	Alaska Stat §§ 45.65.010–.070	The Label of Authenticity Rules (2000)
Aims of the certification scheme	– Distinguish Maori arts and crafts from other arts and crafts – Promote Maori arts and artists nationally and internationally	– Protect consumers – Improve the economic position of Alaska Native Artists	– Maintain the cultural integrity of Aboriginal and Torres Strait Islander (ATSI) art – Ensure a fair and equitable return to ATSI communities and artists

Table 4.2 Continued

	Toi iho™ certification mark	Alaska's Silver Hand programme	Indigenous arts certification mark
	– Assist Maori to retain ownership and control of their knowledge, imagery and design – Maintain the integrity of Maori art culture		– Maximise consumer certainty as to the authenticity of ATSI-derived works/produce – Maximise multiplicity and diversity of ATSI art – Promote an understanding of ATSI cultural heritage and art
Certification marks available	– The toi iho™ Maori Made Mark – The toi iho™ Mainly Maori Mark – The toi iho™ Maori Co-Production Mark – The toi iho™ Licensed Stockist Mark	– The Silver Hand identification seal	– The Label of Authenticity – The Collaboration Mark
Conditions that must be fulfilled in order to be allowed to use the certification mark	– Maori descent – Quality of the works	– Alaskan Native with a blood quantum of one-fourth or greater – 18 years of age or older – Full-time resident of	– Aboriginal or Torres Strait Islander descent – Authenticity – Specify the works and/or services in respect of which he/she intends

		Alaska	
		– Submit application form and supporting documents	to use the Label of Authenticity – Submit application form
Cost of applying	N/A	US$20 handling charge	AUS$30 for one year
Duration of the licence or permit	One year	Two years	One year
Available for joint works with non-indigenous artists or businesses	Yes – toi iho™ Mainly Maori Mark – toi iho™ Maori Co-Production Mark	N/A	Yes – The Collaboration Mark
Object of the certification system	A product	A product	A product or a service
Rights granted with the certification mark	Right to use the words 'toi iho™ Maori Made mark', 'toi iho™ Mainly Maori mark', 'toi iho™ Maori Co-Production mark' or 'toi iho™ Licensed Stockist mark', in association with the relevant logo for a one-year period	Right to use the Silver Hand identification on catalogues, letterheads, business cards, in-store and other advertising and for other similar purposes related to an artist's handicrafts	Right to use the Label of Authenticity

Table 4.2   Continued

	Toi iho™ certification mark	Alaska's Silver Hand programme	Indigenous arts certification mark
Register of artists	Yes	Yes	Yes
Participation of indigenous people in the setting up of the certification system	The toi iho™ marks were introduced in response to calls from Maori to assist them to retain ownership and control of their knowledge, imagery and design. They were created in consultation with Maori artists		The Label of Authenticity Rules capture and implement elements of the definition of authenticity developed by indigenous people during the consultation stage
Dispute resolution	N/A	N/A	Yes
Percentage of approved applications	75% (April 2004)		25% (July 2000)

5. Fair trade labelling

Fair trade bridges artisans' needs for income, retailers' goals for transforming trade, and consumers' concerns for social responsibility through a compatible, nonexploitive, and humanising system of international exchange.[1]

5.1 INTRODUCTION

Having examined the possibility of protecting TCEs with certification marks and collective marks in the previous chapter, this chapter reviews the success story of the fair trade labelling system, as opposed to national initiatives of TCEs protection with labels of authenticity. First, it examines the development of the fair trade movement, the aims and impacts of fair trade, and the functioning of the fair trade labelling system. The chapter then moves on to assess the protection that can be gained for TCEs by the fair trade labelling of handicrafts and the possibility of creating an international system of certification, inspired by the fair trade label, that could be used by indigenous people around the world for the marketing of their products.

5.2 WHAT IS FAIR TRADE?

5.2.1 Definitional Considerations and Historical Development

Fair trade is an alternative approach to conventional international trade. Over the past 40 years, there have been various definitions of fair trade. However, in 2001, four of the main fair trade networks agreed a common definition as part of a broader cooperation strategy. According to this definition:

> Fair Trade is a trading partnership, based on dialogue, transparency and respect, which seeks greater equity in international trade. It contributes to sustainable development by offering better trading conditions to, and securing the rights of, marginalised producers and workers – especially in the South. Fair Trade organisations

---

[1]   Mary Ann Littrell and Marsha Ann Dickson, *Social Responsibility in the Global Market, Fair Trade of Cultural Products* (Sage Publications: London, 1999) 4.

(backed by consumers) are engaged actively in supporting producers, awareness raising and in campaigning for changes in the rules and practice of conventional international trade.[2]

The concept of fair trade began to take shape in Europe after the Second World War, when charities based in Western Europe, such as Oxfam, began to import handicrafts from producers in Eastern Europe to support their economic recovery. At the same time, the US development NGO, Mennonite Central Committee, started importing embroidery from Puerto Rico and other popular crafts as a way of improving the livelihoods of the artists and set up the SELF-HELP Crafts of the World organisation, which would later be known as Ten Thousand Villages. These initiatives relied on the common assumption that traditional business models were fundamentally flawed and that the only way to make them fairer was to set up a parallel or alternative trading model. In the 1970s, alternative trade organisations (ATOs) were established with the aim of offering producer organisations in the South the opportunity to trade with importers in the developed world through a shortened supply chain, without the intervention of middlemen. Products would thus be purchased directly from the producers in developing countries and be sold through networks or 'Third World shops' or catalogues, mainly in Europe and North America. During the 1980s, agricultural products began to be added to the product range of the ATOs and to be sold through sympathetic or socially-oriented retail businesses, such as the Co-operative Group in the United Kingdom, in that way promoting fair trade to a larger consumer base. At the same time, the development of fair trade certification marks allowed the concept of fair trade to get more recognition, as well as mainstream market access. In the 1990s, sales of fair trade products grew significantly in the mainstream markets with the participation of big players such as Costa Coffee, Starbucks or Sainsbury's. Over the past few years, the fair trade volume has been growing steadily because supermarket chains in Europe and the United States have started handling fair trade products and some have even launched their own fair trade labelled products.[3]

---

[2]   Definition of the FINE alliance. FINE brings together the Fair Trade Labelling Organisation International (FLO), the International Federation for Alternative Trade (IFAT), the Network of European World Shops (NEWS) and the European Fair Trade Association (EFTA).

[3]   For more information on the historical development of fair trade, see Andy Redfern and Paul Snedker, *Creating Market Opportunities for Small Enterprises: Experiences of the Fair Trade Movement*, SEED Working Paper No. 30 (ILO: Geneva, 2002) 4–10 and Alex Nicholls and Charlotte Opal, *Fair Trade, Market-Driven Ethical Consumption* (Sage Publications: London, 2005) 19–20.

5.2.2 Fair Trade Aims and Facts

The main objectives of fair trade are:

- to improve the livelihoods and well-being of producers, by improving market access, strengthening producer organisations, paying a better price, and providing continuity in the trading relationship;
- to promote development opportunities for disadvantaged producers, especially women and indigenous people, and to protect children from exploitation in the production process;
- to raise awareness among consumers of the negative effects on producers of international trade so that they exercise their purchasing power positively;
- to set an example of partnership in trade through dialogue, transparency and respect;
- to campaign for changes in the rules and practice of conventional international trade; and
- to protect human rights by promoting social justice, sound environmental practices and economic security.[4]

Other aims of fair trade include environmental protection and sustainability,[5] the maintenance of cultural diversity and contributing to the development of stronger trade relations between countries in the southern and northern hemispheres. In order to achieve these aims, all stakeholders along the trade chain must cooperate and share information, as well as engage in campaigns to raise consumer awareness.

In 2003, worldwide sales of all fair trade products amounted to approximately US$895 million, up from an estimated US$600 million in 2002. In 2006, consumers worldwide spent US$2.2 billion on fair trade certified products.[6] Despite these figures, fair trade still represents a tiny percentage of the

---

4   See Redfern and Snedker, *supra* note 3, 11.
5   Fair trade producer organisations' management policies often include provisions that they must comply with national and international legislation on the protection of the environment (such as natural waters, the virgin forest and other ecosystems of high ecological value), erosion, waste management and the use and handling of hazardous chemicals. In addition, producers are encouraged to work towards organic practices, such as using organic fertilisers and biological disease control. See Fairtrade Foundation, The Fairtrade Mark, Core Standards and Practice behind the Five Guarantees, www.fairtrade.org.uk/downloads/pdf/five_guarantees.pdf
6   See Fairtrade Labelling Organisation International, 'Global Fairtrade Sales Increase by 40% Benefiting 1.4 Million Farmers Worldwide', press release 25 July 2007.

volume of international trade. However, its social and economic impact should not be underestimated. Fair trade involves more than 569 certified producer organisations in 57 countries in Asia, Africa and Latin America, representing over 1.4 million farmers and workers and their families, and there are over 100 fair trade import organisations working with producer groups providing goods to consumers via 45,000 sales outlets worldwide, so that overall, five million people are benefiting from fair trade.[7]

There are various types of groups working for a fairer trade. They can be divided into four main categories:[8]

- the producer organisations in developing or Southern countries which supply the products;
- the buying organisations or ATOs in developed or Northern countries, which act as importers, wholesalers and retailers of the products;
- the umbrella bodies;[9]
- a range of conventional organisations, such as supermarkets, that engage in fair trade and are becoming increasingly important players in the retailing of fair trade products.[10]

---

[7]   See Fairtrade Foundation statistics available at www.fairtrade.nett/figures.html

[8]   See Geoff Moore, 'The Fair Trade Movement: Parameters, Issues and Future Research' (2004) 53 *Journal of Business Ethics* 75–6.

[9]   The umbrella bodies consist of five main organisations: (i) the Fairtrade Labelling Organisation International (FLO) (see *infra* para. 5.3.2); (ii) the International Fair Trade Association (IFAT), which was established in 1989. IFAT is a global trade association for both fair trade producers and traders that has a worldwide membership. Its objectives are to develop the market for fair trade, to build trust in fair trade and to speak out for fair trade, see www.ifat.org; (iii) the European Fair Trade Association (EFTA), which was established in 1990. EFTA is an advocacy and research body consisting of a network of 11 fair trade organisations in nine European countries. Its objectives are to make fair trade importing more efficient and to promote fair trade to commercial and political decision-makers, see www.eftafairtrade.org; (iv) the Fair Trade Federation, which is a US-based trade association of fair trade wholesalers, retailers and producers whose members are committed to providing fair wages and good employment opportunities to economically disadvantaged artisans and farmers worldwide, see www.fairtradefederation.com; and (v) the Network of European World Shops (NEWS), which aims to promote fair trade by stimulating, supporting and linking world shops in Europe that retail fair trade products. NEWS is a network of 15 national World Shop associations in 13 countries, together representing about 2,500 World Shops in Europe, see www.worldshops.org

[10]   In 2004, it was estimated that around 43,000 supermarkets across Europe and 7,000 supermarkets in the United States and Canada were stocking fair trade products. A number of supermarkets are even starting to sell their 'own brand' fair trade products sourced directly from producers, without involving ATOs. See Moore, *supra* note 8, 76.

5.2.3 Fair Trade Philosophy, Economics and Principles

As a philosophy, fair trade attempts to correct market failures by promoting empowerment and improved quality of life for producers through an integrated and sustained system of trade partnerships amongst producers and retailers. Minimum wages and the payment of a social premium are the primary mechanisms for achieving this goal. Fair trade relies on the assumption that consumers are willing to pay a premium price for fair trade products because of the moral satisfaction they derive from the assurance that the fair trade label provides. It contends that a 'survival of the fittest model' on an international scale is neither moral nor defensible in modern society and argues that producers should be paid 'as much as possible' rather than 'as little as possible', thus providing a dramatic contrast with mainstream business models, in which attention is directed towards meeting consumer demand and expanding shareholder profits.[11]

Fair trade is seen as a political reaction to the rise of free trade, capitalism and the power of transnational corporations. It has been characterised in the economics literature as being a third way between free trade, on the one hand, and protectionism, on the other.[12] Under classical free trade theory,[13] countries should export what they are relatively good at producing and they should import what they cannot produce sufficiently. Supporters of free trade argue that the unfettered movement of goods, services and finance between countries offers the most efficient model of transactional business, thus making it a win-win situation in which everyone benefits. Attempts to liberalise world trade and to bring the benefits of free trade to all countries began after the Second World War when the General Agreement on Tariffs and Trade (GATT) attempted to arbitrate between international trade disputes via a series of 'rounds' of negotiations to promote free trade and international deregulation. However, while the volume of international trade has increased significantly over the last 30 years, global inequity has also grown, implying that the benefits of free trade have not been evenly spread. This was partly due to market imperfections within developing countries that compromised the ability of trade to lift them out of poverty. These include a lack of market access, imperfect information, the lack of

---

[11]   See Littrell and Dickson, *supra* note 15, 5 and Redfern and Snedker, *supra* note 3, 4.

[12]   See Moore, *supra* note 8, 76.

[13]   Classical free trade theory has its origins in Adam Smith's and David Ricardo's theories of comparative advantage. According to *Black's Law Dictionary*, free trade is defined as 'the open and unrestricted import and export of goods without barriers, such as quotas or tariffs, other than those charged only as a revenue source, as opposed to those designed to protect domestic businesses'. See Bryan A. Garner (ed.), *Black's Law Dictionary* (Thomson West: St Paul MN, 2004) 691.

access to financial markets, the lack of access to credit, the inability to switch to other sources of income generation, corruption and weak legal systems and enforcement of laws. Fair trade supporters argue that because of these market imperfections, the global trade system cannot work for everyone. Instead, by providing a profitable relationship to all those in the supply chain, fair trade offers a sustainable market-based solution to global trade failures.[14] In addition, it must be highlighted that fair trade does not involve government intervention. It is a consumer choice trading model that operates entirely within the free market system. In that way, fair trade is a sub-set of free trade and functions within the broader free market trading system.[15] In particular, fair trade philosophy is reflected in a series of fair trade principles on which fair trade stakeholders operate.

Direct trade with producers
The first requirement of the fair trade model is that importers must, wherever possible, buy directly from producers, whether they are in the farming or craft sector. While estates, plantations and large-scale craft and textile manufacturers have historically enjoyed access to export markets, small-scale producers are typically isolated from direct export access unless organised into cooperatives or similar group-selling structures. Farmers in developing countries often live in isolated rural areas with few or no roads and often do not have the possibility to take their product to the market. They are therefore reliant on middlemen to come to their farms and buy their product and have a very limited bargaining power, as competition by buyers is rarely achieved. Middlemen will often agree not to compete with each other on price, so that farmers receive only one price offer.[16] In order to develop an alternative approach to these trading practices, ATOs established a practice whereby they would buy directly from and build relationships with producers in developing countries. They set up business and supply chain structures that allowed them to ship the goods from producer to customer via their own warehousing and often through their own shops, relying on mainstream services, such as shipping and packaging, only when they had no other choice.[17]

Long-term trading relationships
The aims behind the long-term trading relationship principle are to allow for long-term planning and sustainable production practices.[18] Long-term trading

---

[14] See Nicholls and Opal, *supra* note 3, 17–19.
[15] Ibid. 53–4.
[16] See Nicholls and Opal, *supra* note 3, 33–4.
[17] See Redfern and Snedker, *supra* note 3, 21.
[18] See FLO FairTrade Standards, www.fairtrade.net/sites/standards/general.html

relationships allow farmers to benefit from a predictable income flow and to correct market information failures by allowing information exchange to take place between producers and importers regarding supply and quality require-ments. This principle, however, is difficult to enforce in practice because there are no clear rules as to how long the 'long-term relationship' must be, with most purchase contracts being initially set up for a duration of six months to one year only, and with importers having the possibility to switch suppliers once their contract expires.

The minimum price and the social premium
The fair trade minimum price is calculated to cover the costs of sustainable production,[19] the cost of sustainable livelihood and the cost of complying with fair trade standards.[20] The application of a minimum price to the fair trade model was inspired by the Keynesian model of economics where price should be more closely linked to the cost of production. According to Keynes, one should not pay less for a product than the cost of its production, plus the cost of a decent standard of living for the producer.[21]

The additional social premium, on the other hand, is intended for investment in social, commercial or environmental development projects. It guarantees that producers earn a little extra to invest in improving their social condition or the quality of their natural environment. In other words, the social premium repre-sents the 'development agenda' of fair trade.[22] FLO inspections check that the social premium is spent on social development projects chosen by the commu-nity through a democratic process and monitors the progress of these projects and the way they benefit the community. FLO does not, however, make judge-ments as to the value of the chosen use of the social premium.

5.3 FAIR TRADE LABELLING

5.3.1 Development of Fair Trade Labelling

The concept of fair trade as such has existed for over 40 years. Fair trade

---

[19] The costs of production include land, labour and capital costs of sustainable production. They are calculated based on surveys of producers. See Nicholls and Opal, *supra* note 3, 40.

[20] The costs of complying with fair trade standards include, for example, those of belonging in a cooperative, organising a worker's assembly, paperwork associated with inspections and reporting to FLO. Ibid.

[21] See Redfern and Snedker, *supra* note 3, 4 and Nicholl and Opal, *supra* note 3, 41–2.

[22] See Nicholls and Opal, *supra* note 3, 47.

labelling, on the other hand, emerged in 1988 at the initiative of Mexican coffee farmers together with a Dutch development agency named Solidaridad.[23] Coffee imported to the Netherlands under fair trade principles was labelled by Solidaridad under the name Max Havelaar.[24] After this first initiative, fair trade retailers realised that by sharing a mark that identified their fair trade business practices, they could benefit from joint marketing and education around the fair trade label and grow more quickly. Other national fair trade labellers such as TransFair and the Fairtrade Foundation soon followed in Solidaridad's footsteps, covering a growing range of products. The formalisation of the fair trade process into a label relied on one important principle: independent third party standard-setting and certification. Indeed, not for profit organisations who licensed the use of a label had to guarantee that producer groups were democratically organised and transparent and that the importer paid them the fair trade price.[25] All the National Initiatives[26] started individually and each defined for their own market the fair trade consumer label they wanted on their products. In 1997, 17 National Initiatives founded an umbrella organisation, the Fairtrade Labelling Organisation International (FLO), recognising the need for a single logo. They believed that a single logo would increase clarity for consumers and facilitate cross-border trade. The logo was not introduced straightaway because of the financial cost of such an operation, the difficulty in finding a mark that would work in all countries, and the risks involved in losing trust and awareness vested in the former logos. However, over the past few years, following an increasing interest in fair trade labelling and facilitated cross-border trade from international companies, FLO has started the process of harmonising the different labels into one international certification mark by proposing the use of this newly developed certification mark to countries that wish to move forward to a common approach. The new mark, which is now available, will be replacing the existing labels at different speeds in different countries.[27]

---

23   Solidaridad is a Dutch development organisation for Latin America, Asia and Africa. It was founded in 1969. Its two main objectives are sustainable economy and fair trade, and human rights and society building. For more information see www. solidaridad.nl

24   The label was called 'Max Havelaar' after an 1860 novel by Multatuli called *Max Havelaar, or the Coffee Auctions of the Dutch Trading Company*, which played a key role in Dutch colonial policy in the Dutch East Indies in the nineteenth and early twentieth centuries.

25   See Nicholls and Opal, *supra* note 3, 128.

26   The National Initiatives are labelling organisations that issue fair trade labels to importers and verify that fair trade standards for specific products are met. National Initiatives are not involved in trading products. They certify products, select, verify and monitor fair trade producers, and promote fair trade products to retailers and consumers.

27   For more information see www.fairtrade.net/sites/aboutflo/faq.html

Figure 5.1   Max Havelaar logo

Figure 5.2   FLO fair trade mark

Fair trade labelling works as a certification system. It provides an independent guarantee to consumers that producers and traders have abided by all fair trade conditions, that fair trade products have been produced and traded according to pre-defined social, contractual and sometimes environmental standards, and that fair trade workers and artisans benefit from a higher price, stable income, fairer trading relations and decent production conditions.

5.3.2   The Fairtrade Labelling Organisation International

FLO is the coordinator of the fair trade labelling system. It is a standard setting and certification agency for fair trade importers and producers. It gives credibility to the fair trade label by providing an independent, transparent and competent certification of social and economic development. Its mission is: (i) to improve the position of the poor and disadvantaged producers in the developing world by setting up fair trade standards and by creating a framework that enables trade to take place at conditions respecting their interests; (ii) to guarantee the integrity of the fair trade mark and certification process; (iii) to facilitate the business of fair trade by helping to match supply and demand; and (iv) to offer producers support and consultancy to improve their business strategies.

Figure 5.3 shows the functioning of the FLO.

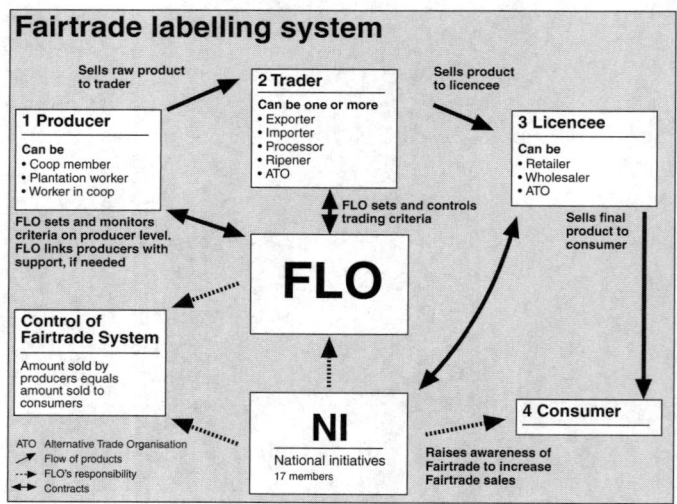

Source: FLO.

Figure 5.3   Fair trade labelling system

At the producers level: FLO sets out the criteria that have to be met by producers to be listed in the fair trade producers register which is distributed to traders. FLO inspects producer groups to certify them for compliance with fair trade standards, including democratic organisation, financial transparency, adequate working conditions and progress regarding social and community development goals. Furthermore, FLO offers support to producers through the Producer Business Unit.[28]

At the traders level: traders sign a contract with FLO to determine the way fair trade works and to give FLO the right of inspection to ensure that the rules have been respected. Traders act as a link between producers and licensees.

At the licensees level: licensees sell the final product to consumers. They are the only stakeholder, in the fair trade chain, who are authorised to use the fair trade label. In return for that right, licensees pay a fee to the National Initiatives. The licensees can be retailers, wholesalers or ATOs.

At the National Initiatives level: the National Initiatives encourage industry and consumers to support a fairer trade and to purchase the products that carry a fair trade label, as an independent consumer guarantee that producers in the developing world are getting a better deal.[29]

5.3.3 Fair Trade Standards

FLO has developed a set of fair trade standards for producer groups and traders that it enforces by inspecting producers and conducting audits of fair trade supply chains. The International Fairtrade Standards were developed by the FLO Standards Committee for all products currently labelled[30] in conjunction with stakeholders from FLO's member organisations, producer organisations, traders and external experts. The standards operate at all levels along the trade chain.

There are two categories of fair trade standards.

Standards for producers: As the problems experienced by producers and workers in developing countries differ greatly depending on the size and structure of the producer entity, the FLO Standards Committee has developed two sets of generic producer standards. The first set applies to cooperatives of

---

[28]   The Producer Business Unit (PBU) offers an introduction to fair trade and its advantages to interested applicants and a follow up on certification decisions. See www.fairtrade.net/sites/support/support.html

[29]   See www.fairtrade.net/sites.aboutflo/why.html

[30]   Coffee, tea, rice, fresh fruit, juices, cocoa, sugar, honey, sports balls and wine. FLO International is currently exploring the possibility to extend the fair trade product range to other products such as flowers and textiles. See www.fairtrade.net/sites/products/productdev.html

small-scale family farmers organised with a democratic, participative structure. It guarantees that they receive a fair price for their products. The second
set applies to organised workers on plantations and in factories. It guarantees
that employers pay decent wages, the right to join trade unions, to be provided
with good housing when relevant, minimum health and safety as well as the
prohibition of child or forced labour. In addition, the generic standards distinguish between minimum requirements,[31] which producers must meet to be
certified 'fair trade' and progress requirements that encourage producer organisations to improve working conditions and product quality, increase the environmental sustainability of their activities and invest in the development of
their workers.[32]

Standards for traders: Traders must buy directly from an FLO-registered
trading association, pay the FLO-determined minimum price that producers
can invest in development, pay a social premium to cover the costs of sustainable production and living, make partial advance payments when producers
ask for it, and sign contracts that allow for long-term planning and sustainable
production practices.[33]

5.3.4   Certification

In order to become certified and participate to the fair trade system, producer
groups must be inspected by a third party, the certifier,[34] for compliance with
the International Fairtrade Standards. Producers must contact FLO and fill in
a questionnaire. After evaluation of the questionnaire, an inspection visit is
performed by an FLO-trained inspector,[35] who spends one or two weeks on
site, depending on the size and type of the producer organisation. Producer

---

[31]   Minimum requirements are meant to ensure that fair trade benefits reach the
small farmers and workers, that the farmer organisation has potential for development,
and that the fair trade instruments can take effect and lead to a development that cannot
be achieved otherwise.

[32]   See www.fairtrade.net/sites/standards/standards.html

[33]   Ibid.

[34]   The certification process is operated by FLO-Cert Ltd on the basis of ISO
standards for certification bodies (ISO 65). FLO-Cert Ltd is a limited company that was
established separately from FLO, to make fair trade certification and auditing operations more transparent. See www.fairtrade.net/sites.certification/certification.html

[35]   In order to ensure that producer groups comply with fair trade standards, FLO
works with a network of independent inspectors who regularly visit all producer organisations. In addition, it uses a specially developed trade auditing system to monitor
traders' and retailers' compliance with fair trade conditions and make sure that every
fair trade-labelled product sold to a consumer has indeed been produced by a certified
producer organisation which has been paid the fair trade price. See www.fairtrade.net/
sites/aboutflo/tasks.html

groups that are already in the system are re-inspected annually and any certified group may also receive surprise visits from FLO inspectors at any time. After visiting the producers, the inspector writes a report assessing the compliance with FLO standards for a specific product. The report is then discussed by an independent certification committee which takes the decision to certify or not. Once approved for certification, a contract is signed between the producer organisation and FLO.[36]

5.4 FAIR TRADE LABELLING FOR HANDICRAFTS

5.4.1 The Fair Trade Market for Craft Products

After agriculture, crafts constitute the second largest sector of rural employment in the developing world. This is mainly due to the difficulty of having access to land as a source of income and to the limited access to other income alternatives. In that context, programmes and business models, such as the fair trade model, that provide new markets for crafts are vital for artisans as they can grant them access to new markets by exporting crafts and expanding cultural products enterprises beyond local markets.

The type of crafts that are involved in fair trade are products that convey a distinctive cultural meaning that has evolved from long-standing patterns of daily and ritual use within a community. Such products embody indigenous colours, motifs and designs, and use locally available raw material such as clay, wood, grasses and cotton. They can be apparel, accessories, jewellery, household goods, decorative objects, toys and musical instruments and are usually produced using dyeing, weaving, sewing, basketry, wood turning, carving, metal smithing, paper making and painting technologies.[37] Generally, the crafts involved in fair trade present many similarities with the subject matter of TCEs.[38] They are transmitted from one generation to another, they are produced within a community, often using raw materials and they reflect the community's social and cultural identity.

ATOs are increasingly using consultants in product development to match a group's skills and available materials with market trends and act as a link between the needs of the artisan producers and consumers. ATOs' approach towards product development vary greatly in the extent to which they become involved with producers in product design and development. They range from limited intervention to ATO-directed intervention strategy in which ATO staff

---

36   For more information, see www.fairtrade.net/sites/aboutflo/tasks.html
37   See Littrell and Dickson, *supra* note 1, 13.
38   See definition and characteristics of TCEs, *supra* para. 1.1.

or consultants participate to develop products aimed at satisfying Western consumers.[39] In addition, ATOs will usually aim at developing products for a contemporary market, while maintaining the traditions of the artisan group. However, while tradition is usually emphasised to provide continuity and enhance the artisan's cultural identity, at other times, tradition represents a marketing strategy of product differentiation or a way to accommodate trade restrictions.[40]

Over the years, strategies for product development have become an integral part of a successful fair trade business plan and unless artisan groups have an extensive understanding of the export market and know how to use market-related information to generate product development, it is unlikely that they can improve their skills without the help of a 'culture broker'. However, there are increasing concerns that product development strategies may influence the characteristics of the product itself and that such practices may lead to the erosion of cultural traditions and have an impact on artisan producers, their communities and products. It is feared that there may be a shift of local standards for quality and beauty when artisans turn to products that meet outsiders' interests in the exotic, or their perception of what constitutes an ethnic look in apparel or household products. In addition, it has been suggested that the involvement of ATOs in product design and development and the tampering with traditional skills and designs to meet customers' preferences could trigger a neo-colonial relationship of dependency on ATOs for success.[41] In this perspective, it is important to maintain a balance between the need to develop new products to meet market demands and the preservation of cultural identity.

One approach that is increasingly taken by ATOs is to use culture brokers to collaborate with artisan producers in developing products for current consumer tastes. For that purpose, culture brokers work with the artisans on a sustained basis, seeking their input, while at the same time helping them acquire higher skill levels.[42] This approach can be compared to that of the New Zealand toi iho™ Maori Co-Production Mark and the Australian

---

[39]   See Littrell and Dickson, *supra* note 1, 13–14 and 252–3.

[40]   Products that can be qualified as handicrafts represent a business advantage for the exporting country as they are exempt from quota restrictions. For example, the amounts of cotton textile products that can be exported to the United States from India are restricted by quotas that are arranged through bilateral agreements falling under the Multi-Fiber Arrangement. If the products involved are handicrafts, they are exempt from the quota restrictions. Therefore, by choosing to make products falling under the definition of handicrafts, artisans are able to retain a level of control on how much they export. Ibid. 253 and 255.

[41]   Ibid. 13 and 258.

[42]   Ibid. 258.

Collaboration Mark that were examined in the previous chapter, and that acknowledge and encourage the growth of innovative and collaborative ventures between indigenous and non-indigenous people.[43]

5.4.2 Fair Trade Labelling of Craft Products

Even though the initial focus of fair trade as such was on textiles and handicrafts,[44] fair trade labelling was mainly used on agricultural commodities, such as coffee or bananas, which have the most widespread impact on the livelihoods of small producers and workers in developing countries. In recent years, however, the growth of consumer and industry interest in fair trade labelled products has created new opportunities to expand the scope of fair trade labelling to also cover handmade and manufactured products, such as jewellery, apparel, gifts, textiles and handicrafts.

One of these initiatives involves hand-made rugs and carpets, where some NGOs and other organisations, such as Rugmark[45] and STEP,[46] have used a series of tools including standard-setting, external verification, labelling and support to producers and their communities in order to eradicate child labour and

---

[43] See *supra* paras 4.4.2 and 4.6.2.

[44] The concept of fair trade developed after the Second World War, when charities in Western Europe began to import handicrafts from producers in Eastern Europe to support their economic recovery. Simultaneously, the Mennonite Central Committee in the United States began to develop a market for embroidery from Puerto Rico by setting up the SelfHelp Crafts of the World organisation that would later become known as Ten Thousand Villages. See Nicholls and Opal, *supra* note 3, 19–20.

[45] Rugmark is a global not for profit organisation established in 1994, working to end illegal child labour and offer educational opportunities for children in India, Nepal and Pakistan. It does so through loom and factory monitoring, consumer labelling and running schools for former child workers. It uses the RUGMARK label as an assurance that no illegal child labour was employed in the manufacture of a carpet or rug. To be certified RUGMARK, carpet-manufacturers must sign a legally binding contract to produce carpets without illegal child labour, register all looms with the RUGMARK foundation and allow access to looms for unannounced inspections. Each carpet is then individually numbered so as to enable its origin to be traced back to the loom on which it was produced. To date, more than 4 million carpets carrying the RUGMARK label have been sold in Europe and North America since 1995 and it is estimated that child labour on South Asia's carpet looms has dropped from 1 million to 300,000 since the launch of RUGMARK. For more information, see www.rugmark.org

[46] STEP is a foundation which was established in 1995 and is guided by Swiss NGOs and representatives of the carpet industry. It is dedicated to improving working and living conditions of the people in regions where hand-woven carpets are made, to fighting abusive child labour and to promoting ecologically harmless production methods. STEP provides a fair trade label to retailers of hand-made carpets who commit themselves to actively work towards providing socially just conditions in the carpet industry. The fair trade label STEP certifies that companies ensure fair conditions of

encourage compliance with the ILO conventions in ways that have many similarities with the fair trade philosophy and approach. In April 2006, FLO commissioned a feasibility study on the fair trade labelling of rugs and carpets to explore
the possibility of cooperation between Rugmark, STEP and NGOs, on the one
hand, and FLO on the other. The aim of the study is to recommend options for
cooperation in view of sustainable poverty reduction and empowerment and
development of producers and workers in the hand-made carpet industry.[47]

Generally speaking, fair trade labelling is increasingly used in relation to
handicrafts and market opportunities are emerging for many new goods
coming from developing countries. Fair trade handicrafts are sold in thousands
of fair trade shops in Europe, in the United States, Canada and Japan, and
some ATOs, such as SERRV International,[48] have established special
programmes to promote fair trade handicrafts. According to Nicholls and
Opal, there could be clear market opportunities in rethinking the development
and distribution patterns of handicrafts and in considering applying the fair
trade mark to these products. For example, whereas the European market for
fair trade handicrafts that are sold through world shops was estimated at
US$107 million in 2003, the European market for 'exotic gifts' that are sold
through private sector companies is estimated to be worth about US$6.3
billion. Nicholls and Opal note that unlike fair trade foods, there is currently
no strategy for fair trade producers to address such a potential demand in handicrafts. They argue that there would be an opportunity for fair trade handicrafts
to enter the mainstream by following the lead set by food. In order to do so,
the first step would be to understand the needs of the 'premium' gifts market
and then fit the design and quality control process to target this, by following
a systematic approach to raising skill levels amongst fair trade producers. The
second step would then be to create new distribution networks in partnership
with sympathetic private sector branches.[49]

---

production, pay fair prices, fight abusive child labour, promote ecologically viable
production methods and authorise independent verification. As of January 2006, there
were 101 points of sales for STEP hand-made carpets across Switzerland, Austria and
France, ten registered licensed importers and 288 producers verified within the STEP
programmes. For more information, see www.step-foundation.ch

  47   Ibid.

  48   SERRV International is a not for profit trade and development organisation
that was established in 1949. Its mission is to promote the social and economic progress
of people in developing regions of the world by marketing products in a just and direct
manner. SERRV International works with thousands of small-scale artisans in Africa,
Asia, Latin America and other developing regions of the world by purchasing and
marketing their handicrafts, as well as to assist them in becoming economically self-
sufficient through product design, training, information, technical assistance and
market access. For more information, see www.agreatergift.org/Default.aspx

  49   See Nicholls and Opal, *supra* note 3, 236.

Even though the incentives behind the fair trade labelling of handicrafts and the use of labels or certification marks to protect TCEs differ, fair trade labelling does provide consumers with a certification that the labelled goods are authentic. In that way, fair trade labelling indirectly serves the purpose of protecting TCEs and can be a complement to an intellectual property system of protection for TCEs.

5.5   AN INTERNATIONAL CERTIFICATION SYSTEM TO PROTECT TCES INSPIRED ON THE FAIR TRADE LABEL

In a paper commissioned by UNCTAD in 2004,[50] Peter Drahos suggests that an international treaty on the protection of traditional group knowledge and practice should help develop a system of certification that could be used by indigenous people around the world for the marketing of their products. He argues that the members of a treaty on traditional knowledge should draw on the experience and success of the fair trade label and use the treaty as a means of developing a coordinated approach to labelling and certification.[51]

Drahos suggests that it would be more efficient to develop a single international sign of indigenous identity, or global brand to act as a certification mark for the protection of TCEs, rather than have a series of national labels of authenticity. When commenting on the success story of the fair trade label, he draws the conclusion that 'it pays to think big' and that TCEs holders should take advantage of the fact that trade marks and certification marks can work large-scale effects in wealthy consumer markets. He argues that producers should unite around a few or one highly visible certification mark.[52] As was highlighted in the previous chapter, labelling initiatives that are poorly financed, that do not receive proper government support, monitoring and legal advice, that do not look to global markets and that are isolated, are likely, as in the case of the authenticity mark in Australia, to fail.[53]

Notwithstanding the advantages that can be gained by developing a global

---

[50]   See Peter Drahos, 'Towards an International Framework for the Protection of Traditional Group Knowledge and Practice', UNCTAD–Commonwealth Secretariat Workshop on Elements of National *Sui Generis* Systems for the Preservation, Protection and Promotion of Traditional Knowledge, Innovations and Practices and Options for an International Framework, Geneva, 4–6 February 2004.

[51]   Ibid. 32–3.

[52]   Ibid.

[53]   See *supra* para. 4.8.

label to protect TCEs, one commentator argues that there are also dangers involved in establishing a single international sign of indigenous identity. Matthew Rimmer argues that such a sign would inevitably create tensions between the various indigenous nations and communities it would represent.[54] Developing such a label would also require the creation of a common set of criteria to be fulfilled in order to be able to use the certification mark. This could raise a series of issues, such as how to define indigenous identity[55] and assess the quality of the work, as different indigenous groups have given different answers to these questions in the past.

In addition, while fair trade labels and labels of authenticity are related, they do not fulfil the same consumer and producer objectives (see Table 5.1). While consumers refer to certification marks because they want to get authentic products, the fair trade label is more altruistic. The success of the fair trade label has been driven by a widespread increase in 'ethical consumerism' which embraces consumer concerns over environmental issues and the human element in the retail supply chain. Consumers clearly like fair trade and they buy fair trade products because they are sensitised to the need for greater equity. As a consequence, sales of fair trade products have been growing rapidly worldwide. Similarly, while the objectives of indigenous groups in having a label of authenticity are guided by cultural and economic considerations, such as to prevent misappropriation, to preserve a group's cultural identity and integrity, to fight against the proliferation of fakes in local markets and to ensure a fair and equitable return to indigenous artists for their products,[56] the objectives of the fair trade label are of a political and economic nature. In this light, it is questionable whether the label of authenticity and the fair trade label can be compared and whether the success of the fair trade labelling system justifies the establishment of an international certification system for the protection of TCEs, inspired by it.

The difficulties that would arise in establishing a single international sign of indigenous identity for TCEs should nonetheless be balanced against the advantages of having a global label. First, there would be an increase of clarity

---

[54]   See Matthew Rimmer, 'Australian Icons: Authenticity Marks and Identity Politics' (2004) 3 *Indigenous Law Journal* 176.

[55]   While some regulations define members of indigenous groups narrowly, with the consequence that some individuals might be excluded from the scope of the definition, others make it easier for a larger range of people to prove indigenous status. In addition, whereas some systems require proof of a certain blood quantum, others simply require a written statement of acceptance from the indigenous community. See *supra* para. 4.4.4 and *infra* para. 7.5.4.

[56]   See *supra* para. 1.2.

for consumers. Consumers would benefit from having only one phrase or one logo when searching for authentic products, in that way avoiding the label fatigue that arises when they are faced with too many labels. Secondly, TCEs holders could benefit from using a label that other TCEs holders use, as it could help increase brand equity behind the global label and benefit all products that carry the label. Having such a label appear on a wide variety of TCEs would also increase consumer awareness and education by repeating brand impression. Finally, a global label could help TCEs gain recognition beyond local markets. This would help promote indigenous crafts internationally and increase financial profits for indigenous groups, thus satisfying some of the objectives of TCEs holders. In addition, the increased recognition of a single sign would facilitate consumer education and in the long run would also help fight the misappropriation of TCEs.

5.6 CONCLUSION

Despite the conceptual success of the fair trade model over the past decades, the fair trade sector has remained small in financial terms. From a political perspective, however, the impact of fair trade has been more wide-reaching. On the one hand, the fair trade movement has made a strong statement about the iniquities in the mainstream trading system. On the other, it has created a business model that could have a positive impact on the lives of farmers and artisans in developing countries. While there is only limited data available on the impact of fair trade on poverty and the ways in which fair trade affects workers and artisans,[57] the evidence available seems to suggest that the fair trade model has had positive developmental impacts on producers and artisan groups, such as an increase in income, improved education, female empowerment, the preservation of indigenous cultures and producer empowerment.[58]

Fair trade labelling is not directly concerned with TCEs. However, this

---

[57] Recent studies include fair trade impact assessment carried out by the Natural Resources Institute at the University of Greenwich in the United Kingdom and Colorado State University in the United States, and ATOs impact assessment of some of their fair trade projects. However, there are very few impact studies on how fair trade affects workers and artisans and there is only limited information on how the livelihoods of fair trade participants compare to those of similar producers or artisans who do not have access to fair trade markets. This is mainly due to the difficulty of quantifying social impacts and the high cost of longitudinal studies. See Nicholls and Opal, *supra* note 3, 203–4.

[58] Ibid.

chapter has shown the benefits of fair trade labelling for producer and artisan groups and has highlighted the analogies with the certification schemes and the advantages that could be gained from having a single international sign of indigenous identity to protect TCEs.

Table 5.1   Comparative analysis of labels of authenticity and fair trade labels

	Labels of authenticity	Fair trade labels
Operating since	1960s	1980s
Still in operation	While some labels of authenticity, such as the toi iho™ Certification Mark and Alaska's Silver Hand programme are still in operation, the Indigenous Arts Certification Mark is not	Yes
Scope	National	National, regional or international
Nature of administrative body	National organisations or government agencies	National or international organisations
Objectives of consumers when buying the labelled product	Desire to buy 'the real thing'	Ethical consumerism
Objectives of producers and artisans using the label	– To distinguish indigenous craft from other craft; – to promote indigenous craft nationally and internationally; – to assist indigenous artists retain ownership and control of their knowledge, imagery and designs; – to maintain the integrity of an indigenous culture; – to ensure a fair and equitable return to indigenous artists for their cultural produce; – to maximise consumer certainty as to the authenticity of indigenous art.	To achieve the aims of fair trade: – to improve the livelihoods and well-being of producers and artisans by improving market access, strengthening producer organisations, paying a better price and providing continuity in the trading relationship; – to promote development opportunities for disadvantaged producers; – to raise awareness amongst consumers of the negative effect on producers of international trade so that they exercise their purchasing power positively; – to set an example of partnership in trade through dialogue, transparency and respect; – to campaign for changes in the rules and practice of conventional international trade; – to protect human rights by promoting social justice, sound environmental practices and economic security.

6. The protection of traditional cultural expressions with geographical indications

6.1 INTRODUCTION

Geographical indications (GIs) have traditionally been associated with agricultural products, foodstuff, wines and spirits. However, in recent years, GIs have been said to be 'potentially useful' in protecting TCEs. At the fifth session of the WIPO Intergovernmental Committee on Intellectual Property and Genetic Resources, Traditional Knowledge and Folklore, it was pointed out that some TCEs, such as handicrafts made using natural resources, may qualify as 'goods' which could be protected by GIs.[1] In addition some TCEs, such as indigenous and traditional names, signs and other indications, may themselves be GIs.

This chapter will assess whether TCEs can be protected by GIs, examine practical examples involving GI protection of TCEs at the international, regional and national level, and examine the possibility of incorporating TCEs under the GIs regime established under Articles 22–24 of the TRIPS Agreement.

6.2 TCES AS SUBJECT MATTER OF GEOGRAPHICAL INDICATIONS

Article 1(a)(iv) of the Substantive Provisions of the WIPO Revised Provisions for the Protection of Traditional Cultural Expressions/Expressions of Folklore provides that 'traditional cultural expressions' or 'expressions of folklore' can be tangible expressions, such as productions of art, in particular, drawings, designs, paintings (including body-painting), carvings, sculptures, pottery, terracotta, mosaic, woodwork, metalware, jewellery, baskets, needlework,

---

[1]   See WIPO, Consolidated Analysis of the Legal Protection of Traditional Cultural Expressions, Document WIPO/GRTKF/IC/5/3, 52.

Table 6.1   Characteristics of GIs and TCEs

GIs	TCEs
GIs identify a good produced by a number of different producers	TCEs are usually produced within a community
GIs are often based on traditional formulas and processes	TCEs are produced according to traditional methods
The know-how attached to GIs is transmitted from one generation to another	The know-how attached to TCEs is transmitted from one generation to another
GIs are granted for products which have a relationship with the land, local resources or the environment	TCEs are generally linked to a specific place where a certain product is made or to traditional methods or conditions used in a specific place for making a product, often using raw material from sustainable resources
Many years are required to produce the link between a product and its geographical origin	There is an element of time in the creation of TCEs
The value of GIs is linked to their origin	The value of TCEs is linked to the knowledge that a particular community from a particular region or place has produced it

textiles, glassware, carpets, costumes, handicrafts, musical instruments and architectural forms.

These tangible expressions or 'handicrafts' may qualify as goods which could be protected by GIs if they present the necessary qualities for GI protection. Such qualities would usually include a symbolic association between the handicraft or artisanal product and a particular culture, which acknowledges the influence of tradition in its creation. Furthermore, these handicrafts would be produced either completely by hand, or with the help of hand-tools or mechanical means, as long as the direct manual contribution of the craftsman remains the most substantial component of the finished product. They would be produced using raw materials from sustainable resources, and their distinctive features could be utilitarian, aesthetic, artistic, creative, culturally attached, decorative, functional, traditional or have a religious or social symbolic. Finally, the creative activity would occur within a small group or a community-based environment.[2]

The common features shown in Table 6.1 above can be identified between GIs and the goods they relate to on the one hand, and TCEs on the other.

6.3   GEOGRAPHICAL INDICATIONS PROTECTION OF TCES AT THE INTERNATIONAL, REGIONAL AND NATIONAL LEVEL

In order to assess the feasibility of a system based on GIs to protect TCEs, the following paragraphs will look at examples, at the international, regional and national level, of situations where GIs have been used or could potentially be used to protect TCEs.

6.3.1   International Agreements

At the international level, there are some indications that TCEs could be protected with GIs in the 1958 Lisbon Agreement for the Protection of Appellations of Origin and their International Registration. The Lisbon Agreement established an international system of registration and protection of appellations of origin. It was a substantial step in the field of GI protection and the first international agreement to provide a definition of an appellation of origin.

Article 2(1) of the Lisbon Agreement defines an appellation of origin as:

> The geographical name of a country, region or locality, which serves to designate a product originating therein, the quality and characteristics of which are due exclusively or essentially to the geographical environment, including natural and human factors.

This definition provides that an appellation of origin serves to designate a product. However, it does not specify what types of products are concerned. According to WIPO statistics on appellations of origin under the Lisbon

---

[2]   See UNESCO and ITC, International Symposium on Crafts and the International Market: Trade and Customs Codification, Manila, Philippines, 6–8 October 1997, *Final Report*, 6; Kunal Basu, 'Marketing Developing Society Crafts: A Framework for Analysis and Change' in Janeen Arnold Costa and Gary J. Bamossy (eds), *Marketing in a Multicultural World: Ethnicity, Nationalism and Cultural Identity* (Sage Publications: Thousand Oaks, CA, 1995) 261; Dev Saif Gangjee, 'Geographical Indications Protection for Handicrafts under TRIPS' (MPhil Thesis, University of Oxford, 2002) 5, available at http://users.ox.ac.uk/~edip/gangjee.pdf

Agreement, protected products under the Lisbon Agreement include, amongst others, wines, spirits, agricultural products, cheeses, ornamental products, tobacco and cigarettes, mineral water and beer and malt.[3] Since ornamental products can obtain GI protection under the Lisbon Agreement and since some TCEs, such as handicrafts, can be qualified as ornamental products, it is therefore possible for those TCEs to obtain GI protection under the Lisbon Agreement.

6.3.2 Regional Agreements

Further evidence of the possibility of protecting TCEs with GIs can be found at the regional level, where 'crafts' or 'handicrafts' have been referred to as being products that can be protected with GIs in the 1977 Bangui Agreement which established the African Organisation of Intellectual Property, and in the Andean Community Decision 486.

The 1977 Bangui Agreement provides a definition of geographical indications which states that 'product' means any natural, agricultural, craft cr industrial product and that 'producer' means any producer of agricultural products or any other person exploiting natural products, any manufacturer of products of craft or industry or any trader dealing in such products.[4] Similarly, Article 212 of the Andean Community Decision 486 provides that the use of appellations of origin with respect to natural, agricultural, handicraft or industrial products from the Member Countries shall be reserved exclusively for producers, manufacturers and craftsmen with production or manufacturing establishments in the locality or region within the Member Country identified or evoked by that appellation.

6.3.3 National Legislation

At the national level, examples of the registrations of geographical indications

---

[3]   Ornamental products protected under the Lisbon Agreement would roughly correspond to the following descriptive class headings from the Nice Agreement concerning the International Classification of Goods and Services for the purpose of registration of marks: class 20 for furniture, mirrors, picture frames, goods of wood, cork, reed, cane, wicker, horn, bone, ivory, whalebone, shell, amber, mother-of-pearl, meerschaum and substitutes for all these materials, or of plastic; class 21 for household or kitchen utensils and containers; class 24 for textiles and textile goods; class 26 for lace and embroidery, and class 28 for games and playthings. See Sergio Escudero, *International Protection of Geographical Indications and Developing Countries* (South Centre, 2001) 18 and 46–7.

[4]   See Annex VI, Title I, Art. 1.

with respect to TCEs can be found in many countries, including India, Mexico,[5] Portugal[6] and the Russian Federation.[7]

In India, while many traditional Indian products, such as Darjeeling tea or Mysore Sandalwood oil, have enjoyed worldwide recognition for a long time, India's initiative towards the statutory protection of geographical indications is fairly recent and can be traced to its accession to the WTO in 1995 and to some highly publicised attempts by third parties to free-ride[8] or obtain intellectual property rights on some traditional Indian products in various jurisdictions.[9]

On 30 December 1999, India enacted the Geographical Indications of Goods (Registration and Protection) Act, 1999,[10] which came into force on 15 September 2003. The Act is a detailed law that establishes a public right in the

---

[5]   In Mexico, there are seven protected appellations of origin, three for spirits, two for craft products, Olinalá and Talavera, one for coffee and one for a semi-precious stone. The appellation of origin Olinalá was applied for in 1993 by the Union of Craftsmen of Olinalá. It relates to craft products, such as chests and crates made of wood in the Municipality of Olinalá, in the State of Guerrero. The manufacture of Olinalá craft products is a local tradition which involves wood from the Aloe tree, which is endemic to the Upper Balsas region, and a lacquering process using additional raw materials such as fats of insect origin and mineral powders. Similarly, the appellation of origin Talavera was applied for in 1994 by the company La Talavera de Puebla SA de CV for craft products manufactured with raw materials from the judicial districts within the zone of Talavera. See Documents WIPO/GRTKF/IC/5/3, 53 and WIPO/GEO/MVD/01/7.

[6]   Examples from Portugal include the registration of Madeira embroidery. See Document WIPO/GRTKF/IC/5/3, 53.

[7]   Examples from the Russian Federation include the registration of Rostov enamel and Kargopol clay toys. See Document WIPO/GRTKF/IC/5/3, 54.

[8]   See the example of Darjeeling tea. Darjeeling tea enjoys a reputation as one of the best teas for flavour and quality and is considered the 'Champagne of teas' on account of the unique geographical location, the type of tea plant and the processing method. However, it is estimated that 80 per cent of internationally traded Darjeeling tea is counterfeit, with most of the tea being passed off as Darjeeling actually coming from Kenya, Sri Lanka and Nepal. See Dwijen Rangnekar, 'The International Protection of Geographical Indications: The Asian Experience', UNCTAD and ICTSD Regional Dialogue in collaboration with IDRC, University of Hong Kong, November 2004.

[9]   See for example US trade mark application of RiceTec Inc, a Texas based corporation, for TEXMATI and US patent nb 5663484 on 'Basmati Rice Lines and Grains' granted in September 1997 to the same company. Following India's protest, RiceTec withdrew four of its 20 claims in September 2000. In March 2001, the USPTO approved three of the 20 initial claims and issued RiceTec with a varietal patent to market the types of Basmati developed by itself alone, as opposed to the ones cultivated and developed by farmers in India and Pakistan.

[10]   The text of the Act is available at http://ipindia.nic.in/ipr/gi/gi_act.PDF

geographical indication, which is officially included on a public register, overseen by the Controller General of Patents, Designs and Trade Marks of India. Registration under the Act is valid for a period of ten years, after which it needs to be renewed.[11] The Act regulates the recognition, administration and enforcement of geographical indications. The protection available to the registered proprietor or authorised user is greater than that contained in the TRIPS Agreement and includes the possibility of civil and criminal penalties.

Table 6.2   Distribution of geographical indications registered in India by types of products

Type of product	Number of registered geographical indications	Percentage
Textiles	13	46.4
Handicrafts	3	10.1
Horticulture products	3	10.7
Tea	3	10.7
Incense sticks	1	3.6
Metal mirror	1	3.6
Essential oil	1	3.6
Soap	1	3.6
Wet grinder	1	3.6
Painting	1	3.6
Total	28	100

Article 1(1)(e) of the Act provides that:

> 'geographical indication' in relation to goods, means an indication which identifies such goods as agricultural goods, natural goods or manufactured goods as originating, or manufactured in the territory of a country, or a region or locality in that territory, where a given quality, reputation or other characteristic of such goods is essentially attributable to its geographical origin and in case where such goods are manufactured goods one of the activities of either the production or of processing or preparation of the goods concerned takes place in such territory, region or locality, as the case may be.

The article then moves on to define 'goods' as meaning 'any agricultural, natural or manufactured goods or any goods of handicraft or of industry and includes food stuff',[12] thus explicitly allowing the registration of TCEs as geographical indications.

---

[11]   See art. 18(1).
[12]   See art. 1(1)(f).

As of 9 November 2006, 28 Indian products were registered with the Geographical Indications Registry,[13] the vast majority of which were TCEs, such as handicrafts or traditional textiles (see Table 6.2).

6.3.4   Bilateral Agreements: Switzerland and the Protection of the Lötschental Masks

Bilateral agreements have been used on many occasions to protect GIs internationally.[14] Switzerland has used bilateral agreements to protect, amongst other things, some of its TCEs, including the Lötschental masks, as products of the industrial arts in a series of bilateral treaties on 'indications of source, appellations of origin and other geographical indications'.

Switzerland has one of the biggest traditions of carnival in the world. There are more than 200 traditional carnivals across the country and each has its own history that was transmitted from generation to generation. Whereas a large part of Western Europe has lost many of its regional customs, Switzerland has managed to maintain its regional disparities while at the same time adapting to the modern world.[15] One of these carnivals comes from the region of Lötschental. It is especially well-known for the Lötschental carnival masks, which today form part of Switzerland's folklore.

---

[13]   See Government of India, Ministry of Commerce and Industry, Department of Commerce, Press Release 9, November 2006, http://commerce.nic.in/pressrelease/ pressrelease_detail.asp?id=1840

[14]   Examples include agreements between Germany and France for the protection of indications of source, appellations of origin and other geographical indications in 1960; between the European Union and Hungary on trade and wines in 1992; between Australia and the United States on the reciprocal protection of wine names and related provisions in 1994; between Australia and the European Union on trade in wine in 1994; between the European Union and Mexico on a mutual recognition and protection of designations for spirits (including wine spirits) in 1997, and between the European Union and South Africa on free trade covering industrial and agricultural goods in 1999.

[15]   This is due to many factors. First, there was a strong 'romantic' reaction, especially in the German part of Switzerland, at the end of the eighteenth century, against the Cult of Reason of the Enlightment period, which was the outcome of the 'de-Christianisation' of French society during the Revolution. This reaction required a return to spontaneity and respect for the traditions of the rural communities, which had safeguarded their ancient customs. Secondly, during the industrial expansion of the nineteenth and twentieth centuries, the ideology of which disregarded the rural communities as being 'primitive', a sense of patriotism developed, which helped them remain close to their origins and ancient traditions and therefore become the custodians of the national identity. Thirdly, the fact that Switzerland does not have a central authority, but a federal system, helps maintain each region's particularities and keep local customs alive. Finally, Switzerland is made up of small communities, which allows the transmission of tradition through contact between generations. See Oleg Kochtchouk, *Carnaval, Rites, Fêtes et Traditions* (Editions Cabédita: Yens sur Morges, 2001) 15–19.

Figure 6.1   Lötschental mask

Lötschental is a region of Switzerland which is situated in Valais at an altitude of 1,300 metres. It is a very remote region with tough living conditions. Villagers live in a close relationship with their ancestors. They believe that goods and laws come from them and that everything is ruled by them. They believe that the ancestors come back during carnival. During carnival, masks allow people to pretend to be the dead, the spirits, the animals. They are worn by the young single people of the Lötschental society. Masks are made out of cows' teeth, wood and hair. The rest of the costume is made out of goat or sheep skin. Before the carnival became more civilised in Lötschental, men used to cover themselves with a mixture of ashes and blood.

The Lötschental masks are protected as 'products of the industrial arts' in a series of bilateral treaties concluded by Switzerland on 'indications of source, appellations of origin and other geographical indications' with the Federal

Republic of Germany (7 March 1967),[16] the Socialist Republic of Czechoslovakia (16 November 1973),[17] the Spanish State (9 April 1974),[18] the French Republic (14 May 1974)[19] and Portugal (16 September 1978).[20] Even though the contracting states to the bilateral treaties were all party to the 1883 Paris Convention for the protection of industrial property and to the 1891 Madrid Agreement for the repression of false or deceptive indications of source on goods, they considered that these conventions had disadvantages. Multilateral treaties often have to satisfy the diverging interests of a plurality of states and cannot take into account the specific situation and needs of each state. In addition, the protection provided by these treaties is largely restricted by the liberty that the courts of the contracting states have when deciding whether a GI is an indication of source or a descriptive sign. Such a solution does not take into account the law and the conception of the country from where the GI originates and goes against a harmonious protection of GIs at the international level.[21] As a consequence, the bilateral treaties were seen as a more efficient way to protect GIs, at least in the short term, as work on the establishment of a multilateral convention to replace both the Madrid and Lisbon Conventions proceeded very slowly.[22]

The treaties are based on the principle of reciprocity and their aim is to protect the GIs of a contracting state against abusive use and acts of unfair competition in the other contracting states.[23] Article 1 of each treaty provides that:

---

16   Feuille Fédérale (1968) I 225; RO (1969) 538.
17   Feuille Fédérale (1974) II 1178; RO (1975) 1657 and 2422.
18   Feuille Fédérale (1974) II 1178; RO (1975) 1657; RO (1976) 515.
19   Feuille Fédérale (1974) II 1178; RO (1975) 1657.
20   Feuille Fédérale (1978) I 353.
21   Bilateral agreements are not uncommon in the field of GI protection. They are often seen as a more efficient way of protecting products in other jurisdictions. This is mainly due to the limited membership of the international treaties regulating GIs and the impasse in the TRIPS negotiations in Cancun. In recent years, the European Union, for example, has entered into a number of bilateral agreements to protect agricultural products and foodstuffs.
22   See François Dessemontet, 'Protection of Geographic Denominations under Swiss Law' in Jehoram Herman Cohen (ed.), *Protection of Geographic Denominations of Goods and Services*, Monographs on Industrial Property and Copyright Law (Sijthoff & Noordhoff: Alphen aan den Rijn, 1980) 122.
23   Note that following the conclusion of the 1968 Treaty between Switzerland and Germany, Austria, Spain, France, Italy, Greece, Portugal and Germany also concluded similar treaties amongst themselves, that were often based on the text of the 1968 Treaty between Switzerland and Germany.

Each contracting state shall take the necessary measures to efficiently protect:

1. Natural and manufactured products which originate on the territory of the other contracting state against unfair competition in industrial and commercial activities

2. Names, designations and graphical representations [mentioned in the treaty] and designations mentioned in annexes A and B of the present treaty.

All these treaties are almost identical in their legal provisions.[24] They comprise the actual treaty, a protocol and annexes. The treaty contains basic principles relating to the protection of indications of source. The protocol deals with the application of some specific aspects of the treaty. The annexes contain the lists of GIs of each contracting state, which are methodically classified by category of goods, respectively wine, food and agricultural and industrial products.

In Switzerland, characteristics of renowned industrial products derive from the traditions, consciousness and know-how of local manufacturers and manpower. The right to affix a given GI is not usually subject to any requirement about the source of the raw material, even though the use of local raw material can be an additional characteristic of the product.[25] Industrial products listed in the Swiss annex include the following categories: glassworks and porcelain; products of the industrial arts; machines and hardware; paper articles; games, toys and musical instruments; pottery, stones, earths; and textile products. Besides the Lötschental masks, protected handicrafts under the treaties include carved wood sculptures and small clocks from Brienz, furniture and hand-woven textiles from Saas, and musical boxes from Sainte-Croix.

6.4   THE PROTECTION OF TCES WITHIN THE GEOGRAPHICAL INDICATIONS REGIME OF THE TRIPS AGREEMENT

The TRIPS Agreement, which is one of the most significant intellectual property treaties of the twentieth century, was the first multilateral text dealing with GIs. It is perhaps the most important international treaty in that field, due to its broad membership, the application of minimum standards and its detailed rules on enforcement through a strong dispute settlement mechanism. Indeed, even if some previous international treaties, such as the Paris Convention, the Madrid Agreement and the Lisbon Agreement, dealt with the protection of

---

24   See the Governmental Message for the Swiss–German Treaty, Feuille Fédérale (1968) I 225 and for the three following, Feuille Fédérale (1974) II 1178.
25   See Dessemontet, *supra* note 22, 111–12.

indications of source or appellations of origin, the protection provided was often inadequate because, on the one hand, the provision of the Paris Convention was too general on this matter, and on the other, the Madrid Agreement and Lisbon Agreement had only limited membership.[26]

It is particularly relevant to examine the possibilities of protection of TCEs within the GIs regime of the TRIPS Agreement, because it provides a definitional starting point for GIs in which TCEs can be incorporated, and also because it provides a framework within which there is a practical and potentially efficient opportunity for the protection of TCEs.

The protection of TCEs, or more specifically 'the protection of folklore' was expressly mentioned in the Doha Ministerial Declaration. Paragraph 19 of the Declaration reads in part as follows:

> [Ministers] instruct the Council for TRIPS, in pursuing its work programme ... to examine, *inter alia*, the relationship between the TRIPS Agreement and the Convention on Biological Diversity, the protection of traditional knowledge and folklore, and other relevant new developments raised by members pursuant to Article 71.1.

In recent years, issues related to the protection of TK and TCEs have progressively acquired importance in global discussions concerning intellectual property and trade. Reasons for that include the fact that many countries, which are rich in TK and TCEs, believe that they have not derived great benefits from 'traditional' forms of intellectual property. In addition, indigenous communities have gained political importance in many countries and are pushing for the protection of TK and TCEs.[27]

Some aspects of TK and TCEs, such as undocumented sacred TK, are not considered trade related, and therefore are outside the scope of the negotiations. On the other hand, it has been acknowledged that certain intellectual property rules, such as collective/certification marks and GIs,[28] can and do apply without any modification to certain forms of TK and TCEs, especially knowledge that is commercially exploitable.

6.4.1 Definitional Considerations

As there is not a single definition or terminology accepted worldwide for the

---

[26]   As of 31 December 2004, the Madrid Agreement had a membership of 34 signatory states and the Lisbon Agreement had a membership of 22 states.

[27]   Daniel Gervais, *The TRIPS Agreement, Drafting History and Analysis* (2nd edn, Sweet & Maxwell: London, 2003) 57.

[28]   See Lionel Bently and Brad Sherman, *Intellectual Property Law* (2nd edn, Oxford University Press: Oxford, 2009) 976; Gervais, *supra* note 27, 62.

concept of GIs, it is important to distinguish the term 'geographical indications' from 'indications of source' or 'appellations of origin'. 'Indications of source' are a broad concept covering any indication pointing directly or indirectly to a country or place of origin, without need to show that a particular quality, reputation or characteristic follows from the 'source'. 'Appellations of origin', which are probably the narrowest concept, are defined in Article 2(1) of the Lisbon Agreement, as referring to the geographical name of a country, region or locality, which serves to designate a product originating therein, the quality and characteristics of which are due exclusively or essentially to the geographical environment, including natural and human factors. Finally, 'geographical indications', as defined in Article 22(1) of the TRIPS Agreement, are indications which identify a good as originating in the territory of a Member, or a region or locality in that territory, where a given quality, reputation or other characteristic of the good is essentially attributable to its geographical origin.

In order to assess whether TCEs qualify for protection under the TRIPS definition of GIs it is necessary to look at the different elements of the definition of a GI.

First, under the TRIPS Agreement, GIs are any 'indication' pointing to a given country, region or locality. This differs from the definition of appellations of origin under the Lisbon Agreement, which provides that appellations of origin are necessarily 'geographical names' of a country, region or locality. Although Article 22(1) does not provide what forms indications can take, it is accepted that an indication is not expressly limited to the name of a place. A word or a phrase, for example, may serve as a GI without necessarily being the name of a territory and so may 'evoke' the territory.[29] A product name, such as the name of a TCE, known to be associated with a place may therefore qualify for protection. In addition, while a word may be an indication, other types of symbols, such as pictoral images, icons or emblems,[30] may also serve as identifiers.[31]

Secondly, whereas appellations of origin designate a product, the name of which is usually the same as the appellation of origin, it is well established that GIs, for the purpose of TRIPS, apply to any good, be it natural, agricultural, agri-industrial or manufactured, in respect to which an appropriate

---

[29]   For example 'Basmati' is known as an indication for rice coming from the Indian sub-continent, although it is not a place name as such. Similarly, Santa Clara Valley in California is more well known as 'Silicon Valley'.

[30]   For example the symbol of the Eiffel Tower to designate French products.

[31]   See UNCTAD and ICTSD, *Resource Book on TRIPS and Development* (Cambridge University Press: Cambridge, 2005) 289.

geographical link is made. They can therefore also apply to TCEs. However, they do not apply to services, which do not come under Article 22(1) of the TRIPS Agreement.[32]

Thirdly, GIs identify a good 'originating' in the territory of a Member, or a region or locality in that territory. This should be understood as referring to goods that must be mined, grown or manufactured in that territory.[33]

Fourthly, under TRIPS, 'quality, reputation or other characteristics' of a good can each be a sufficient basis for eligibility as a GI, where they are 'essentially attributable' to the geographical origin of the good in question. The word 'attributable' seems to suggest an objective criterion. However, while this might be possible for a quality or characteristic, reputation suggests a subjective element.[34] Indeed, the reference to quality refers to physical characteristics of the good. On the other hand, the reference to reputation makes clear that identification of a particular objective attribute of the good is not a prerequisite to conferring protection. It is enough that the public associates a good with a territory because the public believes the good to have desirable characteristics.[35]

Finally, the words 'essentially attributable' to the geographical territory are intended to establish the link between the product and the relevant territory. While a literal reading of 'territory' would suggest that the link must be physical, that is, that the product must embody certain characteristics because of the soil conditions, weather or other physical elements in a place, the terms 'reputation' and 'essentially attributable' allow flexibility. Therefore, 'essentially attributable' can be understood also to refer to human labour in the place or to goodwill created by advertisement[36] in respect to the place.[37] This also seems to be confirmed by the drafting history of TRIPS. In the 1990 draft,[38]

---

[32]   See Jacques Audier, *TRIPS Agreement Geographical Indications* (Office for Official Publications of the European Communities: Luxembourg, 2000) 16.

[33]   This suggests that licences for the use of GIs cannot be protected under the TRIPS Agreement.

[34]   Note that in the Lisbon Agreement, the test is that the quality and characteristics are 'due to' the geographical environment. The wording of TRIPS therefore appears intended to be less strict.

[35]   Indeed, GIs, like trade marks, may be built up through investment in advertising. The drawback is that the public may be deceived as to the quality of goods and their territorial link through false or misleading advertisement. See UNCTAD and ICTSD, *supra* note 31, 290.

[36]   However, it is considered that the reputation of GIs has generally been acquired over a lengthy period by the product's own merits rather than clever public relations. Even though advertising can be used to promote GIs in the same way as brands, the products have to speak for themselves. See Audier, *supra* note 32, 17.

[37]   See UNCTAD and ICTSD, *supra* note 31, 290–1.

[38]   Draft of 23 July 1990 (W/76) para. 2.

the quality, reputation or other characteristic of the product had to be attributable to its geographical origin, including natural and human factors. The qualification 'natural and human factors' did not, however, reappear in the final text of TRIPS, which uses the broader term of 'geographical origin'.[39] In addition, it should be highlighted that TCEs can also be influenced by the geography of the region, both at the pragmatic level of raw material provision, as well as at the more subtle level of inspiration and creative direction. Therefore, the development of a TCE can be dependent on the conditions of a geographical area.

6.4.2 Framework of Protection Provided under Article 22 of the TRIPS Agreement

The TRIPS provisions on geographical indications reflect the delicate compromise reached on one of the most sensitive areas of negotiations during the Uruguay Round, which led to the TRIPS Agreement. The sensitivity of the matter was due a variety of factors, including: (i) the fact that geographical indications were a relatively new area of intellectual property for a great majority of countries, while being well anchored in the systems of many European countries; (ii) the diversity of systems used to protect them; (iii) the divergence of views regarding the most appropriate system of protection; (iv) the economic and trade stakes; and (v) the fact that some delegations in the Uruguay Round considered the protection of geographical indications as a trade-off with concessions they would have to make in the area of agriculture.[40]

Article 22(2) of the TRIPS Agreement establishes the general standard of protection that must be available for all geographical indications. This is the standard of protection which is available to TCEs. It provides that 'legal means' must be provided to interested parties to prevent the use of geographical indications which mislead the public as to the geographical origin of the goods. It also requires that legal means must be provided to prevent use which constitutes an 'act of unfair competition' within the meaning of Article 10*bis* of the Paris Convention. However, while it is mandatory for Member States to provide protection for geographical indications, they are free to determine the appropriate method of protection, when implementing the provisions of the Agreement within their own legal system and practice.[41]

---

[39] See Gervais, *supra* note 27, 188–9.
[40] See WIPO, 'Geographical Indications in the International Arena: The Current Situation', Presentation by Mrs Thu-Lang Tran Wasecha, Counsellor, Intellectual Property Division, World Trade Organisation (WTO), WIPO/GEO/BEI/07/15.
[41] Article 1(1) of the TRIPS Agreement.

Over the past decade, a variety of different legal concepts have been used to protect geographical indications at the national and regional levels. These include, in particular, laws of unfair competition and passing off, protected appellations of origin and registered geographical indications, collective and certification marks and administrative schemes of protection.[42] The choice of a protection mechanism or a combination of systems of protection will usually depend on the legal tradition and historical and economic conditions of the jurisdiction concerned. However, the differences between these systems will have a bearing on important questions, such as conditions of protection, entitlement to use and scope of protection. The legal means must be provided to 'interested parties'. In this context, 'interested parties' should be understood in a broad sense. It can therefore apply to indigenous communities that hold the TCEs.

Misleading indications (Article 22(2)(a))

Article 22(2)(a) requires WTO Member States to provide the legal means for interested parties to prevent:

> the use of any means in the designation or presentation of a good that indicates or suggests that the good in question originates in a geographical area other than the true place of origin in a manner which misleads the public as to the geographical origin of the good.

Article 22(2)(a) provides a negative right, that is, a right to prevent, rather than a positive right, such as the right to authorise use. Therefore, the burden of proof rests on the GI holder, who must show that the public has been misled.[43]

The question as to under what circumstances a designation will be understood to 'mislead the public' raises a couple of interesting issues. First, to whom does 'the public' refer? It could refer to ordinary consumers with limited knowledge, to a more specialised group of consumers, who regularly purchase the product in question, or to members of the trade or experts. Secondly, how strong does the association need to be to establish that the public has been misled? Finally what degree of error is needed for the public to be misled? It has been argued that even though consumers may be unaware of the characteristics or even the existence of the genuine product, they may still be misled.[44] In addition, will the public still be considered to be 'misled' if there is information about the true origin of the product on the labelling or

---

[42]   See UNCTAD and ICTSD, *supra* note 31, 291.
[43]   This is due, in part, to the fact that the system does not rely on a registration or certification system. See Gervais, *supra* note 27, 192.
[44]   See Audier, *supra* note 32, 21.

packaging? Most often, discretion is in the hands of national authorities to determine how the 'public' should be defined and how strong an association there must be for the public to be 'misled'.[45] Finally, the degree of error required also raises questions. If, for example, the consumer is misled about the particular Indian tribe that produced the handicraft but not the fact that the handicraft is 'Indian made', is the designation or presentation a misrepresentation?

Act of unfair competition (Article 22(2)(b))

Article 22(2)(b) requires WTO Member States to provide the legal means for interested parties to prevent 'any use which constitutes an act of unfair competition within the meaning of Article 10*bis* of the Paris Convention (1967)',[46] with respect to GIs.

Under the Paris Convention, an act of unfair competition is defined as 'any act of competition contrary to honest practices in industrial or commercial matters'.[47] Besides the general mandate of Article 10*bis,* that the countries of the Union are bound to assure to nationals of such countries effective protection against unfair competition, the following acts are, in particular, prohibited under that article: (1) all acts of such a nature as to create confusion by any means whatever with the establishment, the goods or the industrial or commercial activities or a competitor; (2) false allegations in the course of trade of such a nature as to discredit the establishment, the goods or the industrial or commercial activities of a competitor; and finally (3) indications or allegations the use of which, in the course of trade, is liable to mislead the public as to the nature, the manufacturing process, the characteristics, the suitability for their purpose or the quantity of the goods. This last category of acts especially applies to geographical origin.

It is interesting to note that most cases that constitute a violation of Article 10*bis* of the Paris Convention are also covered by Article 22(2)(a). One of the reasons brought forward for the inclusion of two separate sections is that they are based upon different interests protected by unfair competition law. Whereas Article 22(2)(b) protects the interests of producers and merchants, Article 22(2)(a) is aimed at representations misleading the public, i.e. consumers.[48] Another explanation brought forward is that the reference to Article 10*bis* of the Paris Convention may be intended to indicate that Article

---

45   See UNCTAD and ICTSD, *supra* note 31, 293.

46   As last revised in Stockholm on 14 July 1967 and as amended on 28 September 1979.

47   Paris Convention, Art. 10*bis*(2).

48   See Albrecht Conrad, 'The Protection of Geographical Indications in the TRIPS Agreement' (1996) 86 *TMR* 11–46, 36.

22(2)(a) should not be understood as a limitation on causes of action previously available under Article 10*bis* of the Paris Convention. Also, it has been argued that Article 22(2)(b) extends the scope of protection provided under Article 22(2)(a) because it protects against misleading the public regarding the 'nature or characteristics of goods'[49] in addition to the geographical origin of the good.

In conclusion, the flexibility left to Member States on how to achieve protection under Article 22(2) allows various approaches to the protection of TCEs, which can be adapted to the specific situations and needs of each Member State.

Misleading trade marks (Article 22(3))

Article 22(3) states that a Member shall, *ex officio*, if its legislation so permits or at the request of an interested party, refuse or invalidate the registration of a trade mark which contains or consists of a GI with respect to goods not originating in the territory indicated, if use of the indication in the trade mark for such goods in that Member is of such a nature as to mislead the public as to the true place of origin.

The criterion used to determine if the registration of a trade mark should be refused or invalidated is the perception of the public, who need to be misled as to the true place of origin of the goods bearing that trade mark. In that sense, Article 22(3) uses the wording and the approach of Article 22(2). Article 22(3) provides that action against a misleading trade mark can be taken either *ex officio*, or at the request of an interested party, which in theory allows TCEs holders to request the trade mark registration authorities of a Member State to refuse or invalidate the registration of a trade mark.

The scope of Article 22(3) is, however, limited by Article 24(5) which provides two exceptions for trade marks that have been applied for or registered in 'good faith', or trade marks that have been acquired through use in good faith.

The first exception is for trade marks that were registered in good faith before the TRIPS Agreement. The criterion of 'good faith' is not defined in the Agreement. According to *Black's Law Dictionary*, one of the meanings of 'good faith' is 'a state of mind consisting in … absence of intent to defraud or to seek unconscionable advantage'. In the context of Article 24(5), a possible interpretation of good faith was that the applicant or registrant had a reasonable belief that their actions were not contrary to existing legal principles within their own jurisdiction or that they did not know of the rights of other

---

49   See UNCTAD and ICTSD, *supra* note 31, 294.

parties.[50] However, 'good faith' should rather be interpreted to mean that the applicant or registrant had no intention to take unfair advantage of a competitor, or in other words, that they acted without deceptive or misleading intent.

The second exception is for trade marks that were registered before the geographical name was protected in its country of origin. This might raise issues for countries that do not yet have a system of protection of GIs, or whose system of protection is very recent, as they may find that their geographical names have already been registered as trade marks in other countries. As a consequence, this exception has been said to give an unwarranted advantage to the countries which have long recognised GIs.[51]

According to some commentators,[52] the exception provided in Article 24(5) might go even further, as they consider that prior trade marks can continue to exist and may also provide grounds to invalidate later GIs. Indeed, the 'right to use' a trade mark, which is stated in Article 24(5), combined with the 'right to exclude' of Article 16(1),[53] which deals with trade marks and the rights conferred thereby, could allow a trade mark owner to prevent the protection of a later GI. In addition, they consider that Article 2(1), incorporating the main principles of the Paris Convention, and more specifically the 'first in time, first in right' principle as the basis for resolving conflicts between intellectual property rights, should be taken into account. They consider that this principle lays the foundation for the primacy of trade marks over GIs. In the words of Gevers (1999, 154–6):

> The TRIPS Agreement does not exclude the possibility of a trade mark owner excluding the protection of a later coming geographical indication (identical or similar) on condition that the geographical indication is used or has been registered in bad faith or that its use constitutes an act of unfair competition.

---

50   See UNCTAD and ICTSD, *supra* note 31, 304–5.
51   See Conrad, *supra* note 48, 42–3.
52   See Florent Gevers, 'Topical Issues of the Protection of Geographical Indications' in WIPO, *Symposium on the International Protection of Geographical Indications in the Worldwide Context, Eger, Hungary, 24–25 October 1997* (WIPO: Geneva, 1999) 154–6; Henning Harte-Bavendamm, 'Geographical Indications and Trademarks: Harmony or Conflict?' in WIPO, *Symposium on the Protection of Geographical Indications, Somerset West, Cape Province, South Africa, 1–2 September 1999* (WIPO: Geneva 2000) 65–7.
53   Article 16(1) states that 'the owner of a registered trade mark shall have the exclusive right to prevent all third parties not having the owner's consent from using in the course of trade identical or similar signs for goods or services which are identical or similar to those in respect of which the trademark is registered where such use would result in a likelihood of confusion'.

In light of the above, it appears that the only exception is when the trade mark misleads the public.

True but misleading geographical indications (Article 22(4))
Article 22(4) provides that the protection under Article 22(1), (2) and (3) shall be applicable against a GI which, although literally true as to the territory, region or locality in which the goods originate, falsely represents to the public that the goods originate in another territory. This paragraph applies to geographical homonyms in situations where, for example, immigrants have brought names from their homeland and used them when establishing new communities.

6.4.3   Future of the Protection of TCEs within the Geographical Indications Regime of the TRIPS Agreement

The compromise that led to the adoption of the geographical indications provisions of the TRIPS Agreement left some unfinished business to be addressed during subsequent negotiations. In particular, differences between Member States arose in relation to three issues. The first was the extension to other products of the higher level of protection which the TRIPS Agreement currently affords to geographical indications for wines and spirits. The second was the establishment of a multilateral system of notification and registration of geographical indications for wines. The third was a proposal by the European Communities that a list of names currently used by producers of agricultural products other than the right holders in the country of origin, and treated as generic, should be established in order to prohibit such use. This section will focus on the first issue.

Article 23 of the TRIPS Agreement provides additional protection for geographical indications for wines and spirits only, which is expressed in two ways. First, Article 23(1) states that Member States shall provide the legal means, for interested parties, to prevent use of a geographical indication identifying wines and spirits not originating in the place indicated by the geographical indication. This protection should be available even where such use would not mislead the public, would not amount to unfair competition, where the true origin of the goods would be indicated or where the geographical indication would be used in translation or accompanied by expressions such as 'kind', 'style', 'imitation' or the like. Secondly, Article 23(2) permits the refusal or invalidation of trade marks for wines and spirits which contain or consist of a geographical indication, where such wines and spirits do not have the stated origin. Here again, the additional protection would also be granted in situations where the public is not misled.

On 9 July 1999, Turkey proposed to extend the ongoing negotiations within the TRIPS Council regarding the additional protection for GIs, and the multilateral registration system for GIs of wines and spirits to other products, as it considered that the concept of additional protection for GIs is one of the essential elements of the TRIPS Agreement, and that confining this concept narrowly just to wines and spirits would not constitute a fair and equitable treatment of the rights and the interests of the Members.[54] Such an extension would provide the more effective protection of Article 23, currently available only for GIs of wines and spirits, for GIs of all other products, including TCEs.

The Turkish proposal was endorsed by the African group of countries, which considered that the negotiations envisaged under Article 23(4) of the TRIPS Agreement concerning the establishment of a multilateral system of notification and registration of GIs for wines should be extended to other categories of products recognisable by their geographical origin, such as agricultural, food and handicraft products.[55] The proposal was also adopted by a number of developing countries, including India, Indonesia, Pakistan and Sri Lanka, which considered that an extended geographical indication regime would facilitate market differentiation for a variety of commodities such as tea, coffee and rice.

Following the Doha Ministerial Conference of 2001, the issue of the extension was included on the Doha Work Programme. In paragraph 18 of the Doha Ministerial Declaration, Ministers agree to negotiate the establishment of a multilateral system of notification and registration of GIs for wines and spirits by the Fifth Session of the Ministerial Conference. They note that issues related to the extension of the protection of GIs provided for in Article 23 to products other than wines and spirits will be addressed in the Council for TRIPS pursuant to paragraph 12 of this Declaration which deals with implementation related issues and concerns.

On 9 July 2003 a proposal was made by a group of countries on how extension could be implemented in the TRIPS Agreement with regard to Article 23.[56]

---

[54] See WTO, General Council, Preparations for the 1999 Ministerial Conference, Agreement on TRIPS: Extension of the Additional Protection for Geographical Indications to Other Products, Communication from Turkey, WT/GC/W/249.

[55] See WTO, General Council, Preparations for the 1999 Ministerial Conference, The TRIPS Agreement: Communication from Kenya on Behalf of the African Group, WT/GC/W/302.

[56] See WTO, Trade Negotiations Committee, Geographical Indications for Significances of Extension in the TRIPS Agreement and its Benefits for WTO Members, TN/C/W/14, Annex. Proposal by Bulgaria, Cyprus, the Czech Republic, Estonia, the European Communities, the Former Yugoslav Republic of Macedonia, Georgia, Hungary, India, Jamaica, Kenya, the Kyrgyz Republic, Latvia, Liechtenstein, Malta, Morocco, Poland, Romania, the Slovak Republic, Slovenia, Sri Lanka, Switzerland, Thailand and Turkey.

They submitted that the implementation of the extension would require only minor modifications of the text of Article 23 and corresponding changes in Article 24. The limitation to wines and spirits should be deleted and replaced with a neutral reference to products, thereby extending the more effective protection of this article to GIs for all products.[57]

On 13 June 2005, the European Communities submitted a radical proposal[58] to amend Section 3 of the TRIPS Agreement with a view to extending the current regime of protection available to geographical indications on wines and spirits to geographical indications on all products, and in addition a proposal for the inclusion of an annex to the TRIPS Agreement establishing a multilateral system of notification and registration of geographical indications.[59]

On the issue of extension, the European Communities argued that the proposal would also meet the needs of developing countries:

> Developing countries would find this proposal more tailored to their needs since it covers geographical indications on other products like coffee, rice and teas. Furthermore, it advances a protection system that is easy to apply. It is sufficient to determine whether the good has the origin referred to by the geographical indications. The suggested changes are important given that the current system cannot be used by poor producers as it requires costly evidence (e.g. consumer surveys) that the public is misled.[60]

To date, no compromise has been reached on the extension of the protection of Article 23 and the Members of the WTO remain divided on this issue.

Proponents of the extension, who are often collectively referred to as the 'Friends of GIs',[61] argue as follows:

- The level of protection provided by Article 22 of the TRIPS Agreement for geographical indications of products other than wine and spirits is not sufficient. In particular, they argue that (i) the 'misleading test' enables free-riding by other producers on the reputation of a geograph-

---

57   See Document TN/C/W/14, 2
58   See WTO, General Council, Trade Negotiations Committee, Council for Trade-Related Aspects of Intellectual Property Rights, Special Session on Geographical Indications, Communication from the European Communities, 14 June 2005, WT/GC/W/547, TN/C/W/26, TN/IP/W/11
59   Ibid. 1.
60   Ibid. 2.
61   See for example Marscha A. Echols, *Geographical Indications for Food Products* (Wolters Kluwer: Alphen aan den Rijn, 2008) 286 and UNDP, *Geographical Indications as Trade-Related Intellectual Property: Relevance and Implications for Human Development in Asia-Pacific*, Discussion Paper (January 2007) 18.

ical indication, as they can profit from the use of a famous geographical indication and argue at the same time that it is not misleading the consumer; (ii) over time, this gap puts geographical indications at risk of becoming generic; (iii) the requirement of the 'misleading test' results in legal uncertainty as to the enforcement of protection as it is up to national courts and national administrative authorities to decide whether or not the public has been misled and the way national authorities interpret the discretionary element of 'misleading the public' differs from country to country; and (iv) Article 22 puts the burden of proof on the producer entitled to use a geographical indication, to prove that the public had been misled, or that there has been an act of unfair competition, which is complicated and expensive.[62]

- There is no substantive justification for providing two different levels of protection for geographical indications in the TRIPS Agreement. They argue that the geographical origin, from a commercial point of view, has the same importance for all products.[63]
- The extension of the protection of geographical indications for wines and spirits to one uniform level of protection is necessary to conform to the goals contained in the TRIPS Agreement and general WTO principles.[64]

In addition, it has been argued that the extension of protection would be especially beneficial for developing countries, as it would provide them with a more efficient tool to protect their investment and compete with mass-produced products in the global market.[65]

On the other hand, opponents of the extension, which include both developing and developed countries, argue as follows:

- A delicate balance has been struck in the TRIPS Agreement, which should not be disturbed, and that the existing level of protection is adequate, and often not even used.[66]

---

[62]   See WTO, Council for Trade-Related Aspects of Intellectual Property, Proposal from Bulgaria, Cuba, the Czech Republic, Egypt, Iceland, India, Jamaica, Kenya, Liechtenstein, Mauritius, Nigeria, Pakistan, Slovenia, Sri Lanka, Switzerland, Turkey and Venezuela, IP/C/W/247/Rev.1, 3–4.

[63]   Ibid. 5.

[64]   Ibid. 5–6.

[65]   See WIPO, 'Perspectives for Geographical Indications: Extension of the Protection of Article 23 of the TRIPS Agreement to All Products: A Promising Solution for Developing and Appropriate International Legal Framework for the Protection of Geographical Indications', Presentation by Mr Mathias Schaeli, Head, Legal Service, Swiss Federal Institute of Intellectual Property (IFPI), WIPO/GEO/BEI/07/11, 4.

[66]   See WTO, Council for Trade-Related Aspects of Intellectual Property Rights,

- There has been no demonstration that existing protection for GIs under Article 22 of the TRIPS Agreement is not sufficient.[67]
- There is no clear forum, nor mandate to negotiate this issue under the Doha Round of trade liberalisation talks.[68]
- Finally, the implementation of the extended protection could necessitate serious costs to governments, manufacturers and consumers in the form of new administrative mechanisms to implement the broadened standards, relabelling and repackaging, and confusion costs to consumers who would not be able to find the products that they are accustomed to buying.[69]

To date, discussions on the issue did not lead to a consensus to recommend initiation of negotiations on extension. Instead, the issue of extension had been strategically linked to that of creating an international register of GIs for wines and spirits, for which there is both a mandate and a dedicated body.[70] The matter has been extensively discussed in both formal and informal meetings of the Council for TRIPS, in informal consultations held by the Director-General and in technical level consultations on GI extension. More specifically, issues discussed included the objectives, scope and content of the extension proposal, especially in terms of the range of products and the number of GIs, the potential implications of extension for the relationship between trade marks and GIs, the implication of the extension on producers benefiting from a GI, other producers, consumers and government authorities, and the administrative costs and burdens of the procedures associated with the extended protection and any other impacts on governments.

Implications of Article 23 Extension, Communication from Australia, Canada, Guatemala, New Zealand, Paraguay, the Philippines and the United States, IP/C/W/360, 2–3.

[67] See WTO, General Council, Trade Negotiations Committee, Issues Related to the Extension of the Protection of Geographical Indications Provided for in Article 23 of TRIPS Agreement to Products Other than Wines and Spirits, WT/GC/W/546, 3.

[68] The second sentence of para. 18 of the Doha Declaration, which deals with the extension of protection of geographical indications to other products, refers to para. 12 of the Doha Declaration, which provides that: 'Negotiations on outstanding implementation issues shall be an integral part of the [Doha] Work Programme'. While proponents of the extension argue that there is a clear negotiating mandate, opponents claim that there is no agreement to negotiate any extension and that consensus will be required in order to launch the negotiations.

[69] See Document IP/C/W/360, *supra* note 66, 4–7.

[70] See Document TN/C/W/52.

6.5 CONCLUSION: EFFICIENCY AND LIMITATIONS OF GEOGRAPHICAL INDICATIONS TO PROTECT TCES

GIs have been said to represent the best balance between recognising the cultural significance and protecting the consequent commercial value of TCEs, without unduly restricting cross-cultural interaction, that is the lifeblood of ongoing creativity.[71] A GI regime to protect TCEs can offer a series of advantages for the protection of tangible TCEs and satisfy some of the concerns and policy objectives of TCEs holders. Such a regime:

- provides protection that is potentially unlimited in time, as long as the distinctive link between the TCE and the place is maintained and that the indication has not fallen into genericity; this is particularly relevant as many TCEs holders believe that TCEs should be protected in perpetuity;
- is consistent with the nature of TCEs in that GIs work as a collective right, and there is no provision for a right to assign; in addition, the product-quality-place link underlying GI protection also prohibits the transfer of the indication to producers outside the demarcated region;[72]
- protects the goodwill accumulated over time, provides TCEs holders with a means to differentiate their products and use GIs as a barrier to entry into a niche market segment; GIs can in that way help TCEs holders get increased recognition for their TCEs and benefit from their commercialisation;
- recognises the cultural significance of TCEs, helps enhance the development of rural communities and enables product differentiation in markets, by enhancing the association of the product with the craftsmen of a particular place in the consumers' mind;[73]
- protects consumers who wish to buy genuine products.

---

[71] See Gangjee, *supra* note 2, 5.

[72] See Dwijen Rangnekar, *The Socio-Economics of Geographical Indications: A Review of Empirical Evidence from Europe* (ICTSD and UNCTAD: Geneva, May 2004) 18.

[73] Indeed, according to Rangnekar, 'by emphasising the intertwined relationship between place and product and between geography and culture, communities producing regionally distinctive goods can develop a niche in the market', see Dwijen Rangnekar, 'Geographical Indications: A Review of Proposals at the TRIPS Council' in UNCTAD and ICTSD, *Capacity Building Project on Intellectual Property Rights and Sustainable Development* (UNCTAD and ICTSD: Geneva, 2002) 14.

However, GIs also present some limitations:

- a GI regime to protect TCEs would only protect tangible TCEs;
- the knowledge associated with the GI is not protected and remains in the public domain; as a consequence, such knowledge is open to misappropriation by third parties;
- the level of protection of Article 22 of the TRIPS Agreement is currently insufficient. In this perspective, the proposal for a multilateral register and Article 23 levels of protection should be encouraged to provide better protection.

Finally, it should be noted that while a successful GI can bring a number of economic and social benefits to TCEs holders, the value and benefits of a GI will depend on the way it is exploited, marketed and policed.

First, the economic and social benefits attributed to GIs through the creation of value in the marketplace require investment, such as in production methods, the development of reliable supplies of raw materials and quality controls. These costs, which may be significant, are to be borne by the owners of GIs.

Secondly, the exploitation of a GI needs to be accompanied by appropriate marketing strategies to guide and develop consumer perception of the good-place-quality link attached to the GI and securing consumer's loyalty. The importance of marketing in achieving market penetration was highlighted in a study on the link between origin labelled products (OLPs) and local production systems by Albisu:

> [The] marketing of many OLPs is often one of the weakest links in the chain. Many firms belonging to an OLP supply chain tend to be more product oriented than market oriented. Pride of the product and loyalty to the traditional production technique may generate highly valuable product qualities, but it is definitely not a guarantee for a sound and successful sale strategy.[74]

Therefore, appropriate marketing strategies taking into account the tangible features of the final product, as well as communication, pricing and distribution strategies,[75] are essential to the successful exploitation of a GI.

Finally, there needs to be oversight by an authority in order to ensure that the characteristics and quality of the goods comply with established standards.

---

[74]   See Luis Miguel Albisu, Work Programme 2 (Link between origin labelled products and local production systems, supply chain analysis), *Final Report* (July 2002) as reported in Rangnekar, *supra* note 8, 33.

[75]   See Rangnekar, *supra* note 8, 7.

This might take the form of sampling and testing, and may require the involvement of a number of trained people to undertake inspections and penalise deviations from approved standards, while at the same time ensuring that such standards are controlled and applied in a uniform manner.[76]

---

[76] For more information and examples of systems of verification, see Carlos Correa, *Protection of Geographical Indications in Caricom Countries* (September 2002) 21–2.

7. The protection of traditional cultural expressions with passing off and laws against misrepresentation

7.1 INTRODUCTION

This chapter will examine the protection of TCEs with passing off and laws against misrepresentation. It will examine how the elements of the action for passing off, and more particularly the extended passing off action, can provide protection for TCEs. Also, it will focus on some aspects of the US law of passing off and unfair competition and on section 43(a) of the Lanham Trademarks Act, and see how these influences combined led to the creation of the Indian Arts and Crafts Act, which is the object of the case study of this chapter.

7.2 PASSING OFF

7.2.1 Introduction

In the early nineteenth century, passing off[1] developed in British and American common law as an offshoot of the legal action based on fraud and the torts of deceit and misrepresentation.[2] The term passing off first appeared in 1842 in *Perry v Truefitt,*[3] where Lord Langdale stated the principle that:

> A man is not to sell his own goods under the pretence that they are the goods of another man; he cannot be permitted to practise such a deception, nor to use the

---

[1]   On passing off, see John Drysdale and Michael Silverleaf, *Passing Off Law and Practice* (2nd edn, Butterworths: London, 1995); J. Thomas McCarthy, *McCarthy on Trade Marks and Unfair Competition* (loose-leaf, Thomson West: New York) 25-5–25-23; Frank I. Schechter, *The Historical Foundation of the Law Relating to Trade Marks* (Columbia University Press: New York, 1925); Christopher Wadlow, *The Law of Passing-Off: Unfair Competition by Misrepresentation* (3rd edn, Sweet & Maxwell: London, 2004).

[2]   See Wadlow, *supra* note 1, 16.

[3]   *Perry v Truefitt* (1842) 6 Beav. 66.

means which contribute to that end. He cannot be allowed to use names, marks, letters, or other indicia, by which he may induce purchasers to believe that the goods which he is selling are the manufacture of another person.[4]

In the United States, the concept of passing off (also called palming off) developed into a modern claim for trade mark infringement and has been used by the courts to refer to at least three different and distinct situations: (i) the substitution of one brand of goods when another brand is ordered; (ii) trade mark infringement where the infringer intentionally meant to defraud and confuse buyers; and (iii) trade mark infringement where there is no proof of fraudulent intent, but there is a likelihood of confusion of buyers.[5]

In the United Kingdom, the jurisprudence took a different path, developing into two separate bodies of law, trade mark law, which is restricted to infringement of registered marks, and passing off, which is restricted to common law liability for unregistered marks and trade dress.

7.2.2 Elements of the British Action for Passing Off

Stated generally, the action for passing off allows a trader A to prevent another trader B from passing off their goods as if they were A's. In order to succeed in an action for passing off, the claimant must establish that (i) he has goodwill; (ii) the defendant made a misrepresentation that is likely to deceive the public; and (iii) the misrepresentation damages the goodwill of the claimant.[6]

Goodwill
Goodwill is a form of intangible property that is difficult to define. It was described by Lord Macnaghten as 'the benefit and advantage of the good name, reputation, and connection of a business' and 'the attractive force which brings in custom'.[7] Goodwill can take a variety of forms. It is established that

---

4   Ibid. 73.
5   See McCarthy, *supra* note 1, 25-5.
6   It is difficult to formulate the precise requirements of the action for passing off. In *Erven Warnink BV v J. Townend & Sons (Hull) Ltd (No. 1)* [1979] AC 731, [1980] RPC 31, per Lord Diplock, the five characteristics that must be present to create a valid cause of action in passing off are: (i) a misrepresentation; (ii) made by a trader in the course of trade; (iii) to prospective customers of his or ultimate consumers of goods or services supplied by him; (iv) which is calculated to injure the business or goodwill of another trader; and (v) which causes actual damage to a business or goodwill of the trader by whom the action is brought or will probably do so. In *Reckitt & Colman Products Ltd v Borden Inc.* [1990] 1 WLR 491, 499, [1990] RPC 341, Lord Oliver reduced the elements of the action to reputation, deception and damage.
7   See *Inland Revenue Commissioners v Muller & Co.'s Margarine Ltd* [1901] AC 217, 223.

goodwill can arise in relation to the name, symbol or logo that is employed by a trader, as well as the packaging, get-up, trade dress of products, and advertising style.[8]

Goodwill could therefore arise in the name used to designate a particular TCE or type of TCE, such as 'katchina doll', 'Navajo rug' or 'Hopi jewelry'; a symbol or logo used to designate a TCE, be it of indigenous origin, such as a Maori '*koru*'[9] or '*moko*'[10] or not, for example the use of a feather to indicate Indian origin; or finally the packaging, get-up or trade dress, or the advertising style of a TCE.

In order to demonstrate goodwill in an action for passing off, the claimant must be a trader operating in trade. In the vast majority of cases, this requirement will not cause problems in the context of TCEs, as many TCEs holders operate in trade by manufacturing and selling handicrafts. Case law indicates that this requirement is to be construed widely as the courts have been generous in deciding whether someone is engaged in business. Indeed, it seems that any person who derives an income from the provision of goods or services can be said to be a trader: 'the word "trade" is widely interpreted and includes persons engaged in a professional, artistic or literary occupation'.[11] In addition, very slight trading activities have been held to suffice in order to constitute trading.[12]

Misrepresentation: the 'origin related' element

Misrepresentation is the core element of the tort of passing off.[13] A misrepresentation occurs where the defendant says or does something that indicates (expressly or impliedly) that the defendant's goods or services derive from (or are otherwise economically connected with) the claimant. There are no formal restrictions as to the type of misrepresentations that are actionable.[14] In the

---

[8]   See Lionel Bently and Brad Sherman, *Intellectual Property Law* (3rd edn, Oxford University Press: Oxford, 2009), 729–34.

[9]   A '*koru*' is a fern fond symbolising life. It is a typical Maori design.

[10]   A '*moko*' is a Maori form of tattoo.

[11]   See *Kean v McGivan* [1982] FSR 119, 120.

[12]   See *Sheraton Corp. of America v Sheraton Motels* [1964] RPC 202.

[13]   See *Spalding v Gamage* (1915) 32 RPC 273, per Lord Parker: '[T]he basis of a passing-off action being a false representation by the defendant, it must be proved in each case as a fact that the false representation was made ... the point to be decided is whether, having regard to all the circumstances of the case, the use by the defendant in connection with the goods of the mark, name, or get-up in question impliedly represents such goods to be the goods of the plaintiff, or the goods of the plaintiff of a particular class of quality, or, as it is sometimes put, whether the defendant's use of such mark, name or get-up is calculated to deceive'.

[14]   Ibid. per Lord Parker: 'it would be impossible to enumerate or classify all the possible ways in which a man might make the false representation relied on'.

case of TCEs, misrepresentation will most often be as to the source of manufacture of the goods, i.e. the defendant suggests that the claimant is the source of their goods. In that way, the defendant attempts to ride on the back of the claimant's reputation.

Damage

In order to sustain an action for passing off, a claimant must prove that they have suffered, or are likely to suffer, damage as a result of the defendant's misrepresentation. In the case of TCEs, damage will usually take one of two forms:

- destruction damage: where the goodwill is destroyed, damaged or depreciated; this can arise, for example, when low quality imitations are sold as original indigenous TCEs;
- loss of existing or potential trade and profit: where TCEs holders lose profits and future earnings on the sale of their TCEs because the misrepresentation diverts trade and profit from the claimant to the defendant.

7.2.3   Extended Passing Off

In the 1960s, the courts developed a variant of the classic passing off action examined above, called 'extended passing off'. The extended form of passing off was first recognised and applied by Danckwerts J in the Champagne case, *Bollinger v Costa Brava Wine Co. Ltd*[15] and later approved and elaborated in *Warnink v Townsend*[16] and *Chocosuisse v Cadbury*.[17]

Extended passing off recognises that a class or group of traders may share goodwill in a name or other indicator that is distinctive of a particular class of goods. Protection is given to a name or word which has come to mean a particular product rather than a product from a particular trader. The word can therefore be entirely descriptive of the product. In the Champagne, Sherry and Scotch whisky cases, the descriptive term referred to the geographical provenance of the goods, and the class entitled to the goodwill in the term was

---

[15]   *Bollinger v Costa Brava Wine Co. Ltd* [1960] RPC 16, [1960] Ch. 262. This extended form of passing off was also the object of the Sherry case, *Vine Products Ltd v Mackenzie & Co. Ltd* [1969] RPC 1; the Scotch Whisky case, *John Walker & Sons Ltd v Henry Ost & Co. Ltd* [1970] RPC 489; and in the more recent Elderflower Champagne case, *Taittinger SA v Allbev Ltd* [1993] FSR 641.

[16]   *Erven Warnink BV v J. Townend & Sons (Hull) Ltd (No. 1)* [1979] AC 731, [1980] RPC 31.

[17]   *Chocosuisse Union des Fabricants Suisses de Chocolat v Cadbury Ltd* [1998] RPC 117 and *Chocosuisse Union des Fabricants Suisses de Chocolat v Cadbury Ltd* [1999] RPC 826.

accordingly restricted to those supplying on the English market goods produced in the locality indicated by it. In *Warnink v Townsend*, however, the House of Lords held that extended passing off was not confined to drinks, or to indications of origin, but could apply equally where any product had a particular characteristic or quality. The misrepresentation in that case lies in marketing the goods in a way which will lead a significant section of the public to think that those goods have some attribute or attributes which they do not truly possess.[18] Finally, while likelihood of damage remains a prerequisite of the extended passing off action, it is not essential for a claimant to demonstrate that they would have been damaged individually.[19]

The extended form of passing off is particularly relevant in the case of TCEs as they are often communal in nature and it is difficult to identify a specific author or authors, or quantify the individual damage suffered by each craftsperson. Rather, the reduction of the distinctiveness of the descriptive term will usually harm the community as a whole.

7.3   THE MISAPPROPRIATION DOCTRINE

The misappropriation doctrine[20] is a judge-made common law form of unfair competition that developed in the United States in the early twentieth century. It is usually invoked by a plaintiff when the defendant has copied or appropriated some commercially valuable item or creation which is not protected by either patent law, copyright law, trade mark law, or any other traditional theory of exclusive rights. Thus, the argument behind the misappropriation doctrine is that the plaintiff's item or creation deserves recognition by the common law of a 'property right' which was illegally 'misappropriated' by the defendant. In that way, protection against misappropriation of intangible values ensures an incentive to invest in the creation of intangible assets and prevents the potential unjust enrichment that may result from the appropriation of the investment made by another.

---

[18]   See *Chocosuisse Union des Fabricants Suisses de Chocolat v Cadbury Ltd* [1999] RPC 826, 837.

[19]   See *Erven Warnink BV v J. Townend & Sons (Hull) Ltd (No. 1)* [1979] AC 731, 756, [1980] RPC 31.

[20]   On the misappropriation doctrine, see Douglas G. Baird, 'Common Law Intellectual Property and the Legacy of International News Services v Associated Press' (1983) 50 *U Chi. L Rev.* 411; McCarthy, *supra* note 1, 10-89–10-94; Richard A. Posner, 'Misappropriation: A Dirge' (2003–04) 40 *Hous. L Rev.* 621–41; American Law Institute, *Restatement of the Law (Third) of Unfair Competition* (American Law Institute Publishers: St Paul MN, 1995) 407–24.

The misappropriation doctrine was born in 1918 in the US Supreme Court decision of *International News Service v Associated Press*.[21] In that case, the plaintiff, Associated Press (AP) spent considerable amounts of money and time in gathering information on the First World War that was raging in Europe, and passing the information to its headquarters in the United States. The International News Service (INS) was barred at the time by British and French censors from sending war dispatches to the United States, because its owner had offended the British and French by siding with Germany at the outset of the war. To circumvent this boycott, INS paraphrased AP's war dispatches in the East coast newspapers in which they appeared first, and telegraphed them to INS-affiliated newspapers on the West coast for publication in competition with western members of AP.

The 'appropriation' of the war dispatches did not fit into any previous category of unfair competition. It was not an appropriation of confidential information, as the defendant took the stories from New York newspapers available to the public. It was not the classic form of passing off, since the INS was not misrepresenting its products as AP products. Finally, there was no copyright infringement because AP had not copyrighted the dispatches, and in any case INS was copying the facts reported in AP's dispatches rather than the dispatches themselves.

The majority of the Supreme Court held that INS' actions constituted a new kind of unfair competition called 'misappropriation' and that while AP had no monopoly right in the war dispatches against the public at large, it had a 'quasi-property' right against its competitors for as long as the dispatches remained hot news. [22]

The following three elements are necessary to succeed in a case of misappropriation:

(1)   the plaintiff has made a substantial investment of time, effort and money in creating the thing misappropriated, such that the court can characterise that 'thing' as a kind of property right;

---

[21]   *International News Service v Associated Press*, 248 U.S. 215 (1918).

[22]   Justice Holmes partially agreed with the majority but based his decision on the implied misrepresentation that AP was copying from INS. Justice Brandeis, on the other hand, dissented and argued that news stories are in the public domain and should be free for all to use. As such, the acts of the defendant did not contravene any traditional category of unfair competition. In addition, he argued that it is not for judges to create new forms of exclusive rights, which must come from legislation drafted by Congress, rather than by judge-made modifications of the common law of unfair competition. See *International News Service v Associated Press*, *supra* note 21, 262–7.

(2)   the defendant has appropriated the 'thing' at little or no cost, such that the court can characterise the defendant's actions as 'reaping where it has not sown'; and

(3)   the defendant's acts have injured the plaintiff, such as by a direct diversion of profits from the plaintiff to the defendant or a loss of royalties that the plaintiff charges to others to use the thing misappropriated.[23]

Over the years, the *International News Service v Associated Press* misappropriation doctrine has generated controversy and enjoyed mixed reception by courts and commentators. Moreover, the *INS* decision and the misappropriation doctrine have had little enduring effect. In most of the areas in which the misappropriation doctrine has been expansively applied, its application has been supplanted by legislation.[24] Recently, however, the misappropriation doctrine has regained some attention in *National Basketball Association v Motorola, Inc.*, which clarified the doctrine by outlining the necessary elements that need to be fulfilled in order to succeed in a claim under the doctrine. Accordingly, it was held that:

> The surviving 'hot-news' *INS*-like claim is limited to cases where: (i) a plaintiff generates or gathers information at cost; (ii) the information is time-sensitive; (iii) a defendant's use of the information constitutes free-riding on the plaintiff's efforts; (iv) the defendant is in direct competition with a product or service offered by the plaintiff, and (v) the ability of other parties to free-ride on the efforts of the plaintiff or others would so reduce the incentive to produce the product or service that its existence or quality would be substantially threatened.[25]

The misappropriation doctrine, together with the influence of the law of passing off and section 43(a) of the Lanham Act, has set the basis and the conceptual framework of the Indian Arts and Crafts Act. Indeed, even though there are differences in the policy objectives of the misappropriation doctrine[26] and the Indian Arts and Crafts Act,[27] they both aim at providing protection to a

---

23   See McCarthy, *supra* note 1, § 10.51. Some courts also said that the plaintiff and the defendant need to be in direct competition for a misappropriation claim to be possible. See *United States Golf Ass'n v St Andrews Systems, Data-Max, Inc.*, 749 F.2d 1028, 224 USPQ 646.

24   See American Law Institute, *supra* note 20, 410.

25   *National Basketball Association v Motorola, Inc.*, 105 F.3d 841, 845; 41 USPQ.2d 1585.

26   Policy objectives behind the misappropriation doctrine are to provide a competitor with the incentive to invest in the creation of intangible assets and to prevent unjust enrichment of a competitor that may result from the appropriation of the investment made by another.

27   Policy objectives behind the Indian Arts and Crafts Act are the protection and

competitor against a misappropriation of intangible commercially valuable items.

7.4 SECTION 43(A) OF THE LANHAM ACT

Section 43(a) of the Lanham Act[28] is the federal law used for asserting claims in private litigation against two types of unfair competition:[29] (i) infringement of unregistered trade marks, trade names and trade dress, and (ii) false advertising and product disparagement.

Section 43(a) provides as follows:

> False designations of origin and false descriptions forbidden:
> (a) Civil action.
> (1) Any person who, on or in connection with any goods or services, or any container for goods, uses in commerce any word, term, name, symbol, or device, or any combination thereof, or any false designation of origin, false or misleading description of fact, or false or misleading representation of fact, which
> (A) Is likely to cause confusion, or to cause mistake, or to deceive as to the affiliation, connection, or association of such person with another person, or as to the origin, sponsorship, or approval of his or her goods, services, or commercial activities by another person, or
> (B) In commercial advertising or promotion, misrepresents the nature, characteristics, qualities, or geographic origin of his or her or another person's goods, services, or commercial activities,
> shall be liable in a civil action by any person who believes that he or she is or is likely to be damaged by such act.

7.4.1 'False Designation of Origin': The 'Origin Related' Element

Section 43(a) of the Lanham Act was originally envisioned as a federal anti-false advertising statute and the phrase 'false designation of origin' was thought to

---

promotion of Indian arts and crafts, the promotion of Indian self-sufficiency, as well as the protection of consumers. See *infra* para. 7.5.2.

[28] On s. 43 of the Lanham Act, see J. Thomas McCarthy, 'Lanham Act § 43(a): The Sleeping Giant is Now Wide Awake' (1996) 59 *Law and Contemp. Probs* 45–74; Charles E. McKenney and George F. Long, *Federal Unfair Competition: Lanham Act § 43(a)* (West Group: St Paul MN, 1989); Henry R. Veenstra, 'Section 43(a) of the Lanham Act: A Federal Unfair Competition Remedy' (1975–76) 25 *Drake L Rev.* 228–38.

[29] Section 43(a) is narrower than the general unfair competition prohibitions of some state statutes and of the Federal Trade Commission Act (FTC Act § 5(a), 15 USCS § 45). It is not a federal codification of the law of unfair competition and is only limited to a prohibition against some forms of false designation or misleading representation. See McCarthy, *supra* note 28, 50–1.

be limited to false advertising of geographic origin.[30] However, in 1963, in *Federal-Mogul-Bower Bearings, Inc. v Azoff*,[31] the Court of Appeals for the Sixth Circuit held that 'origin' did not only refer to geographic origin but also to 'origin of source of manufacture'. In this perspective, section 43(a) can cover claims or suggestions by a competitor that a product is of Indian origin.

7.4.2   False Advertising

The false advertising prong of section 43(a) has been very successful since the 1960s as a legal tool in a wide range of industries where a plaintiff felt a competitor was engaging in false advertising. Unlike the common law rule on false advertising where, in order to sue, a competitor had to be the 'single source' of the product that the defendant was falsely advertising, in the 1960s, the courts adopted the view that section 43(a) created a new *sui generis* statutory federal tort, which only required a showing that the plaintiff was 'likely to be damaged'.[32]

The federal cause of action for false advertising of section 43(a) of the Lanham Act can be used to enforce a Native American tribe's rights in the case of fraudulent misuse of a descriptor, for example 'Hopi' for jewelry that are cheap imitations.[33] In order to benefit from this provision, TCEs holders must prove that: (i) a false statement of fact has been made by the defendant in a commercial advertisement about its own or another's product; (ii) the statement actually deceived or has the tendency to deceive a substantial segment of its audience; (iii) the deception is material, in that it is likely to influence the purchasing decision; (iv) the defendant caused its false statement to enter interstate commerce; and (v) the plaintiff has been or is likely to be injured as a result of the false statement, either by direct diversion of sales from itself to the defendant, or by a loss of goodwill associated with its products'.[34]

False advertising claims are intended to protect interests of a purely commercial nature[35] and are therefore not open to defrauded consumers. Such a claim would be open, however, to a Native American tribe as it is in direct

---

30   See McCarthy, *supra* note 28, 58.

31   *Federal-Mogul-Bower Bearings, Inc. v Azoff*, 313 F.2d 405; 136 USPQ 500.

32   See *L'Aiglon Apparel, Inc. v Lana Lobell, Inc.*, 214 F.2d 649, 651; 102 USPQ 94.

33   Note that a competitor who argues that 'Hopi jewelry' merely refers to the style of the jewellery rather than its origin will also face the argument that the statement is misleading. See *Castrol Inc. v Pennzoil Co.*, 987 F.2d 939; 25 USPQ.2d 1666.

34   See *United Industries Corp. v Clorox Co.*, 140 F.3d 1175; 46 USPQ.2d 1337.

35   *Colligan v Activities Club of New York, Ltd*, 442 F.2d 686, 692; 170 USPQ 113.

competition with the defendant. The tribe would not need to prove a likelihood of confusion, but only that the defendant's statement was deceptive and was likely to influence the purchasing decision. In that case, the damage results in lost goodwill when consumers buy inferior quality products that they believe to be genuine.

Section 43(a) of the Lanham Act is in line with the policies of the IACA, which is a 'truth in advertising' law.

7.5   THE UNITED STATES EXPERIENCE

This process of white dabbling in American Indian spiritual rituals represents the ultimate absorption. Native American spirituality becomes a commodity in the Euroamerican market place, to be bought and sold alongside other 'New Age' items.[36]

Our elders and traditional teachers want to share the beauty of Native cultures, the Native way. But appropriation is not sharing. Appropriation exploits and commercializes Native cultures, and is harmful to innocent people.[37]

7.5.1   Introduction

Historical considerations

In primitive Indian culture, there was no art separate from function. All objects were created for a practical purpose until the first European conquerors began to view these Indian artefacts as art in the Western sense of the word.[38] As more settlers migrated to America, the Indian tribes began to produce more arts and crafts, to be traded with the white man.[39] During the 1940s and 1950s, however, the development of Indian arts and crafts was slowed down because of the government's policy of assimilation, one of the aims of which was to

---

[36]   Ward Churchill (Creek/Cherokee Melis), 'Fantasies of the Master Race' (1992). See www.sonomacountyfreepress.com/features/native.html

[37]   Chief Oren Lyons (Onondaga). See ibid.

[38]   Native American pottery, for example, was created for practical use rather than aesthetic purpose. The shape of the pottery was dependent on what purpose the pottery was to serve, be it to hold water, store grains or preserve seeds for the next planting season. The pieces were plain and usually unsymmetrical until it became important to Native American Indians to decorate their pots. See www.indians.org/articles/native-american-pottery.htm

[39]   Jon Keith, 'Regulation of Counterfeit Indian Arts and Crafts: An Analysis of the Indian Arts and Crafts Act of 1990' (1993) 18 *American Indian Law Review* 497–503, 488.

stifle all Indian expressions of tribalism and traditionalism. Up until the 1960s, the Southwest was the only region where buyers could purchase Indian arts and crafts, and prior to the 1970s, Indian arts and crafts were considered to be merely a tourist industry and were not held in high esteem by the American public.[40] By the late 1980s, however, American Indian arts and crafts became very popular in American culture causing a huge demand for such products and foreign companies started marketing products, which appeared to be Indian arts and crafts, but were actually mass-produced overseas. According to a study mandated by the US Department of Commerce, annual sales of Native American jewellery and handicrafts were estimated at US$400 to US$800 million in 1985.[41] By 2000, Indian arts and crafts had become a billion dollar industry in the United States and it was estimated that imported imitations of Indian arts and crafts from countries such as the Philippines, Mexico, Thailand, Pakistan and China amounted to an average of US$30 million annually, which combined with domestically produced imitations represented an estimated US$400 to 500 million in revenue that could otherwise belong to Indian artisans.[42] The results of the study, together with a growing American Indian lobby in Washington, prompted the introduction of legislation to amend the powers of the existing federal Indian Arts and Crafts Board that had been created in 1935, 'to put real teeth'[43] into the 1935 Indian Arts and Crafts Act.

The Indian Arts and Crafts Act of 1935

The Indian Arts and Crafts Act of 1935[44] created the Indian Arts and Crafts Board, a separate entity of the Department of the Interior. Under the 1935 Act, the function of the Indian Arts and Crafts Board was to promote the economic welfare of the 'Indian wards of the Government' through the development and expansion of the Indian arts and crafts industry in the United States.[45] This was clearly a nurturing mandate. There were no civil remedies in the Act and criminal penalties were negligible. The Act provided for penalties for counter-

---

[40]   Ibid. 488–9.

[41]   Department of Commerce, International Trade Administration, *Study of Problems and Possible Remedies Concerning Imported Native American-Style Jewelry and Handicrafts* (US Department of Commerce: Washington, 1985).

[42]   See Testimony of the Council for Indigenous Art and Culture presented by Andy P. Abeita, submitted to the US Senate Committee on Indian Affairs' Oversight Hearing on the Implementation of the American Indian Arts and Crafts Protection Act, Public Law 101-644, 17 May 2000, available at www.doi.gov/iacb/pdf/iacbtestimony. pdf

[43]   See William J. Hapiuk, 'Of Kitsch and Kachinas: A Critical Analysis of the Indian Arts and Crafts Act of 1990' (2000–01) 53 *Stan. Law Rev.* 1018.

[44]   Pub. L No. 74-355.

[45]   See s. 2 of the 1935 Act.

feiting the government trade mark and misrepresenting goods as Indian made. However, in 1948, the provisions about counterfeiting the IACB trade mark and misrepresentation were moved to the Crimes and Criminal Procedure Section of the United States Code. The Act authorised the establishment of a government trade mark for genuine Indian products and provided misdemeanour penalties for the counterfeiting of the government trade mark and the misrepresentation of goods as Indian made.[46] However, in the 55 years that these criminal penalties have been enacted, there has been no conviction under the Act. This lack of convictions was blamed on the difficulty of proving 'wilfulness' and 'intent'.[47] In addition, it was considered that penalties were not severe enough to deter violations.[48]

The Indian Arts and Crafts Act of 1990

The Indian Arts and Crafts of 1990[49] (IACA) succeeds the original Act of 1935.[50] It was adopted by Congress to expand the powers of the Indian Arts and Crafts Board in order 'to protect Indian artists from unfair competition'[51] arising from the growing sales of arts and crafts products misrepresented as being made by Indians. The 1990 Act increased criminal penalties and created civil remedies for violations. The IACA is a truth-in-advertising law that prohibits the marketing of products as Indian made when such products are not made by Indians. It is intended to protect Indian artists and craftspeople, Indian tribes, Indian-owned businesses and consumers, and covers all Indian

---

46   25 U.S.C. § 305(d)–(e) (1988). These sections were repealed in 1948 and the penalty provisions were moved to the criminal code in 18 U.S.C. §§ 1158–1159 (1988).
47   Both the counterfeiting and misrepresentation provisions provided for penalties of misdemeanour status subject to prerequisite requirement of knowledge and intent.
48   See Parsley, *supra* note 39, 492–3.
49   Pub. L No. 101-644, title I, § 101, 104 Stat. 4662 (codified at 25 U.S.C. §§ 305a, 305d–305e, 18 U.S.C. §§ 1158–1159 (Supp. II 1991).
50   After a long period of insensitivity towards the history and culture of Native Americans, the United States Congress passed the Native American Graves Protection and Repatriation Act of 1990, a statute mandating the repatriation of Native American remains and cultural antiquities, and the Indian Arts and Crafts Act of 1990. These two statutes represent a fundamental change in the political view towards Native American culture. By enacting legislation increasingly protective of Native American interests, the United States Congress has sought, on the one hand, to limit access to historical sites and to reduce the alienability of artefacts already on the antiquities market, and on the other, to promote the economic welfare of Native American artists by encouraging the creation of contemporary artwork and to provide buyers with a means to assure the provenance of artefacts. See Leonard D. DuBoff, '500 Years After Columbus: Protecting Native American Culture' (1992) 11 *Cardozo Arts and Ent. LJ* 43–4.
51   House Report 101-400 (I), 'Indian Arts and Crafts Act of 1990'.

and Indian-style traditional and contemporary arts and crafts produced after 1935.

The Indian Arts and Crafts Enforcement Act

In 2000, the Act was amended again 'to improve the enforcement of the Act for the protection of the economic and cultural integrity of authentic Indian arts and crafts'.[52] The amendment expanded civil enforcement by providing standing for Indian arts and crafts organisations, as well as individual Indians, to file civil suits. In addition, it allowed plaintiffs to file suit against the manufacturers, wholesalers, and others involved in the chain of distribution, and not only against the final retailer.

7.5.2 Aims

The IACA was created to provide a solution to a twofold problem: (i) the flooding of imported imitation American Indian arts and crafts onto the market in the United States sold by dealers as genuine, and (ii) the misrepresentation by some American artists who questionably claimed Indian descent and heritage. As pointed out above, this imitation and misrepresentation resulted in millions of dollars lost to Indian arts and crafts. In addition, it was feared that fakes might also threaten the very existence of the Indian arts and crafts market.

The IACA serves four distinct categories of aims. These are outlined below.

Protection and promotion of Indian arts and crafts

According to some authors, the protection and promotion of Indian arts and crafts is the primary aim of the IACA.[53] Many artists make their living solely by selling arts and crafts. They risk being driven out of business by cheap imitations which can be sold for a much lower price, thus causing their income to decline, and discouraging younger generations from learning traditional techniques and becoming artisans. The IACA seeks to improve business opportunities for Indian artists in order to maintain their interest in producing traditional arts and crafts.

Promotion of Indian self-sufficiency

The IACA provides Indian artists with a means to assert self-determination and to secure economic independence. These objectives are within the broader

---

52   Senate Report 106-452, 'To Improve the Cause of Action for Misrepresentation of Indian Arts and Crafts'.
53   See for example Parsley, *supra* note 39, 495–6.

government goal of Indian self-sufficiency. The Act gives Indians the means by which to pursue redress for themselves through the Act's civil and criminal penalties and promotes an industry which brings millions of dollars into the Indian economy.[54] According to an article in *The Economist*, describing the IACA, the promotion of Indian self-sufficiency is actually the main objective of the Act:

> The law may indeed keep ancestral styles alive – a worthy aesthetic aim – but much of the stuff Indians produce now is already gift shop kitsch, indistinguishable from imports of fakes. The real impetus behind this new legislation is a desire to protect jobs on the Indian reservations. Like bingo games (lucrative thanks to the Indians' exemption from state anti-gambling laws), Indians can profit from autonomous handicraft businesses on their own lands.[55]

Protection of Native American culture and know how

The IACA aims to avoid the loss of know-how in traditional manufacturing techniques. It was feared that the sale of cheap imitation products might drive Indian producers out of the market and cause the loss of traditional techniques and art,[56] which according to a brochure of the Indian Arts and Crafts Board is 'an integral and enduring part of Indian life'.[57] Closely related is also the cultural justice argument that Indians ought to profit, or at least control who profits, from the sales of Indian arts and crafts.[58]

Protection of consumers

The final aim of the IACA is the protection of consumers. The availability of fakes threatens the integrity of the market, leading to an erosion of consumer confidence. Producers and sellers of fake goods commit a fraud on unsuspecting consumers, who spend millions of dollars each year buying products which they believe to be authentic. The provisions of the IACA were expected to act as a deterrent to fraudulent selling techniques and provide additional protection for consumers of Indian arts and crafts.

---

[54] Ibid. 496.

[55] *The Economist*, 'On the Warpath', 5 September 1992, 94.

[56] It was feared that the undercutting of prices may force Indians to cut corners and spend less time on each piece of work, thus diminishing the works' authentic appeal. See Parsley, *supra* note 39, 496.

[57] US Department of the Interior, Indian Arts and Crafts Board, *American Indian and Alaska Native Arts and Crafts* (US Department of the Interior: Washington, 1995).

[58] See Hapiuk, *supra* note 43, 1021–2.

7.5.3   The Indian Arts and Crafts Board

The Indian Arts and Crafts Board (IACB) is an agency of the Department of the Interior.[59] It was created in 1935 by the original Indian Arts and Crafts Act, as part of the so-called Indian New Deal[60] of the Roosevelt administration. Its mandate is to 'promote the economic welfare of the Indian tribes and Indian individuals through the development of Indian arts and crafts and the expansion of the market for the products of Indian art and craftsmanship'.[61] For that purpose, the IACB is entitled to prescribe:

> [R]ules and regulations governing the conduct of its business and containing such provisions as it may deem appropriate for the effective execution and administration of the powers conferred upon it.[62]

Amongst other things, the IACB is authorised to engage in activities such as market and technical research, technical and management assistance, and the making of loan recommendations in view of the production and sale of Indian products.[63] However, its main tasks are the creation of government trade marks of genuineness and quality, the establishment of standards and regulations for the use of such marks by corporations, associations or individuals, the registration of such trade marks in the US Patent and Trademark Office without charge, and the assignment of such trade marks, together with the goodwill associated with them, to an individual Indian or Indian tribe without charge.[64]

Finally, the IACB has the power to refer complaints of violations to the Federal Bureau of Investigation (FBI), to recommend to the Attorney General

---

[59]   Note that the IACB is not part of the Bureau of Indian Affairs.

[60]   The 'New Deal' was the name President Roosevelt gave to the series of programmes between 1933 and 1937, with the goal of relief, recovery and reform of the US economy during the Great Depression. One of these programmes was the Indian Reorganization Act of 1934, also known as the 'Indian New Deal'. The Indian New Deal secured certain rights to Native Americans, such as a reversal of the Dawes Act's privatisation of common holdings of American Indians and a return to local self-government on a tribal basis. In addition, it restored to Native Americans the management of their lands and included provisions intended to create a sound economic foundation for the inhabitants of Indian reservations.

[61]   25 U.S.C. § 305(a).

[62]   25 U.S.C. § 305(b).

[63]   Other activities of the IACB include the running of three regional museums: the Sioux Indian Museum in Rapid City, South Dakota, the Museum of the Plains Indian in Browning, Montana and the Southern Plains Indian Museum in Anadarko, Oklahoma and the publication of a consumer directory of Native American owned and operated arts and crafts businesses.

[64]   25 U.S.C. § 305(a).

of the United States that criminal proceedings should be instituted, and to recommend that the Secretary of the Interior shall refer a matter to the Attorney General for civil enforcement action.

The IACB is composed of five commissioners, appointed by the Secretary of the Department of the Interior,[65] who determine the policies of the IACB. The IACB's activities and programmes, on the other hand, are carried out by executive officers and other employees, headquartered in Washington, DC, whose duties and responsibilities are prescribed by the IACB.[66]

7.5.4 Definitional Considerations

Definition of 'Indian' and 'Indian tribe'
The definition of 'Indian' provided by the IACA is probably the most controversial element of the Act. It raises issues of discrimination, self-determination, tribal sovereignty and freedom of speech.

Under the IACA, an 'Indian' is any individual who is a member of an Indian tribe or is certified as an Indian artisan by an Indian tribe.[67] 'Indian tribe' in turn means: (i) any Indian tribe, band, nation, Alaska native village, or other organised group or community which is recognised as eligible for the special programmes and services provided by the United States to Indians because of their status as Indians, or (ii) any Indian group that has been formally recognised as an Indian tribe by a state legislature or by a state commission or similar organisation legislatively vested with state tribal recognition authority.[68]

Discrimination   Generally speaking, definitions of Indians and Indian tribes in federal law are political. They are adapted to satisfy the political objectives and considerations specific to each law. They determine which groups are considered to be in a quasi-sovereignty relationship with the government and which individuals are eligible for various government programmes.[69] By using a definition that revolves around tribal membership, and by providing

---

65   25 U.S.C. § 305.
66   Ibid. § 305(a).
67   25 U.S.C. § 305(d).
68   25 U.S.C. § 305(d)(4).
69   Such tribes are called 'federally recognised' or 'federally acknowledged'. Their members are usually referred to as 'enrolled'. As the tribes are sovereign political entities, their members are citizens as well as members. Besides federally recognised tribes, there are other tribes that have no sovereign status, and some tribes that are recognised by their state governments only. See Gail K. Sheffield, *The Arbitrary Indian: The Indian Arts and Crafts Act of 1990* (University of Oklahoma Press: Norman and London, 1997) 4–5.

that one must be a member of a federally or state-recognised tribe, some Indian people are excluded from the Act's narrow definition of Indian. However, there are many legitimate reasons for not being an enrolled tribal member, which cause the IACA to have a discriminatory effect. These include persons who were adopted, lost their records, do not believe they should be forced to prove their heritage to the government,[70] whose tribe is not recognised by the government[71] or whose ancestors did not sign the tribal rolls.[72] In addition, differing tribal enrolment standards can also lead to discrimination. This can be the case with situations involving persons who are members of tribes with a matrilineal or patrilineal system of enrolment,[73] or tribal enrolment standards involving blood quantum limits.[74]

Self-determination and sovereignty   Over the years, the scope of tribal sovereignty has shifted in federal policy,[75] statutes, regulations and court decisions with a great deal of inconsistency and the US government, the states and the federally recognised tribes have each time attempted to maximise their legal position with respect to one another. To further complicate matters, the federal government does not act as a single entity as far as Indian policy is concerned but is dependent on Congress, the President and the US Supreme Court, which

---

    [70]   See Parsley, *supra* note 39, 498.
    [71]   In the 1950s, the federal government's policy was to assimilate tribes into 'white culture' by terminating their tribal status. Even though this policy was repealed, of the 113 tribes that were terminated, only 78 have been restored to recognised status, leaving at least 35 tribes without recognition. Ibid. 499.
    [72]   There are a number of reasons why many Native Americans did not, at the time, sign the tribal rolls. Besides a general distrust of the white government, many Native Americans lived far from were the rolls where to be signed or never even became aware of the signing of the tribal rolls. In addition, many were afraid of the ramifications that could result from claiming their true Indian heritage. Ibid. 499.
    [73]   In matrilineal or patrilineal systems of enrolment, the enrolment of a child onto the tribe's rolls would follow the tribe of either the mother or the father depending on the tribe. This would cause problems in the case of a person whose mother came from a patrilineal tribe and whose father came from a matrilineal tribe, as he or she would be 100 per cent Indian, but would be ineligible for enrolment into either tribe. Ibid. 498.
    [74]   Different tribes often require different blood quantum limits. For example, while one tribe might require only one sixty-fourth blood quantum for enrolment, another might require up to one-half Indian blood to qualify for tribal membership. This can result in one person qualifying as 'Indian' while another person with equal or greater Indian blood in a different tribe not qualifying. Ibid. 499.
    [75]   On Indian policy, see Rennard Strickland, 'Introduction to Indian Law Symposium, Indian Law and Policy: The Historian's Viewpoint' (1978–79) 54 *Wash. L Rev.* 475–8; David Wilkins, 'An Inquiry into Indigenous Political Participation: Implications for Tribal Sovereignty' (1999–2000) 9 *Kan. JL and Pub. Pol'y* 732–51.

often follow different agendas. In that respect, the federal government has been analogised to 'a ship with three rudders, each controlled by a different helmsman'.[76]

The principle that a federally recognised tribe, being a sovereign entity, should determine its own membership was recognised by the Supreme Court as early as 1897 in *Roff v Burney*[77] and was reaffirmed in subsequent case law[78] and in the Indian Civil Rights Act of 1968,[79] which made applicable some of the Bill of Rights that protects US citizens from arbitrary and unjust actions by state and federal government, to Indian tribal governments.[80]

Indian people consider that they should have control over policies which concern their economic stability, such as the IACA, and therefore feel that the tribal governments should be the entities dealing with the imitation arts and crafts problem. They consider that they should be the ones to determine who has the right to decide who is or is not Indian, and consequently they feel that the IACA is infringing on their right of sovereignty and self-determination.

Freedom of speech   All government restrictions, which might have the effect of tampering with First Amendment freedoms, such as the freedom of speech, must be carried out in the way least restrictive to such freedoms. Statutes, for example, must not be so vague that a person must forgo First Amendment rights for fear of violating an unclear law.[81] It has been argued, in legal literature[82] and in case law,[83] that the IACA might have the effect of decreasing free speech in a number of ways. Because of the narrow definition of 'Indian', artists who are not enrolled members of a tribe, or who are not certified, may be forced to stop calling themselves Indians and stop producing art from fear

---

[76]   See Sheffield, *supra* note 69, 36.

[77]   *Roff v Burney*, 168 U.S. 218 (1897).

[78]   See *Santa Clara Pueblo v Martinez*, 436 U.S. 49 (1978). In that case, a Pueblo woman sued her pueblo in Federal Court, seeking membership for her daughter, and claimed that a membership rule based on patrilineality violated the Equal Protection provision of the Indian Civil Rights Act, since it discriminated on the basis of gender and ancestry. The court dismissed her suit, thus recognising the right of a tribe to determine its own membership.

[79]   Pub. L 90-284, 25 U.S.C.A. §§ 1301–41.

[80]   See Sheffield, *supra* note 69, 47–8.

[81]   See *Scull v Virginia*, 359 U.S. 344 (1959); *NAACP v Button*, 371 U.S. 415 (1963).

[82]   See Parsley, *supra* note 39, 504–6.

[83]   See *Native American Arts, Inc. v Village Originals, Inc.*, 25 F.Supp.2d 876; *Ho-Chunk ex rel. Native American Arts, Inc. v Nature's Gifts, Inc.*, Not Reported in F.Supp.2d, 1999 WL 169319 (N.D. Ill.); *Native American Arts, Inc. v Bundy-Howard, Inc.*, 168 F.Supp.2d 905; *Native American Arts, Inc. v Earth Dweller, Ltd*, Not Reported in F.Supp.2d, 2001 WL 910394 (N.D. Ill.).

of a fine or imprisonment. In addition, they face the risk of devaluation of their work, seen as a fake, and ultimately being driven out of business. In this light, the Act might have the long-term effect of destroying the Indian self-sufficiency it originally sought to protect.[84]

Certification as an 'Indian artisan'

Because of the narrow definition of 'Indian' in the IACA, the federal legislators inserted a certification clause which gives both state and federally recognised tribes the authority to certify artisans who are not entitled, or do not desire, to become enrolled members of a tribe.[85] In order for an individual to be certified by an Indian tribe as a non-member Indian artisan: (i) the individual must be of Indian lineage of one or more members of such Indian tribe, and (ii) the certification must be documented in writing by the governing body of an Indian tribe or by a certifying body delegated this function. Tribes may not impose a fee for certifying an Indian artisan.[86] The specifics of the certification process are left to the discretion of each individual tribe.

Despite its good intent, the certification provision raises some issues. As the certification process is at the sole discretion of the tribes, the Act is open to situations where tribes might arbitrarily refuse to certify someone, either to exclude competition from non-enrolled Indians, or to avoid losing benefits in other areas, thus leaving artists who should have been protected under the Act with no choice but to cease calling themselves Indian artists.[87]

Definition of 'Indian product'

Whereas the Act defines the terms 'Indian', 'Indian tribe' and 'Indian arts and crafts organisation', it leaves it to the regulations to define the terms 'Indian product' and 'product of a particular Indian tribe or Indian arts and crafts organisation'. The definition of 'Indian product' under the 1990 Act's implementing regulations focused on the nature and Indian origin of products covered by the Act. It specified that the term 'Indian product' applied to Indian arts and crafts and not to all products generally. It did not, however, provide

---

84   See Parsley, *supra* note 39, 505–6.
85   The certification as an 'Indian artisan' by a tribe under IACA can be compared to the practice of societies of craftsmen or guilds in Britain between the eleventh and sixteenth centuries, where the craftsman's mark or guild's mark served a regulatory function and appeared on goods to attest to the fact that they were the result of true guild workmanship. On the practice of societies of craftsmen and guilds, see Jeffrey Belson, *Certification Marks* (Sweet & Maxwell: London, 2002) 5–17.
86   See 25 CFR Part 309, s. 309.4.
87   See Parsley, *supra* note 39, 502–3.

specific arts and crafts examples.[88] In 2000, Congress enacted the Indian Arts and Crafts Enforcement Act of 2000 to strengthen the cause of action for misrepresentation of Indian arts and crafts and directed the Indian Arts and Crafts Board to promulgate regulations to include in the definition of the term 'Indian product' specific examples of such products, in order to provide guidance to Indian artisans as well as to purveyors and consumers of Indian arts and crafts. The federal rule of 12 June 2003 therefore provides specific examples of items that may be marketed as Indian products[89] and those that may not, thereby informing the public as to when an individual may be subject to civil or criminal penalties for falsely marketing a good as an 'Indian product'.[90]

7.5.5 Rights Granted

The IACA 1990 builds up on the rights granted by the 1935 Act by increasing criminal penalties and creating civil remedies for violations. The prohibited behaviour for both kind of penalties is the same:

> To offer or display for sale or sell any good, with or without a Government trademark, in a manner that falsely suggests it is Indian produced, an Indian product, or the product of a particular Indian or Indian tribe or arts and crafts organization, resident within the United States.[91]

Criminal penalties

For a first time violation of the Act, individual offenders are subject to fines of up to US$250,000 and/or five years imprisonment. Non-individual offenders,[92] on the other hand, are subject to fines of up to US$1,000,000. Subsequent violations of the Act expose individual offenders to fines of up to

---

88 The term 'Indian product' was defined as any art or craft product made by an Indian, including, but not limited to (i) artworks that are in a traditional or non-traditional Indian style or medium; (ii) crafts that are in a traditional or non-traditional Indian style or medium; (iii) handicrafts, such as objects created with the help of only such devices as allow the manual skill of the maker to condition the shape and design of each individual product (25 CFR part 309).

89 The rule provides specific examples of jewellery, basketry, weaving and textile, beadwork, quillwork, moose hair tufting, apparel, regalia, woodwork, hide, leatherwork, fur, pottery, ceramics, sculpture, carving, pipes, dolls and painting, and other fine art forms that are Indian products. See Federal Register, Vol. 68, No. 113, 12 June 2003, 35169–35171.

90 Ibid. 35164–35171.

91 See 18 U.S.C. § 1159 and 25 U.S.C. § 305e. Note that the language 'falsely suggest' parallels the requirement of the Lanham Act for trade mark infringement.

92 Non-individual offenders can be businesses, wholesalers, shops or galleries.

US$1,000,000 and/or 15 years' imprisonment and non-individual offenders are subject to fines of up to US$5,000,000.[93]

Civil actions

Civil remedies allow plaintiffs to obtain injunctive or equitable relief as well as damages, in the form of either (i) treble damages,[94] or (ii) 'in the case of each aggrieved individual Indian, Indian tribe, or Indian arts and crafts organizations, not less than $1000 for each day on which the offer or display for sale or sale continues'.[95] In addition, the court may award punitive damages and the costs of suit and attorney's fees.[96]

Standing

The IACB is empowered to refer complaints for criminal investigation to the FBI and recommend to the Attorney General that criminal proceedings be instituted for misrepresentation of Indian produced goods and services.[97] In addition it can recommend that the Attorney General sue for civil remedies on behalf of Indian individuals, tribes and arts and crafts organisations. Civil proceedings may also be initiated by an Indian tribe on its behalf, or by an Indian person, on their own behalf.[98]

7.5.6 The Trade Mark Provisions

Under the trade mark provisions of the 1935 Act,[99] the IACB was authorised to create government trade marks of genuineness and quality for Indian arts and crafts products, register them in the United States Patent and Trademark Office (USPTO), and license them to corporations, associations or individuals. However, most artists were not interested in these government-owned trade marks as they did not give them exclusive rights.

The trade mark provisions of the 1990 Act[100] partly rectified this problem

---

93   See 18 U.S.C. § 1159.

94   See 25 U.S.C. § 305e(a)(2)(A).

95   See 25 U.S.C. § 305e(a)(2)(B).

96   See 25 U.S.C. § 305e(b).

97   See 25 U.S.C. § 305d.

98   See 25 U.S.C. § 305e.

99   The trade mark provisions of the 1935 Act authorised the Board 'To create Government trade marks of genuineness and quality for Indian products and the products of particular Indian tribes or groups; to establish standards and regulations for the use of such trade marks; to license corporations, associations, or individuals to use them; and to charge a fee for their use; to register them in the United States Patent Office without charge.' See s. 2(g).

100   The trade mark provisions of the 1990 Act authorise the Board '(1) To create

by authorising the Board to create government trade marks of genuineness and quality for Indian arts and crafts products, register them in the USPTO, and assign them as well as the goodwill associated with them to individual Indians or tribes without charge. However, when drafting the regulations covering the use of the trade mark provisions, the IACB concluded that two ambiguities in the statutory language of the Act prevented it from developing a trade mark registration programme.[101]

First, whereas section 2(g)(1) of the Act authorised the Board to create trade marks of genuineness and quality for individual Indians, Indian tribes and Indian arts and crafts organisations, paragraph (3) of the same section only authorised the Board to assign those trade marks to an individual Indian or Indian tribe, leaving aside arts and crafts organisations and denying them the trade mark benefits anticipated by the Act.

The second issue concerned a conflict between the Act's trade mark registration provisions and the trade mark ownership requirements of the Lanham Act. Under the 1990 Act, the Board is authorised 'to register any such trademark owned by the Government in the United States Patent Office without charge and assign it and the goodwill associated with it to an individual Indian or Indian tribe'. Consequently, rights on such trade marks would first belong to the government and then be transferred to an individual Indian or tribe. Under the Lanham Act, however, an applicant to register a trade mark must be the owner of the mark or, if the application is filed on an intent-to-use basis, must be entitled to use the mark and have a *bona fide* intention to use the mark in commerce.[102] Therefore, if the named applicant is not the owner of the mark at the time of registration, the registration would be defective under the Lanham Act and thus void.[103] Such a defect could not be cured with an amendment substituting the true owner at a later stage.

---

for the Board, or for an individual Indian or Indian tribe or Indian arts and crafts organization, trademarks of genuineness and quality for Indian products and the products of an individual Indian or particular Indian tribe or Indian arts and crafts organization; (2) to establish standards and regulations for the use of Government-owned trademarks by corporations, associations, or individuals, and to charge for such use under such licenses; (3) to register any such trademark owned by the Government in the United States Patent and Trademark Office without charge and assign it and the goodwill associated with it to an individual Indian or Indian tribe without charge; and (4) to pursue or defend in the court any appeal or proceeding with respect to any final determination of that office.' See s. 2(g).

[101] See Oversight Hearing on Indian Arts and Crafts, *supra* note 42, 5.
[102] See 25 U.S.C. § 1051 (1994).
[103] Ibid.

7.5.7   Case Law

Under the IACA of 1935, the only sanction for violating the false advertising provision was of a criminal type, and there has been not one single prosecution. Under the IACA of 1990, government and private law suits were authorised by Congress alongside criminal ones. Since then, there have been two federal indictments and a few law suits, of which most were at District Court level, and one reached an appellate court.

Federal indictments
Investigations by federal prosecutors under the criminal provisions of the IACA have led to the filing of indictments in two separate cases. In the first one, the Office of Inspector General (OIG) of the US Department the Interior investigated allegations that a South Dakota jeweller was falsely selling his work as Indian made.[104] In 1998, a federal grand jury indicted him on two counts of misrepresentation of Indian-produced goods and one charge of illegally collecting feathers from a protected species. According to prosecutors, the man, who called himself 'Eagleboy' was not an enrolled member of any federally recognised tribe and had violated the IACA by selling artwork he had created and by falsely suggesting that it was 'Indian-made'. The man, who was sentenced to a year of probation and a fine of US$250 for possession of golden eagle parts, agreed to remove the word 'Indian' from the goods he sold and to cease making claims that he was Indian.[105] In the second case, a manufacturer/wholesaler was indicted by a federal grand jury in Utah on two counts of misrepresenting and selling to retail stores dream-catchers as being Indian-made 'genuine articles', whereas they were made by Vietnamese workers.[106]

Law suits
Surprisingly, the first civil cases filed under the IACA did not involve importers of imitation arts and crafts from overseas or unenrolled Indians, but big-name national retailers such as J.C. Penney and Wal-Mart. In 1998, the Ho-Chunk Nation and Native American Arts, Inc. (NAA), an Indian arts and

---

[104]   See Hugh O'Gara, 'Who Makes Indian Art? Rapid City Man is First to be Prosecuted under Indian Arts and Crafts Act of 1990', *Rapid City Journal* (SD), 19 September 1999, A1; 'Man Charged with Selling Fake Goods', *Rapid City Journal* (SD), 23 December 1998, as cited in US Department of the Interior, Office of Inspector General, *Indian Arts and Crafts: A Case of Misrepresentation* (US Department of the Interior: Washington, 2005) 8.

[105]   Note that although this case resulted in a criminal conviction, it was not a conviction under the IACA.

[106]   See 'Business Digest: Ex-Utahn Indicted under Indian Arts & Crafts Act', *Salt Lake Tribune*, 25 May 2000, C1, as cited in Hapiuk, *supra* note 43, 1038.

crafts organisation comprising Indians from the Ho-Chunk Nation, filed 12 separate law suits against a mix of retail stores alleging that they had represented items for sale as Indian-made when they were not. While most of the cases were settled by 2000, some have produced judicial opinions. Most of those, however, were concerned with questions of standing and routine motions to dismiss.[107]

In a case brought against it in 1998 by the NAA,[108] national retailer Village Originals challenged the constitutionality of the IACA arguing that it violated the First Amendment because its language was overly broad and vague. The plaintiffs argued that the over-breadth doctrine[109] was inapplicable to commercial speech. The District Court agreed with the plaintiffs and rejected Village Original's argument. It held that commercial speech is protected by the First Amendment in so far as it serves an informational function, but loses its protection if it deceives, misleads or constitutes fraudulent activity.[110] It further found that the IACA:

> was not unconstitutionally vague; IACA did not restrict artistic quality of retailer's merchandise, but rather, merely regulates the means through which such merchandise is marketed, prohibiting retailer from representing to the public that its merchandise was made by Native Americans when, in fact, it was not.[111]

---

[107]   See *Native American Arts, Inc. v Chico Arts, Inc.*, 8 F.Supp.2d 1066; *Native American Arts, Inc. v J.C. Penney Co., Inc.*, 5 F.Supp.2d 599; *Native American Arts, Inc. v Moon Raven Intern., Inc.*, Not Reported in F.Supp., 1998 WL 325245 (N.D.Ill.). In each of these cases, the District Court ruled, interpreting the ambiguous language of the Act, that the NAA did not have standing under the Act and held that only the Attorney General or an Indian tribe could bring the cause of action. The later Indian Arts and Crafts Enforcement Act of 2000 clarified the language of the IACA 1990 and confirmed that Indian arts and crafts organisations have standing to bring a civil action under the Act.

[108]   See *Native American Arts, Inc. v Village Originals, Inc.*, 25 F.Supp.2d 876.

[109]   Plaintiffs relied on the *Hoffman Estates* two-step test for determining whether a statute is void for over-breadth or vagueness. First, the court must determine whether the statute reaches a substantial amount of constitutionally protected conduct. If not, then the over-breadth challenge fails. Next, assuming that the statute implicates no constitutionally protected conduct, the court must uphold the challenge only if the statute is impermissibly vague in all of its applications. See *Village of Hoffman Estates v Flipside Hoffman Estates, Inc.*, 455 U.S. 489 (1982).

[110]   See *Native American Arts, Inc. v Village Originals, Inc.*, 25 F.Supp.2d, 876, 880.

[111]   Ibid. 881. In later cases, the courts relied on Village Originals to reject similar constitutional challenges to the Act. See *Ho-Chunk ex rel. Native American Arts, Inc. v Nature's Gifts, Inc.*, Not Reported in F.Supp.2d, 1999 WL 169319 (N.D. Ill.); *Native American Arts, Inc. v Bundy-Howard, Inc.*, 168 F.Supp.2d 905; *Native American Arts, Inc. v Earth Dweller, Ltd*, Not Reported in F.Supp.2d, 2001 WL 910394 (N.D. Ill.).

Besides cases involving national retailers, there have been a few law suits involving individual offenders. In *Native American Arts, Inc. v Aquino*,[112] the NAA brought an action against Emma Aquino and Mohammad Rahman, the owners of a small retail business through which they sold artwork, crafts and jewellery, alleging they falsely represented that goods they sold were Indian-made in violation of the IACA. In that particular instance, defendants were granted a motion to dismiss for failure by the plaintiffs to plead fraud with particularity.[113] The court held that fraud is the *sine qua non* of an action brought under the IACA and that '[i]n all averments of fraud … the circumstances constituting fraud … shall be stated with particularity'.[114] This means stating the identity of the person making the misrepresentation, the time, place and content of the misrepresentation, and the method by which the misrepresentation was communicated to the plaintiff.[115]

Finally, the first law suit to go beyond the District Court level was an appellate case of 2005. In *Native American Arts, Inc. v Waldron Corp.*,[116] the NAA brought a suit for damages against a non-Indian manufacturer of Indian-style jewellery which was advertised under names such as 'Navajo', 'Crow', 'Southwest Tribes' and 'Zuni Bear', and sold with tags giving facts about the tribes, and identifying the designer of the jewellery as Trisha Waldron, who is not an Indian. The case was tried by a jury and the verdict was for the defendants, following which the plaintiffs appealed.

The plaintiffs challenged the soundness of the District Court judge's ruling that the 'unqualified use'[117] regulation infringes freedom of speech and is constitutionally vague and overbroad, and argued that they were entitled to give the jury instructions on the regulation. On the first argument, the court found for the plaintiffs and said that:

> [The district court judge was] indeed wrong … A non-Indian maker of jewelry designed to look like jewelry made by Indians is free to advertise the similarity but if he uses the word 'Indian' he must qualify the usage so that consumers aren't confused and think they're buying not only the kind of jewelry that

---

[112]   See *Native American Arts, Inc. v Aquino*, Not Reported in F.Supp.2d, 2004 WL 2434260 (N.D. Ill.).

[113]   Ibid. 3.

[114]   Fed.R.Civ.P. 9(b).

[115]   See *Native American Arts, Inc. v Aquino*, Not Reported in F.Supp.2d, 2004 WL 2434260 (N.D. Ill.) 2.

[116]   *Native American Arts, Inc. v Waldron Corp.*, 399 F.3d 871; 74 USPQ.2d 1221.

[117]   According to the regulation implementing § 305e 'the unqualified use of the term "Indian" or … of the name of an Indian tribe … in connection with an art or craft product is interpreted to mean … that the art or craft product is an Indian product'. See 25 C.F.R. § 309.24(a)(2).

Indians make, but jewelry that Indians in fact made. There is no constitutional infirmity.[118]

On the second argument, however, the court held that the litigants were not entitled to jury instructions on how to interpret a sufficient proof of false advertising.[119] While the court affirmed the judgment for the defendant, Judge Posner, writing for the court, observed that '[i]n effect, the regulation makes 'Indian' the trademark denoting products made by Indians'[120] thus raising the question whether the Indian Arts and Crafts Act and its implementing regulation created trade mark-like rights in the word 'Indian' and in the names of Indian tribes. This issue is examined in the next paragraph.

7.5.8 Does the Indian Arts and Crafts Act Create Trade Mark Rights in the Use of the Word 'Indian' and in the Names of Indian Tribes?

The proposition of *Native American Arts, Inc. v Waldron Corp.* that the Indian Arts and Crafts Act and its implementing regulation create trade mark-like rights in the use of the word 'Indian' and in the names of Indian tribes is an issue that has been discussed by many commentators,[121] and on which there is not a unanimous view.

In *The Arbitrary Indian*, Sheffield argues that the IACA should be read to create a new category of intellectual property, i.e. a proprietary right in Indian identity. She argues that the statutory language of the Act supports this assumption by providing that the initiation of a civil action and the recovery of damages are not available to consumers but only to an Indian individual, Indian tribe or an Indian arts and crafts organisation for 'the unauthorized appropriation of these parties' "property", their Indian identity'.[122]

Another commentator goes further in that direction and argues that tribal names qualify for trade mark protection as descriptive terms with secondary meaning[123] and that:

---

[118]   See *Native American Arts, Inc. v Waldron Corp.*, 399 F.3d 871; 74 USPQ.2d 1221.

[119]   Ibid. 875.

[120]   Ibid. 873.

[121]   See Thekla Hansen-Young, 'Whose Name is it, Anyway? Protecting Tribal Names from Cybersquatters' (2005) 10 *Va. J L and Tech*. 1–18, 6; J. Kimball, 'The Indian Arts and Crafts Act: Trademark Misfit or Just Missing the Mark?' www.kentlaw.edu/honorsscholars/2006students/writings/Kimball_paper.htm; Sheffield, *supra* note 69, 137–42.

[122]   Ibid. 137–8.

[123]   See Hansen-Young, *supra* note 121, 13–14. Hansen-Young argues that when

> With respect to arts and crafts, the secondary meaning of tribal names has been statutorily prescribed [by the IACA] ... Essentially, the Act makes Indian the trademark denoting products made by Indians.[124]

In contrast, one commentator argues that 'IACA does not expressly create trademark rights by reference to the Lanham Act, but rather creates the functional equivalent of trademark rights then vests those rights into certain ethnic populations'.[125] According to Kimball, the failure of IACA to operate within the Lanham Act, combined with the tying of rights to particular groups of people, create a series of distinct conflicts. He argues that the grant of trade mark-like rights to groups of citizens creates a conflict with the international trade mark regime. First, by providing trade mark protection to particular groups, without requiring those groups to demonstrate that they have acquired these rights in the particular source-identifying mark, the IACA allows for preferential treatment of particular nationals, i.e. Native Americans and Native American tribes and thus violates the national treatment clause of the TRIPS Agreement. In addition, IACA allows statutory damages that are at odds with the remedies available for other US trade mark violations, thus entitling a special class of rights holders to receive greater monetary awards from the US legal system.[126] Secondly, IACA also appears to be in conflict with the Paris Convention. Under the Paris Convention, one of the circumstances where a Member may deny trade mark registration to another Member is when the mark would infringe the rights of third parties within the non-registering country. However, this is understood to apply to trade mark rights rather than the rights acquired by virtue of legislative intervention. Thus, the IACA might not justify the refusal of a foreign trade mark registration that conflicted with its mandate.[127]

Despite the proposition of *Native American Arts, Inc. v Waldron Corp.*, the assumption that the IACA and its implementing regulation create trade mark-like rights in the use of the word 'Indian' and in the names of Indian tribes seems to be far-fetched and limited by the IACA itself. Indeed, if Congress had intended to create statutorily prescribed trade marks for each tribe, there would

---

used in connection with goods and services, tribal names are descriptive as they denote a certain quality or describe the nature of the goods or service. In addition, they identify the source of the good or service. For example, Cherokee beads denote the quality of the goods, as well as the fact that the beads originate from the Cherokee tribe. Secondly, he argues that when used in connection with goods or services, tribal names whose source-identifying quality has been acquired through years of the name being used to identifying a tribe, acquire secondary meaning.

[124]   Ibid. 14–15.
[125]   See Kimball, *supra* note 121, 4.
[126]   Ibid. 4–5.
[127]   Ibid. 5.

have been no need for a separate trade mark section in IACA which authorises the Board to create such trade marks.[128] Furthermore, the creation of trade mark rights in the term 'Indian' would raise problems of ownership and freedom of speech, as there is no constitutionally agreed definition of who is Indian.

7.5.9 Results to Date

Despite its 70-year history, the enforcement record of the IACA is less than outstanding. As reported by a member of staff in June 2005, the IACB receives an average of six complaints per month, and while some are referred to the FBI for investigation, very few lead to actual prosecutions.[129] As noted above, there have been some prosecutions and civil law suits, but none has resulted in a civil or criminal conviction under the Act.

In 2005, the OIG produced a report on 'the evaluation of the Indian Arts and Crafts'.[130] The report consisted of a review of the counterfeit Indian arts and crafts market. It obtained, assessed and verified Indian artists' perspectives on the issue of misrepresentation and counterfeiting in the Indian arts and crafts industry. The conclusion of the report was that:

> While well-intended, the laws that pertain to Indian arts and crafts do little to protect Indian artisans from the unfair competition created by low-priced, mass-produced imitations of their work. The primary law, the Indian Arts and Crafts Act, is practically unenforceable and does not provide adequate authority to the IACB. In addition, the vast majority of imported Indian-style items will be marked as such with removable sticky labels, string tags, or nothing at all due to weak country of origin marking regulations. Enforcement of these laws largely depends upon the cooperation of agencies, such as the U.S. Attorneys Offices, the FBI, and U.S. Customs and Border Patrol, all of which are outside the Department's control. In addition, there are conflicts between the Act and current trademark law, which prevent the IACB from facilitating the registration of trademarks for Indian artisans.[131]

Lack of enforcement

According to the Department of the Interior *Departmental Manual*, 'the top priority of the [IACB] is the enforcement and implementation of the Indian

---

[128]   See s. 2(g) of the IACA.

[129]   Author's transcripts of an interview with Mrs Sheryl Rakestraw, Program Specialist, Indian Arts and Crafts Board, US Department of the Interior, 8 June 2005 ('IACB interview').

[130]   See US Department of the Interior, Office of Inspector General, *supra* note 104.

[131]   Ibid. 7.

Arts and Crafts Act'.[132] The manual further provides that 'the Indian Arts and Crafts Enforcement Staff is responsible for receiving, processing, evaluating, and referring complaints ... to the Department of Justice for investigation and prosecution'.[133] The IACB does not therefore have investigative power of its own, but must rely on the FBI and other government agencies such as the Bureau of Indian Affairs and the OIG to investigate possible violations of the Act. However, these agencies have limited resources and are often unable to accommodate the IACB's requests for assistance. The powers of the IACB are limited to sending letters to alleged violators advising them of the Act's provisions.[134] It does not have the power to revoke licences, suspend operations or levy fines.

As part of its review of evaluation of the Indian arts and crafts industry, the OIG found that the IACB had spent most of its effort focusing on criminal prosecution, the highest and most difficult level of counterfeit. However, it suggested that most behaviour could be corrected with the least amount of activity or force, such as the dissemination of educational brochures or administrative actions and civil remedies, and that criminal charges should only be brought against significant violators who failed to respond to the lesser enforcement efforts.

In 2004, the Senate Committee on Indian Affairs introduced a new Bill, the Native American Technical Corrections Act of 2004[135] 'to make technical corrections to the law relating to Native Americans, and for other purposes'. The proposed Bill intended to allow the IACB to impose administrative fines and penalties of up to 100 per cent of the price of the goods offered or displayed for sale in violation of the Act and to investigate violations of the Act itself rather than referring cases to the FBI and other government agencies. Unfortunately, the Bill was not enacted by the Senate and House of Representatives on that occasion. The new provisions would have been beneficial, however, as they would have given the IACB the authority it lacks to enforce the Act.[136]

---

[132]   See US Department of the Interior, *Departmental Manual*, part 112, ch. 27, s. 27.2.A.

[133]   Ibid. s. 27.3.D.

[134]   See IACB interview, *supra* note 129, 705.

[135]   Senate Bill 2843.

[136]   In its conclusion, the report of the OIG encourages the reintroduction of Senate Bill 2843, saying it would give the IACB the authority to (a) investigate violations of the Act; (b) enforce the Act through the imposition of fines for violations; (c) enforce the Act through injunctive relief; and (d) enter into a reimbursable support agreement with federal, state, tribal, regional and local law enforcement entities. See US Department of the Interior, Office of Inspector General, *supra* note 104, 14.

Other problems with the Act

Many questions relating to the application of the IACA still remain unanswered. Many of these relate to the narrow perception in the IACA of what constitutes an 'imitation' or a 'counterfeit'.[137] While federal law only addresses the misrepresentation of Indian-style products, many believe that these terms denote much broader issues, such as traditional versus modern production methods,[138] the 'borrowing' of artistic or religious traditions from other tribes, and the practice of representing as 'authentic' Indian arts and crafts designed by Indians, but produced overseas,[139] or produced by Indians but using imported materials.[140]

One famous example of 'inter-tribal counterfeiting' is the making of kachina dolls[141] by tribes other than the Hopi. In an ongoing controversy, the Hopi have accused the Navajo of making fake kachina dolls. Under the IACA, the Hopi would have no cause of action since the Navajo are Indians and their work technically meets the letter of the law. For the Hopi, however, kachina dolls have a religious significance and a kachina carved by someone from any other tribe would be considered a counterfeit.

Finally, it was reported by the staff of the IACB that while sales of fake Indian arts and crafts used to take place mainly in retail, they are now rapidly increasing in the Internet environment and the number of Internet related complaints received by the Board has gone up over 40 per cent over the past few years.[142] It was reported that most complaints relate to auction websites such as Ebay, where arts and crafts are put up for sale and advertised as Indian.[143] In addition, fake Indian arts and crafts can also be purchased through Internet retailers on dedicated websites.[144] These practices raise a new set of concerns as

---

[137]   On this issue, see ibid., 6.

[138]   For example, traditional Indian jewellers using only hand tools and rock casts formed from volcanic ash would consider jewellery made with power tools and centrifugal casting as 'counterfeit', even if it was made by Indian artisans. Ibid

[139]   In 1997, award-winning jewellery maker and politician, Ben Nighthorse Campbell, created controversy by offering for sale the 'Spirit of the Thunder Collector's Knife'. Although the knife was designed by Campbell, it was assembled by factory labour in China. See Hapiuk, *supra* note 43, citing Jack Anderson, 'Knife Cuts Campbell's Credibility', *St J- Reg.* (Springfield, Ill.), 22 June 1997, 18.

[140]   This is the case, for example, if Indians use plastic imported beads instead of beads made of natural material when producing jewellery.

[141]   Authentic Hopi kachina dolls are religious icons carved by Hopi artists from cottonwood root and painted to represent figures from Hopi mythology, who act as intermediaries between humans and the gods. Kachina dolls are presented to the women and children of the tribe and are kept in homes as fetish objects.

[142]   See IACB interview, *supra* note 129.

[143]   Ibid.

[144]   In October 2000, the Federal Trade Commission and the IACB joined forces

it is much harder to get information and prosecute the seller of fake arts and crafts on an auction website or to gain personal jurisdiction over an Internet retailer who is often based outside the United States.

7.5.10   Conclusion

Although well-intended, the Indian Arts and Crafts Act does not fully manage to achieve its objectives to protect Indian artists from the unfair competition arising from the sale of arts and crafts products misrepresented as being made by Indians. As pointed out in this case study, the main reasons for that are the difficulty in enforcing the Act, the lack of authority of the IACB, and the inappropriateness of the definition of 'Indian' and 'Indian tribe' in the Act, which raise issues of discrimination, self-determination and sovereignty, and freedom of speech.

However, it remains to be seen how things will develop following the report of the OIG and the possible reintroduction of Senate Bill 2843, the Native American Technical Corrections Act, which will allow the IACB to impose administrative fines and penalties and investigate violations of the Act.

7.6   CONCLUSION: EFFICIENCY AND LIMITATIONS OF LAWS AGAINST MISREPRESENTATION TO PROTECT TCES

Passing off and laws against misrepresentation can be used by TCEs holders as a defence mechanism to prevent the misappropriation of intangible valuable items and provide relief for TCEs holders and consumers against misleading and deceptive conducts in relation to TCEs. In particular, they can be used to:

- allow TCEs holders to prevent the commercial use of their TCEs by third parties and avoid the loss of income that may occur when third parties pass off their goods as being those of TCEs holders;
- offer TCEs holders the possibility to object to false connection claims where non-indigenous products or businesses are promoted by using indigenous or traditional names or signs, in that way misleading

---

to combat the deceptive marketing of arts and crafts products as Indian-made during an awareness-raising event called the 'American Indian Arts and Crafts "Surf Day"'. Representatives from both agencies identified approximately 425 websites that appeared to market American Indian arts and crafts as authentic and notified each site operator of the provisions of the IACA. See News Release www.ftc.gov/opa/2000/10/indianart.htm

consumers by falsely suggesting a connection with a particular traditional community;

- offer TCEs holders the possibility to object to false attribution that occurs when imitation products are presented as genuine TCEs in the marketplace;
- protect consumers who wish to buy authentic products by acting as a deterrent to fraudulent selling techniques.

In addition, passing off and laws against misrepresentation can help protect, promote and preserve TCEs, and allow TCEs holders to benefit economically from their TCEs. Indeed, by reducing the amount of imitation products and the use of indigenous or traditional names and signs to designate non-indigenous products, passing off and laws against misrepresentation can help avoid the loss of know-how that can occur if cheap imitations drive indigenous producers out of the market and discourage younger generations from learning traditional techniques, improve business opportunities for indigenous artists and provide them with a means to secure economic independence.

8. Summary and conclusions

The debate over the protection of TCEs has been on the international agenda since the 1960s. However, differences continue to exist over whether or not TCEs should be protected, and if so, how.

This study argued that origin related intellectual property rights are the best policy option for the protection of TCEs, rather than other policy options that have been proposed, such as a system based on copyright, or the establishment of a new *sui generis* system. As was examined in Chapter 2, even though the rights granted by copyright law seem to address some of the concerns and policy objectives of TCEs holders – in particular, it was shown in the case studies that copyright law may, to some extent, assist in preventing the unauthorised reproduction of TCEs – this will only be possible where they fulfil the conditions for the grant of copyright protection. However, the application of copyright law to TCEs has important limitations. Such limitations relate to the requirements of originality, fixation, identifiable author and limited term of protection. On the other hand, a new *sui generis* system would take a long time to establish and may not in any case be politically feasible.

The study also observed that origin related intellectual property rights share a common heritage and a degree of commonality in the rationale for their protection, that make them compatible and more appropriate for the protection of TCEs. It was also established that because of the multi-faceted nature of TCEs, its broad subject matter, and the varying concerns and policy objectives of TCEs holders, it is difficult if not impossible to find a 'one size fits all' approach for their protection. In this view, it was argued that the protection of TCEs should be considered as part of a wider set of policies based on origin related intellectual property rights, that could provide both positive and defensive protection for TCEs and that would seek to protect as well as promote them. The result would be a complementary, though sometimes overlapping, system offering policy solutions that could be adopted depending on the specific needs of each traditional community.

The following advantages, in particular, were highlighted in favour of a system using origin related intellectual property rights.

Intrinsic characteristics of TCEs: Origin related intellectual property rights are particularly well-suited for the protection of TCEs because of the specific nature of TCEs. Many TCEs holders consider that their TCEs should be protected in perpetuity. As was examined, trade marks, collective marks and certification marks can be renewed perpetually provided the necessary steps are taken. Similarly, geographical indications are protected as long as the good-place-quality link is maintained and the indication has not fallen into genericity. Secondly, many TCEs are communal in nature, and it is often difficult to identify a single author or authors for TCEs. In this view, collective marks, certification marks and geographical indications are suitable for their protection as they allow for collective use.

Economic interests and commercial use: Origin related intellectual property rights can be used as a defensive tool by TCEs holders to prevent or control the unwanted commercial use of their TCEs by third parties. For example, passing off and laws against misrepresentation allow TCEs holders to avoid the loss of income that may occur when third parties pass off their goods as being those of TCEs holders. In addition, trade marks, certification and collective marks and geographical indications can help TCEs holders increase their commercial benefits and ensure that they get fair and equitable returns, as it is generally agreed that distinctive marks are economically valuable. Such marks can help realise the economic potential of TCEs.

Inappropriate and offensive use: Trade mark law can provide defensive protection against offensive and deceptive uses by taking into account cultural offensiveness in the absolute grounds for refusal to register a trade mark or by creating new mechanisms by which the interests of TCEs holders are taken into account during the trade mark registration process. Passing off and laws against misrepresentation, on the other hand, can also be used by TCEs holders as a defence mechanism against misleading and deceptive conducts in relation to TCEs.

Attribution: Passing off and laws against misrepresentation offer TCEs holders the possibility to object to false connection claims where non-indigenous products or businesses are promoted by using indigenous or traditional names or signs and to false attribution that occurs when imitation products are presented as genuine, in that way increasing consumer recognition of authentic indigenous goods.

Identification, preservation and promotion: The use of distinctive signs, such as trade marks, certification marks and collective marks, and geographical indications can assist in the promotion and dissemination of TCEs, especially when combined with an appropriate marketing strategy. Such signs provide TCEs holders with a means to differentiate their products and can act as a barrier to entry into a niche market segment. In particular, geographical indications recognise the cultural significance of TCEs, protect the goodwill accumulated over time, help enhance the development of rural communities, and enable product differentiation in the marketplace by enhancing the association of the product with the craftsmen of a particular place in the consumer's mind. In addition, passing off and laws against misrepresentation can also help protect, promote and preserve TCEs as they contribute to avoid the loss of know-how that can occur if cheap imitations drive indigenous producers out of the market and discourage younger generations from learning traditional techniques.

Protection of consumers: Trade marks, certification and collective marks and geographical indications share a common rationale based on reducing informational asymmetries between buyers and sellers. In this view, the reputation conveyed by such distinctive signs plays an important role in signalling the genuineness of TCEs and helps consumers in their search for reliable information to enable them to make informed decisions. Certification marks and geographical indications can provide an objective guarantee as to the characteristics and/or origin of a product or service, in that way protecting both consumers and indigenous artists from imitation products. In a similar line, passing off and laws against misrepresentation also aim at protecting consumers who wish to buy genuine products. They act as a deterrent to fraudulent selling techniques, as they allow TCEs holders to object to false claims of authorship and false attribution.

As was highlighted throughout this study, origin related intellectual property rights also present some limitations. Trade mark laws, for example, do not prevent the offensive use of TCEs where the user does not seek to register a trade mark. It is not possible for TCEs holders to obtain exclusive rights to trade marks based on TCEs where third parties have already registered such trade marks and the registration or use is not considered offensive, and the requirement that trade marks must be used commercially means that trade marks are not an appropriate mechanism for TCEs holders who do not want to see their words, designs and symbols used in that way. Also, the trade mark system could not offer a comprehensive positive protection mechanism as it would be prohibitively expensive to register all existing works, designs and symbols that TCEs holders may want to see protected as trade marks.

As was established by the case studies on certification marks and the analysis of the fair trade labelling system, the effectiveness of a certification scheme and its ability to meet the concerns and policy objectives of TCEs holders will depend on the way it is set up, implemented and policed. In addition, a successful scheme will need to get the support of the stakeholders and be the object of a public education campaign for the acceptance of the mark. Finally, geographical indications only protect tangible TCEs, and often, the knowledge associated with trade marks, certification and collective marks, and geographical indications is not protected and remains in the public domain.

Despite the existence of limitations, and although the proposed approach does not provide a comprehensive scheme for the protection of TCEs, origin related intellectual property rights provide a quick, practical and effective solution, as most of those rights can be used as such, or with minor adaptations. As such, a system based on origin related intellectual property rights to protect TCEs represents a workable, balanced compromise that can satisfy most of the concerns and policy objectives of TCEs holders.

Bibliography

Aboriginal and Torres Strait Islander Commission (ATSIC) and Office of National Tourism, 'National Aboriginal and Torres Strait Islander Tourism Industry Strategy' (1997) 3 *Aboriginal Law Bulletin* 4–8

Albisu Luis, Miguel, Work Programme 2 (Link between origin labelled products and local production systems, supply chain analysis), *Final Report* (July 2002)

American Law Institute, *Restatement of the Law (Third) of Unfair Competition* (American Law Institute Publishers: St Paul MN, 1995) 407–24

Annas, Marianna, 'The Label of Authenticity: A Certification Trade Mark for Goods and Services of Indigenous Origin' (1997) 3 *Aboriginal Law Bulletin* 4–6

Arts Council of New Zealand Toi Aotearoa, *Annual Report of the Arts Council of New Zealand Toi Aotearoa for the Year Ended 30 June 2005* (Creative New Zealand: Wellington, 2007)

Audier, Jacques, *TRIPS Agreement, Geographical Indications* (Office for Official Publications of the European Communities: Luxembourg, 2000)

Austin, Graeme W., 'Re-Treating Intellectual Property? The Wai 262 Proceedings and the Heuristics of Intellectual Property Law' (2003) 11 *Cardozo J Int'l and Comp. L* 333–63

Australia Council, *Final Report of the Review of the National Indigenous Arts Advocacy Association* (Australia Council: Sydney, 2002)

Australian Department of Aboriginal Affairs, *The Aboriginal Arts and Crafts Industry, Report of the Review Committee* (AGPS: Canberra, 1989)

Bachner, Bryan, 'Comment on the 17 December 2003 Decision of the Beijing Higher People's Court in Case No. 246 (2003) (final)' (2006) 37 *IIC* 488–9

Baird, Douglas G., 'Common Law Intellectual Property and the Legacy of International News Services v Associated Press' (1983) 50 *U Chi. L Rev.* 411–29

Baird, Stephen R., 'Moral Intervention in the Trademark Arena: Banning the Registration of Scandalous and Immoral Trademarks' (1993) 83 *TMR* 661–800

Basu, Kunal, 'Marketing Developing Society Crafts: A Framework for Analysis and Change' in Janeen Arnold Costa and Gary J. Bamossy (eds), *Marketing in a Multicultural World: Ethnicity, Nationalism and Cultural Identity* (Sage Publications: Thousand Oaks CA, 1995)

Behrendt, Kristin E., 'Cancellation of the Washington Redskins' Federal Trademark Registrations: Should Sports Team Names, Mascots and Logos Contain Native American Symbolism?' (2000) 10 *Seton Hall J Sport L* 389–414

Belson, Jeffrey, *Certification Marks* (Sweet & Maxwell: London, 2002)

Bently, Lionel and Sherman, Brad, *Intellectual Property Law* (3rd edn, Oxford University Press: Oxford, 2009)

Blake, Janet, *Preliminary Study into the Advisability of Developing a New Standard-Setting Instrument for the Safeguarding of Intangible Cultural Heritage: Elements for Consideration* (Paris, 2002)

Blakeney, Michael, 'The Protection of Traditional Knowledge under Intellectual Property Law' (2000) 22 *EIPR* 251–61

Blakeney, Michael, 'Communal Intellectual Property Rights of Indigenous Peoples in Cultural Expressions' (1998) 1 *JWIP* 985–1002

Blakeney, Michael, 'Protecting Expressions of Australian Aboriginal Folklore under Copyright Law' (1995) 9 *EIPR* 442–5

Blankenship, Justin G., 'The Cancellation of Redskins as a Disparaging Trademark: Is Federal Law an Appropriate Solution for Words that Offend?' (2001) 72 *U Colo. L Rev.* 415–57

Cassidy, Michael and Langford, Jock, *Intellectual Property and Aboriginal People, A Working Paper* (Minister of Indian Affairs and Northern Development: Ottawa, 1992)

Cazenave, B., 'The African Intellectual Property Organization (OAPI) from Libreville to Bangui' (1989) *Industrial Property* 291–307

Clark Hughey, Rachel, 'The Impact of *Pro-Football, Inc. v Harjo* on Trademark Protection of Other Marks' (2004) 14 *Fordham Intell. Prop. Media and Ent. LJ* 327–67

Conrad, Albrecht, 'The Protection of Geographical Indications in the TRIPS Agreement' (1996) 86 *TMR* 11–46

Dawson, Norma, *Certification Trade Marks, Law and Practice* (Intellectual Property Publishing Ltd: London, 1988)

Dennie, Christian, 'Native American Mascots and Team Names: Throw Away the Key: The Lanham Act is Locked for Future Trademark Challenges' (2005) 15 *Seton Hall J Sports L* 197–220

Dessemontet, François, 'Protection of Geographic Denominations under Swiss Law' in Jehoram Herman Cohen (ed.), *Protection of Geographic Denominations of Goods and Services*, Monographs on Industrial Property and Copyright Law (Sijthoff & Noordhoff: Alphen aan den Rijn, 1980) 97–134

Drahos, Peter, 'Towards an International Framework for the Protection of Traditional Group Knowledge and Practice', paper presented at UNCTAD–Commonwealth Secretariat Workshop on Elements of National *Sui Generis*

Systems for the Preservation, Protection and Promotion of Traditional Knowledge, Innovation and Practices and Options for an International Framework, Geneva, 4–6 February 2004

Drysdale, John and Silverleaf, Michael, *Passing Off Law and Practice* (2nd edn, Butterworths: London, 1995)

DuBoff, Leonard D., '500 Years After Columbus: Protecting Native American Culture' (1992) 11 *Cardozo Arts and Ent. LJ* 43–58

Durie, M.H. and Asher, S. (eds), *The Hirangi Hui: A Report Concerning the Government's Proposals for the Settlement of Treaty of Waitangi Claims and Related Constitutional Matters* (Turanga, 1995)

Endeshaw, Assafa, *Intellectual Property Policy for Non-Industrial Countries* (Dartmouth: 1996)

Escuerdo, Sergio, *International Protection of Geographical Indications and Developing Countries* (South Centre, 2001)

Frankel, Susy, 'Third Party Trade Marks as a Violation of Indigenous Cultural Property: A New Statutory Safeguard' paper presented at the Twelfth Fordham Annual Conference on International Intellectual Property Law and Policy, 15 April 2004

Frankel, Susy and McLay, Geoff, *Intellectual Property in New Zealand* (LexisNexis Butterworths: Wellington, 2002)

Gardiner, Wira, *Haka: A Living Tradition* (Hodder Moa Beckett Publishers Ltd: Auckland, 2001)

Gervais, Daniel, *The TRIPS Agreement, Drafting History and Analysis* (2nd edn, Sweet & Maxwell: London, 2003)

Gevers, Florent, 'Topical Issues of the Protection of Geographical Indications' in WIPO, *Symposium on the International Protection of Geographical Indications in the Worldwide Context, Eger, Hungary, 24–25 October 1997* (WIPO: Geneva, 1999)

Gilson, Jerome, *Trade Mark Protection and Practice* (LexisNexis: Newark, NJ, 1974)

Golvan, Colin, 'Aboriginal Art and Copyright: The Case for Johnny Bulun Bulun' (1989) 11 *EIPR* 346–55

Greenawalt, Kent, 'Insults and Epithets: Are They Protected Speech?' (1990) 42 *Rutgers L Rev.* 287–309

Hall, Michael, 'Case Note: Bulun Bulun v R & T Textiles' (1998) 16 *Copyright Reporter* 124–35

Hansen-Young, Thekla, 'Whose Name is it, Anyway? Protecting Tribal Names from Cybersquatters' (2005) 10 *Va. J L and Tech.* 1–18

Hapiuk, William J., 'Of Kitsch and Kachinas: A Criminal Analysis of the Indian Arts and Crafts Act of 1990' (2000–01) 53 *Stan. L Rev.* 1009–75

Harte-Bavendamm, Henning, 'Geographical Indications and Trademarks: Harmony or Conflict?' in WIPO, *Symposium on the International*

Protection of Geographical Indications, Somerset West, Cape Province, South Africa, 1–2 September 1999 (WIPO: Geneva, 2000)

Hollowell-Zimmer, Julie, 'Intellectual Property Protection for Alaska Native Arts' (2001) 24.4 *Cultural Survival Quarterly* 30

Iguza, Kunio, 'Revitalisation in Asia and Local Revitalization Efforts: A View from One Village One Product (OVOP) Movement in Oita', http://ideaix03.ide.go.jp/English/Ideas/School/pdf/igusa.pdf

International Institute for Environment and Development (IIED), *Traditional Resources Rights and Indigenous People in the Andes* (IIED, 2005)

ITC and WIPO, *Marketing Crafts and Visual Arts: The Role of Intellectual Property – A Practical Guide* (ITC and WIPO: Geneva, 2003)

Janke, Terri, *Minding Culture: Case Studies on Intellectual Property and Traditional Cultural Expressions* (WIPO: Geneva, 2003)

Janke Terri, *Our Culture: Our Future, Report on Australian Indigenous Cultural and Intellectual Property Rights* (report prepared for the Australian Institute of Aboriginal and Torres Strait Islander Studies and the Aboriginal and Torres Strait Islander Commission, 1998)

Janke Terri, 'Protecting Australian Indigenous Arts and Cultural Expressions: A Matter of Legislative Reform of Cultural Policy?' (1996) 7 *Culture and Policy* 14

Jopson, Debra, 'Aboriginal Seal of Approval Loses its Seal of Approval', *Sydney Morning Herald*, 14–15 December 2002

Joubert, Claude, 'Comments on the New Tunisian Law on Artistic and Literary Ownership' (1966–67) 50 *RIDA* 180–223

Kamperman Sanders, Anselm and Maniatis Spyros, 'A Consumer Trade Mark: Protection Based on Origin and Quality' (1993) 11 *EIPR* 406–15

Kimball, Jennifer, 'The Indian Arts and Crafts Act: Trademark Misfit or Just Missing the Mark?', www.kentlaw.edu/honorsscholars/2006students/writings/Kimball_paper.htm

Kitchin, David *et al.*, *Kerly's Law of Trade Marks and Trade Names* (14th edn, Sweet & Maxwell: London, 2005)

Kochtchouk, Oleg, *Carnaval, Rites, Fêtes et Traditions* (Editions Cabédita: Yens sur Morges, 2001)

Kremers, Nancy, 'Speaking with a Forked Tongue in the Global Debate on Traditional Knowledge and Genetic Resources: Is U.S. Intellectual Property Law and Policy Really Aimed at Meaningful Protection for Native American Cultures?' (2004) 15 *Fordham Intell. Prop. Media and Ent. LJ* 1–146

Kutty, Valsala, *National Experiences with the Protection of Traditional Cultural Expressions/Expressions of Folklore: India, Indonesia, the Philippines* (WIPO: Geneva, 1999)

Leicester, John, 'Hand-Crafted Products of Thailand's Village Communities',

Tourism Authority of Thailand News Room e-Magazine, www.tatnews.org/emagazine/2178.asp

Littrell, Mary Ann and Dickson, Marsha Ann, *Social Responsibility in the Global Market, Fair Trade of Cultural Products* (Sage Publications: London, 1999)

Lucas-Schloetter, Agnès, 'Folklore' in Silke von Lewinski (ed.), *Indigenous Heritage and Intellectual Property* (Kluwer Law International: London, 2004) 259–377

Masters, Brooke A. , 'Creative Legal Tactics Used Against Teams with Indian-Themed Names', *Houston Chronicle*, 11 April 1999

McCarthy, J. Thomas, *McCarthy on Trade Marks and Unfair Competition* (loose-leaf, Thomson West: New York)

McCarthy, J. Thomas, 'Lanham Act § 43(a): The Sleeping Giant is Now Wide Awake' (1996) 59 *Law and Contemp. Probs* 45–74

McKenney, Charles E. and Long, George F., *Federal Unfair Competition: Lanham Act § 43(a)* (West Group: St Paul MN, 1989)

Mezghani, Nébila, 'The New Tunisian Body for the Protection of Author's Rights' (1997) 31 *Copyright Bulletin* 30–8

Mezghani, Nébila, 'A New Tunisian Law Relating to Literary and Artistic Property' (1995) 29 *Copyright Bulletin* 26–34

Mezghani, Nébila, 'Letter from Tunisia, Development of the Law on Literary and Artistic Property in Tunisia' (1984) *Copyright* 265–72

Moore, Geoff, 'The Fair Trade Movement: Parameters, Issues and Future Research' (2004) 53 *Journal of Business Ethics* 73–86

New Zealand Ministry of Commerce, Competition Policy and Business Law Division, *Reform of the Trade Marks Act 1953* (Ministry of Commerce: Wellington, 1991)

New Zealand Ministry of Commerce, Competition Policy and Business Law Division, *Review of Industrial Property Rights, Patents, Trade Marks and Designs: Possible Options for Reform, Volume One* (Ministry of Commerce: Wellington, 1990).

New Zealand Ministry of Commerce, Maori Trade Marks Focus Group, *Maori and Trade Marks: A Discussion Paper* (Ministry of Commerce: Wellington, 1997)

New Zealand Ministry of Economic Development, *Review of the Patents Act 1953: Boundaries to Patentability, A Discussion Paper* (Regulatory and Competition Policy Branch, Ministry of Economic Development: Wellington, March 2002)

New Zealand Ministry of Economic Development, *Review of the Plant Variety Rights Act 1987, A Discussion Paper* (Regulatory and Competition Policy Branch, Ministry of Economic Development: Wellington, March 2002)

Nicholls, Alex and Opal, Charlotte, *Fair Trade, Market-Driven Ethical Consumption* (Sage Publications: London, 2005)

Niedzielska, Marie, 'The Intellectual Property Aspects of Folklore Protection' (1980) *Copyright* 339–46

O'Gara, Hugh, 'Who Makes Indian Art? Rapid City Man is First to Be Prosecuted under Indian Arts and Crafts Act of 1990', *Rapid City Journal* (SD), 23 December 1998

Osborn, Andrew, 'Maoris Win Lego Battle', *Guardian Unlimited*, 31 October 2001

Owen, Morgan, 'Protecting Indigenous Signs and Trade Marks: The New Zealand Experiment' (2004) 1 *IPQ* 58–84

Palethorpe, Stephen and Verhulst, Stefaan, *Report on the International Protection of Expressions of Folklore under Intellectual Property Law* (report commissioned by the European Commission's Internal Market, October 2000)

Parsley, Jon Keith, 'Regulation of Counterfeit Indian Arts and Crafts: An Analysis of the Indian Arts and Crafts Act of 1990' (1993) 18 *Am. Indian L Rev.* 487–514

Phillips, Jeremy, *Trade Marks Law: A Practical Anatomy* (Oxford University Press: Oxford, 2003)

Posner, Richard A., 'Misrepresentation: A Dirge' (2003–04) 40 *Hous. L Rev.* 621–41

Rangnekar, Dwijen, *The Socio-Economics of Geographical Indications: A Review of Empirical Evidence from Europe* (ICTSD and UNCTAD: Geneva, 2004)

Rangnekar, Dwijen, 'The International Protection of Geographical Indications: The Asian Experience', UNCTAD and ICTSD Regional Dialogue in collaboration with IDRC, University of Hong Kong, November 2004

Rangnekar Dwijen, 'Geographical Indications: A Review of Proposals at the TRIPS Council' in UNCTAD and ICTSD, *Capacity Building Project on Intellectual Property Rights and Sustainable Development* (UNCTAD and ICTSD: Geneva, 2002)

Redfern, Andy and Snedker, Paul, *Creating Market Opportunities for Small Enterprises: Experiences of the Fair Trade Movement*, SEED Working Paper No. 30 (ILO: Geneva, 2002)

Rimmer, Matthew, 'Australian Icons: Authenticity Marks and Identity Politics' (2004) 3 *Indigenous Law Journal* 139–79

Rhode, John B., 'The Mascot Name Change Controversy: A Lesson in Hypersensitivity' (1994–95) 5 *Marq. Sports L J* 141–61

Ricketson, Sam, *The Berne Convention for the Protection of Literary and Artistic Works: 1886–1986* (Centre for Commercial Law Studies, Queen Mary College and Kluwer: London, 1987)

Schechter, Frank I., *The Historical Foundation of the Law Relating to Trade Marks* (Columbia University Press: New York, 1925)

Shand, Peter, 'Scenes from the Colonial Catwalk: Cultural Appropriation, Intellectual Property Rights, and Fashion' (2002) 3 *Cultural Analysis* 47–88

Sheffield, Gail K., *The Arbitrary Indian: The Indian Arts and Crafts Act of 1990* (University of Oklahoma Press: Norman and London, 1997)

Sherkin, Samantha, 'A Historical Study on the Preparation of the 1989 Recommendation on the Safeguarding of Traditional Culture and Folklore' in *Safeguarding Traditional Cultures: A Global Assessment* (UNESCO and Smithsonian Center for Folklife and Cultural Heritage, 2001) 45

Sims, Calvin, 'It's Not Just How Well You Play the Game ...', *New York Times,* 31 January 1999

Smith, Scott S., 'The Scandal of Fake Indian Crafts', *Cowboys and Indians Magazine*, September 1998

Solomon, Maui, 'Intellectual Property Rights and Indigenous Peoples Rights and Obligations', www.inmotionmagazine.com/nztrip/ms1.html

Spratley, David, *Protecting Aboriginal Knowledge, Culture and Art under Canadian Intellectual Property Laws* (Davis & Company LLP: Vancouver, 2005)

Sterling, Adrian, *World Copyright Law* (2nd edn, Sweet & Maxwell: London, 2003)

Strickland, Rennard, 'Introduction to Indian Law Symposium, Indian Law and Policy: The Historian's Viewpoint' (1978–79) 54 *Wash. L Rev.* 475–8

Te Puni Kokiri, *A Guide to the Principles of the Treaty of Waitangi as Expressed by the Courts and the Waitangi Tribunal* (Te Puni Kokiri: Wellington, 2002)

UNCTAD and ICTSD, *Resource Book on TRIPS and Development* (Cambridge University Press: Cambridge, 2005)

UNDP, *Geographical Indications as Trade-Related Intellectual Property: Relevance and Implications for Human Development in Asia-Pacific*, Discussion Paper (January 2007)

UNESCO and ITC, International Symposium on Crafts and the International Market: Trade and Customs Codification, Manila, Philippines, 6–8 October 1997, *Final Report*

UNESCO and WIPO, *UNESCO/WIPO World Forum on the Protection of Folklore, Phuket, Thailand, April 8 to 10, 1997* (UNESCO and WIPO, 1998)

UNESCO and WIPO, *Model Provisions for National Laws on the Protection of Expressions of Folklore against Illicit Exploitation and Other Prejudicial Actions* (UNESCO and WIPO, 1985)

United Kingdom Patent Office, *Trade Marks Registry Work Manual* (Patent Office: Newport, 1994–)

US Department of the Interior, Indian Arts and Crafts Board, *American Indian and Alaska Native Arts and Crafts* (US Department of the Interior: Washington, 1995)

US Department of the Interior, Office of Inspector General, *Arts and Crafts: A Case of Misrepresentation* (US Department of the Interior: Washington, 2005)

US Department of Commerce, International Trade Administration, *Study of Problems and Possible Remedies Concerning Imported Native American-Style Jewelry and Handicrafts* (US Department of Commerce: Washington, 1985)

Veenstra, Henry R., 'Section 43(a) of the Lanham Act: A Federal Unfair Competition Remedy' (1975–76) 25 *Drake L Rev.* 228–38

Völkwe, Stefan, 'Registering New Forms under the Community Trademark' (2002) 152 *Trademark World* 24–33

Wadlow, Christopher, *The Law of Passing-Off: Unfair Competition by Misrepresentation* (3rd edn, Sweet & Maxwell: London, 2004)

Waitangi Tribunal, *Guide to the Practice and Procedure of the Waitangi Tribunal* (Waitangi Tribunal: Wellington, 2000)

Wendland, Wend, 'Intellectual Property, Traditional Knowledge and Folklore: WIPO's Exploratory Program' (2002) 33 *IIC* 485–504, 606–21

Wendland, Wend, 'Intellectual Property and the Protection of Cultural Expressions: The Work of the World Intellectual Property Organisation (WIPO)' in Molengrafica Series 2002, *Intellectual Property Law, Articles on Cultural Expressions and Indigenous Knowledge* (Intersentia: Antwerp, 2002) 101–38

Wilkins, David, 'An Inquiry into Indigenous Political Participation: Implications for Tribal Sovereignty' (1999–2000) 9 *Kan. J L and Pub. Pol'y* 732–51

Williams, David, *Matauranga Maori and Taonga* (Waitangi Tribunal Publications: Wellington, 2001)

Wilson, Norman, *Submission to the Contemporary Visual Arts and Crafts Inquiry* (Department of Communications, Information Technology, and the Arts: Canberra, 2001)

WIPO, *Intellectual Property and Genetic Resources, Traditional Knowledge and Traditional Cultural Expressions/Folklore, Information Resources* (WIPO: Geneva, 2006)

WIPO, *Consolidated Analysis of the Legal Protection of Traditional Cultural Expressions/Expressions of Folklore* (WIPO: Geneva, 2003)

WIPO, *Intellectual Property Needs and Expectations of Traditional Knowledge Holders, WIPO Report on Fact-Finding Missions on Intellectual Property and Traditional Knowledge (1998–1999)* (WIPO: Geneva, 2001)

WIPO, 'Committee of Governmental Experts to Prepare a Model Law on Copyright for Developing Countries' (1976) *Copyright* 139–52

WIPO, 'Tunis Model Law on Copyright' (1976) *Copyright* 165–86
WIPO, *Records of the Intellectual Property Conference of Stockholm, June 11 to July 14, 1967* (WIPO: Geneva, 1971)
Wiseman, Leanne, 'The Protection of Indigenous Art and Culture in Australia: The Labels of Authenticity' (2001) 23 *EIPR* 14–25
Zlotchew, Ethan G. '"Scandalous" or "Disparaging"? It Should Make a Difference in Opposition and Cancellation Actions: Views on the Lanham Act's Section 2(a) Prohibitions Using the Example of Native American Symbolism in Athletics' (1998)] 22 *Colum.-VLA JL and Arts* 217–46
Zografos, Daphne 'The Legal Protection of Traditional Cultural Expressions: The Tunisian Experience' (2004) 7 *JWIP* 229–42

Index